Bold Experiment

*The Story of Educational Television
in American Samoa*

Bold Experiment

The Story of Educational Television in American Samoa

WILBUR SCHRAMM, LYLE M. NELSON, *and* MERE T. BETHAM

STANFORD UNIVERSITY PRESS

Stanford, California   1981

Stanford University Press
Stanford, California
© 1981 by the Board of Trustees of the
Leland Stanford Junior University
Printed in the United States of America
ISBN 0-8047-1090-2
LC 79-67777

THIS BOOK *is dedicated to the Samoans and the American mainlanders who worked so hard and so unselfishly to upgrade education in American Samoa with this Bold Experiment in the use of school television*

Preface

EVENTS in a far-off corner of the world sometimes turn out to have wide-ranging significance. Such was the case with the coming of television to a remote corner of the South Pacific on October 4, 1964. Introduced in American Samoa as the central feature of a crash program designed to modernize and rapidly upgrade an entire educational system, television soon took on a significance of its own, one that reached far beyond the classroom and also beyond the shores of this chain of tiny islands. For the action represented a historic first in the use of educational technology on such a broad scale.

Because of the significance to education everywhere of Samoa's Bold Experiment, it immediately became the center of worldwide attention, not just in education circles, but also in national planning offices and in "development" efforts in many countries. During the course of those early years, the project was visited by individuals and teams from dozens of countries. Their reports, based mostly on anecdotal evidence and personal observation, probably exceeded everything that had ever been written about Samoa up until then.

The authors of this book contributed their share to that volume of material. In so doing, however, they became convinced of the need for a thorough, carefully documented, longitudinal appraisal of the results of the Samoan experience. This book is the result. We hope that it will be read in the spirit in which it was written—not as an attempt to assess success or failure, but rather as an attempt to cast some light on the significance of developments and the lessons to be learned from them.

We owe much to many individuals and organizations. It is not possible to recognize all of them, but we would like to express our special thanks to the students, teachers, and staff of the schools of American Samoa who participated in the early stages of the project. Without their idealism, dedication, and hard work, often under the most difficult of circumstances, Samoan schools today might be little improved over those of 1964.

More generally, we owe a debt of gratitude to all members of the school system, past and present, who were honest and open about their experiences and willing to share with us freely and fully their observations and records. We could not have asked for more helpful or more responsible cooperation. In particular, we would like to thank Chief Nikolao Pula, for nearly 40 years a member of the Samoan school system and its first Samoan director of education; Roy and Milly Cobb, two of the early pioneers in bringing television to the classrooms of Samoa; and Milton deMello, the last U.S. director of education.

One of the most important contributions to this book was made by Richard Baldauf, whose early studies (for a Ph.D. degree at the University of Hawaii) provided important benchmarks for comparisons of changes in Samoan attitudes and values. We are also grateful to Dean Jamison of the World Bank, for reading the chapter on costs and for his comments thereon.

The cooperation and helpfulness of the National Association of Educational Broadcasters, and its president, James Fellows, also deserves special mention. The NAEB gave us unrestricted access to all its files and records, and President Fellows was unusually helpful in tracking down former project participants who could provide information and answers to complex questions. Additionally, no book of this kind would be complete without mentioning the encouragement and unhesitating support given us by former Governor H. Rex Lee, a dedicated public servant whose desire to do something to redress years of American neglect in Samoa led to what was then—and remains today—a bold, innovative experiment in education.

We also acknowledge with gratitude the thorough and comprehensive review of the manuscript, and the many contributions, by our editor at the Stanford University Press, Barbara Mnookin. Stanford University and the East-West Center contributed much of the time of two of the authors. The contributions of UNESCO and the International Institute of Educational Planning, which commissioned some of the early studies that provided data for this book are also acknowledged.

Finally, this book would not have been possible without the support and encouragement of the Ford and Markle foundations and the Government of American Samoa, whose grants helped make possible much of the research.

W.S.
L.M.N.
M.T.B.

Contents

1. The Project and Its Setting 1
2. The Decision to Use Television 25
3. Introducing the New System 44
4. Coping with Change 69
5. Teachers' and Students' Attitudes Toward Television 92
6. How Much Did the Students Learn? 107
7. How Should We Evaluate This Performance? 127
8. The Impact of Television on the Home Audience 148
9. The Cost of Educational Television in American Samoa 174
10. Lessons from the Samoa Experience 184

Appendixes 201
   A. Supplementary Data on Tests and Opinion Surveys, *201*. B. Survey of Teachers' and Administrators' Preferences on the Use of Educational Television, *215*. C. Surveys of Values in American Samoa, *219*. D. Sample Home Television Schedules of KVZK-TV, American Samoa, 1966–1980, *223*. E. Sample Sizes, 1970–1979, *230*.

Works Cited 235

Index 241

Tables

TEXT TABLES

1. Population of American Samoa, 1900–1977   7
2. Governors and Directors of Education of American Samoa, 1950–1980   10
3. Growth of American Samoa's School System, 1904–1980   18
4. Expansion of American Samoa's Elementary School System, 1964–1973   47
5. Daily Schedule of Classroom Television in American Samoa, 1966   49
6. Progression from Levels to Grades in American Samoa's Elementary Schools, 1964–1974   50
7. Hours Devoted Weekly to Classroom Television in American Samoa by Grade Level, 1966   53
8. Teachers' Attitudes Toward Educational Television in American Samoa, 1972   83
9. Students' Attitudes Toward Educational Television in American Samoa, 1972   84
10. Teachers' and Administrators' Preferences Among Four Proposed Ways of Using Television (Plans A–D) in American Samoa, 1972   85
11. Students' Average Weekly Exposure to Classroom Television in American Samoa, 1965, 1972, and 1975   88
12. Grade Level as a Variable in American Samoa Students' Attitudes Toward Educational Television, 1972   93
13. Comparison of Teachers' Assessment of Educational Television, by Grade Level, in Hagerstown, 1965, and American Samoa, 1972   94
14. American Samoa Students' Changing Attitudes Toward Educational Television Over Time and by Grade Level, 1972–1976   96

15. El Salvador Teachers' Changing Attitudes Toward
    Educational Television, 1969–1972 — 97
16. Educational Preparation as a Variable in American Samoa
    Elementary Teachers' Opinions of Educational
    Television, 1976 — 100
17. Location of Schools as a Variable in American Samoa
    Elementary Teachers' Opinions of Educational
    Television, 1976 — 102
18. Stanford Achievement Test Scores of American Samoa
    Teachers and Students, 1932, 1935, 1954, and 1970 — 111
19. Gates Reading Survey Scores of American Samoa
    Students in Grades 5–12 and Elementary Teachers,
    1967 — 112
20. Oral English Scores of American Samoa Students in
    Grade 7, 1964 and 1968 — 114
21. Oral English Scores of American Samoa Students in
    Grade 7 by Years of Experience with Educational
    Television, 1966 — 115
22. Oral English Scores of American Samoa Students by Age,
    1968 — 116
23. Oral English Scores of American Samoa Students by
    Years of Experience with Educational Television, 1968 — 116
24. Oral English Scores of American Samoa Students in
    Grades 3 and 4, 1969 and 1970 — 117
25. Oral English and Reading Scores of American Samoa
    Students in Schools With and Without Television,
    1972 — 119
26. Comparative Scores in Oral English and Reading of
    Swains Island Students With and Without
    Educational Television Experience, 1972 — 120
27. Stanford Achievement Test Scores of American Samoa
    Students in Grades 3–6, 1971 and 1972 — 121
28. SRA Achievement Test Scores in Reading of American
    Samoa High School Students, Elementary Teachers,
    and High School Teachers, 1972 — 122
29. SRA Achievement Test Scores of American Samoa
    Students in Grade 8, 1970–1979 — 124
30. SRA Achievement Test Scores of American Samoa
    Students in Grade 12, 1972–1979 — 124
31. English as a Foreign Language (TOEFL) Test Scores of
    American Samoa Students in Grade 12, 1976–1978 — 125
32. Expected Rates of Gain on Standardized Tests and Actual
    Rates of American Samoa Students, 1971–1972 — 131

33. Stanford Achievement Test Scores of Fia Iloa Students in Grades 1–4, 1971 — 134
34. Average Correlation Between Cognitive Skills Index and Background, School, and Community Variables for El Salvador Students in Grades 7–9, 1970–1972 — 140
35. Top Ten Programs in Samoa During Survey Week, December 1976 — 155
36. Capital Costs of the American Samoa Television System as of January 1966 — 176
37. Operating Costs of the American Samoa Television System in Fiscal 1966 — 177
38. Estimated Costs of Production, Transmission, and Reception in the American Samoa Television System as of January 1966 — 178
39. Budget Allocations for the American Samoa Television System, 1972 — 180

APPENDIX TABLES

A.1. Stanford Achievement Test Scores of Teachers and Teacher-Candidates, 1932 — 201
A.2. SRA Achievement Test Scores of American Samoa Elementary and High School Teachers, 1972 — 201
A.3. Stanford Achievement Test Scores of American Samoa Students in Grades 4–12, 1935 — 202
A.4. Stanford Achievement Test Scores of American Samoa Students in Grade 9, 1954 — 203
A.5. Stanford Achievement Test Scores of American Samoa Students in Grades 3–6, 1971 — 203
A.6. Stanford Achievement Test Scores of American Samoa Students in Grades 3–7, 1972 — 204
A.7. SRA Achievement Test Scores of American Samoa Students in Grades 7–12, 1971 — 204
A.8. SRA Achievement Test Scores of American Samoa Students in Grades 8–12, 1972 — 205
A.9. Difference in SRA Achievement Test Scores After Four Years of High School, American Samoa Graduating Classes of 1975 and 1976 — 205
A.10. Performance of American Samoa Students in Grades 3–6 on English- and Samoan-Language Versions of a Mathematics Test, 1971 — 206
A.11. Performance of American Samoa Students in Grade 12 on the Michigan Test of English Language Proficiency (MTELP), 1966, 1968, 1970, and 1971 — 206

A.12. Analysis of Variance for Text Tables 22 and 23   207
A.13. Opinions of Educational Television Held by American
      Samoa Elementary and High School Teachers, 1972   208
A.14. Opinions of Educational Television Held by American
      Samoa Teachers and Administrators for Grades 1–8,
      1972–1974 and 1976   209
A.15. Opinions of Educational Television Held by American
      Samoa Upper Elementary and High School Students,
      1972   211
A.16. American Samoa Teachers' Opinions of Educational
      Television by Level of Education, 1976   212
A.17. Opinions of Educational Television Held by American
      Samoa Students in Grades 5–8, 1972–1974 and 1976   213
A.18. Opinions of Educational Television Held by American
      Samoa Students in Grades 5–8 in Pago Pago Bay
      Area and Remote Schools, 1976   214
B.1. Teachers' and Administrators' Preferences Among
     Proposed Ways of Using Television, 1972   216
B.2. Teachers' and Administrators' Preferences Among Types
     of Support Programs Depending on the Way
     Television Is Used, 1972   217
C.1. Intercorrelations of Six Value Scales, American Samoa,
     1972   219
C.2. Factors and Item Loadings for American Samoa Value
     Study, 1977   219
C.3. Effect of Language on Judgments of 40 American Samoa
     Students Taking Value Test in Both Samoan and
     English, 1977   222

Bold Experiment

The Story of Educational Television in American Samoa

ONE

The Project and Its Setting

TELEVISION came to American Samoa on Sunday afternoon, October 4, 1964. It was the first time a developing region set out to use that medium in an all-out attempt to modernize an educational system. Consequently, it was a historic day not only for a group of small islands deep in the South Pacific, but also for many other countries looking to modern technology to speed economic and social development.

In 1964 educational television looked like an idea whose time had come. Economically advanced nations had already begun to make major use of it. As early as 1956 all the public schools of Washington County, Maryland, had been connected by closed-circuit, and some 21,000 students were receiving daily televised instruction from studios in Hagerstown. An airplane was flying lazy circles over the American midwest, broadcasting recorded television lessons to schools in six states that wanted to supplement their own teaching. The Chicago junior college was broadcasting many of its courses so that viewers could do most of the required work for a degree by studying at home. Italy was using television to teach illiterates how to read and write and to bring the classroom to parts of the country where schools were nonexistent or inadequate. Britain, France, Germany, Sweden, Japan, and other affluent countries were all using television in one way or another to supplement instruction.

Developing countries also were experimenting with television. Colombia was beginning to offer courses over its national network. India was broadcasting supplementary courses to schools within reach of the country's only television transmitter in Delhi. And only a few weeks after Samoa's project got under way, the Republic of Niger, in Central Africa, launched a major ETV experiment of its own. The Niger experiment, conducted under French auspices, was intended to demonstrate—using relatively untrained monitors rather than certified teachers in the classroom and highly skilled educators and broadcasters in the studio—an alternative to the country's traditional system of education.

But in the midst of all this interest and activity, the Samoa project was unique. It was like Hagerstown in the sense that it was intended to carry the main load of instruction, rather than to supplement it. But unlike the Hagerstown operation, the Samoa project was not able to draw on the services of teachers who were well trained and could play a full part in designing the courses to be broadcast. Few of the Samoan teachers had gone beyond high school or teaching certificates, and they were accustomed to teaching in one-room native *fales*—huts with no interior or exterior walls—where the pupils sat on the ground and chanted back the words or statements their teacher gave them to learn. In this respect, Samoa was more like Niger, but in another, important respect it was quite different. The project in Niger moved very slowly and carefully. For several years it was restricted to a few classrooms and a few hundred students. Programs were carefully crafted and pretested; instruction began with the youngest students and progressed only one grade a year so that television did not reach the last level of primary school for five years. Not until the 1970's, by which time most of the French experts had been withdrawn, did Niger take steps to extend television beyond the few experimental classrooms to other schools in its national system.

No such slow and cautious beginnings in American Samoa! "There was no time for waiting, no time for armchair patience—there had been too much of that for sixty years," the governor of American Samoa said in 1965, looking back on the introduction of television (Kaser 1965). In part his statement reflects the sense of guilt the U.S. government felt in the early 1960's over not having done more, in the period of its responsibility, to help Samoa move into the modern world. But the problem of conscience was two-edged: rather than doing more to help Samoa develop, perhaps the United States should not "disturb the peace and tranquility of the islands," as the governor put it, by introducing new customs, new goals, new problems, the turmoil of the modern world. Anthropologists and others who knew the Samoan culture well were inclined to argue that the culture should not be tampered with. Beyond that, many of the mainlanders who worked in the Samoa Department of Education for purely educational reasons opposed the introduction of television.

But by the time the Kennedy administration came to Washington in 1961, the balance had swung away from preserving the culture relatively unchanged. Island leaders themselves were asking for better education. There was prodding by the U.N. Trusteeship Council, which had apparently decided that development was good per se. A vigorous and public-spirited new governor, H. Rex Lee, was sent to Samoa in 1961. Thus in the early Kennedy years the pull of conscience over what had *not* been done in the past 60 years began to overbalance the pull of conscience over what the effect of doing it *might* be. And when the decision to use television was reached, then the sheer vigor and audacity of the actions taken drew the attention of the whole educational world to Samoa.

At the same time, education was made universal; previously it had been for a select few. New consolidated schools were built throughout the islands, handsome structures that retained much of the spirit of the native architecture but ended forever the day of the one-room school in Samoa. New classrooms were designed to receive television as soon as it was available. The best in television equipment was provided, including an air-conditioned studio building adjoining the central offices of the

Department of Education and a transmitter building and two television towers set spectacularly on a mountain top, where equipment could be delivered and employees could go to work only by means of a mile-long tramway over an arm of Pago Pago Bay. Teachers with television experience, ETV producers, engineers, and school principals intended to spark a program of in-service education for teachers—these and others were recruited in the States. Television teaching was made available to the six primary grades of most of the schools in the first year and to the full system (through grade 12) a year later. Thus, remarkably, within a matter of months the Samoans had an educational system organized around a medium that was unknown to them as late as July 1964. Two years later, four of every five school-age children were spending one-fourth to one-third of their class time looking at a television picture.

To some observers, this was seen as "typically American go-for-broke behavior," as indeed it was. But it was also a national response to a sense of obligation, for Samoa's destiny was at least partly dependent on the United States. Most of the hundreds of dedicated persons who participated in the project saw it that way, and made a sincere and deeply felt effort to remedy a long history of educational neglect by helping the islands move into the modern world of education. Such mistakes as were made must be seen in that light. And in any case there is nothing to be gained now by evaluating the performance of individuals or attempting to apportion blame for what may in hindsight seem to be errors of policy or practice. Rather, our intention is to try to identify some of the lessons that can be learned from this project concerning the use of television for instruction, and particularly its use on a grand scale for wholesale educational reform and development.

The ambitious goals of the Samoa project, the pace at which it was designed to move, the fact that it was intended for an entire school system separated from others by miles of ocean, and that it inevitably brought an old and relatively changeless culture into confrontation with a new and rapidly changing one—these not only challenged educational television to do what few other projects had asked of it, but also threw a bright and pitiless light on the problems of using this technology as a tool of development. The architects of the Samoa plan said the project should not be evaluated until an entire academic generation—12 years —had passed through the school system. That time has now come. Several of the high school graduates in 1976 were first-graders, six- or seven-year-olds, in October 1964, when television tubes first lighted up in Samoan classrooms; and a still higher proportion of the subsequent graduates began their schooling in television classrooms. It seems an appropriate time, therefore, to look back over what has happened in the intervening years.

Like most such projects, this one had been neither a complete success nor a complete failure. It has fallen short of many of the hopes for it, and some of the recent developments relating to the use of television have been disappointing to observers who believed and still believe in the power of the medium as a teaching device. On the other hand, television has made important differences in Samoa, and the figures on student learning, so far as we can now resurrect them, though not spectacular are far from discouraging. But the important lessons to be learned from Samoa are more specific than general evaluations of the project. As we review the record, it seems to us that four stages in the history of the effort had most to do with its effectiveness or lack of it. These were, first, the decision to use television rather than something else to modernize the school system; second, the pace at which it was introduced; third, the kind of curriculum adopted in relation to the culture in which it had to operate; and fourth, the problem of coping with changes in teachers and students as the new program took hold. In the following pages we shall try first to fill in these chapters in the history of the project and then to see how this pattern of development relates to what we know about the effects of television in Samoa—on the school system itself, on student learning, on student attitudes and teacher attitudes, and on the cultural values of the young people.

But to understand what happened, one must begin with the

geographical, social, economic, and educational setting into which the project was introduced.

The Islands and Their People

The seven islands of Eastern Samoa came under U.S. jurisdiction in 1899, when the United Kingdom, Germany, and the United States resolved a dispute over rights in that part of the Pacific by recognizing America's claim to all islands east of the 171st meridian and Germany's claim to the islands to the west. (Great Britain withdrew its claim in return for a sphere of influence elsewhere in the Pacific.)

The Samoan islands stretch about 600 miles along a line running approximately southeast to northwest, and lie some 12° to 15° south of the equator. They are about 4,150 miles from the continental United States—2,300 miles south and a little west of Hawaii, and 1,600 miles north and a little east of New Zealand. They are primarily volcanic islands whose soaring mountains rise abruptly from the very blue water. They are heavily forested with the typical South Pacific trees, including palm, banana, pandanus, and breadfruit, and their meadows are thickly carpeted with grasses and tropical vegetables like yams and taro, all kept green by 200 inches of rain a year. The temperature seldom falls below 75°F (24°C) or rises above 90°F (32°C). Humidity ranges from 70 percent to 90 percent in the wet season (November–March) and 40 percent to 60 percent in the dry season (April–October).

The American island group, the eastern part of the chain, consists of the main island of Tutuila; a small nearby island, Aunu'u; the Manu'a group of Ta'u, Olosega, and Ofu; Rose Island, an uninhabited coral atoll; and Swains Island, 210 miles to the northwest, which is really part of the Tokelaus rather than the Samoan chain but is included in American Samoa for administrative convenience. The total land area of these islands is only 76 square miles, slightly larger than the District of Columbia. The estimated population in 1977 was 30,600, roughly 80 percent of whom live on Tutuila. This population, which has grown rapidly

TABLE 1

Population of American Samoa, 1900–1977

Year	Population	Percent increase
1900	5,679	—
1912	7,251	27.7%
1920	8,056	11.1
1930	10,055	24.8
1940	12,908	28.4
1950	18,937	46.7
1960	20,051	5.9[a]
1970	27,769	38.5
1977	30,600	10.2

SOURCE: 1900–1970, U.S. censuses. 1977 estimate, *The World Almanac, 1979,* p. 704.

NOTE: Since 1930 the censuses have supplied data as of April 1. The 1900 and 1920 census figures are for June 1 and January 1 of those years, respectively. The precise date for the 1912 figure is unknown.

[a] The smaller gain is due to the dismantling of the Naval Administration after 1950, which took with it many Samoan "support" personnel and their families.

since the islands came under American jurisdiction (see Table 1) presents special problems not only because there is too little arable land to support so many people, but also because there are not enough job opportunities for the young, many of whom consequently emigrate to Hawaii or the mainland.

The Samoans are ethnically Polynesians with little mixture of other strains. Their language, which is considered the oldest Polynesian tongue in existence, is closely related to the Maori, Tahitian, Marquesan, Tongan, and Hawaiian languages. Many Polynesian legends have the world beginning in Samoa, and it is likely that the present Polynesian world did begin here, that these islands were the first of the Polynesian group to be settled by that hardy breed of mariners who are thought to have sailed large two-hulled canoes across thousands of miles of the open Pacific when the Egyptians were still building pyramids and the Europeans just beginning to venture cautiously out on the Mediterranean.

Samoan society has long been based on an intricate pattern of traditional family relationships, which Margaret Mead saw as "an amalgamation and recombination of several distinct principles: the principle of hereditary rank; the functions and privileges of relationship groups; and the recognition of the organized village community with rights and privileges of its own" (Mead 1934: 10).

One characteristic of this leadership (*matai*) system is that almost all land in American Samoa is communally owned by extended families (called *aiga*, pronounced ah-inga). It cannot be bought or sold, or attached for delinquent debts. A few small tracts are owned by churches and related organizations, but from the earliest days the prevailing doctrine—recognized by the United States in all its dealings with the Samoan people and stated officially in the Senate Interior and Insular Affairs Committee Report of 1961—has been "Samoan lands for the Samoans."

However, the matai system is far more than a means of landholding. As a social structure it extends into virtually every phase of Samoan life, controlling the economic as well as the social relationships of the Samoans. The matai, who may hold either of two titles, chief (*ali'i*) or orator (*tulafale*), is responsible for the family members under his control. The matai title is bestowed by the family itself. In many cases, it passes from father to son, though that custom has undergone considerable change over the years (Grattan 1948).

Once chosen, the matai has in the past—much less so today—had great authority over all members of the family. By Samoan custom he controlled their economic activities and the disposal of all the group's wealth. In return, he was responsible for their material and moral welfare and was expected to apportion the wealth for the benefit of the group as a whole.

Association with Western cultures over the years has had a substantial impact on the matai system as it existed when Margaret Mead and Felix Keesing wrote their classic books on the culture of American Samoa. The prevalence of salaried jobs, the increasing tendency of young people to leave the family village in search of these jobs, and a growing reluctance to "bank with the matai" (that is, to turn over one's income for communal use) have placed new strains on family relationships. Rapid population growth also has played a role, encouraging many young people (up to 50 percent of a high school graduating class) to leave the islands, temporarily or permanently.

Although American rule may have been characterized by neglect in some fields, health and medical care were not among them. Largely as a result of improved public health standards and facilities, but also because of migration from Western Samoa, the population of American Samoa increased 253 percent between 1900 and 1960. This growth rate, one of the highest in the world, created problems that were largely ignored. Accordingly, more and more young people went to Hawaii or the mainland, to return with new values that were often inconsistent with the traditional culture. In turn, this caused confusion in the goals of education and conflict over what those goals should be.

The Islands' Political Status

American Samoa is an unincorporated Territory of the United States. Its inhabitants are American nationals, but not citizens, who may visit or emigrate to the United States without passport. No organic legislation for the Territory has been enacted by Congress, partly because of concerns that to do so would open up Samoan lands for ownership by other than Samoans.

In 1900, and again in 1904, the Samoan chiefs in effect ratified the agreement of 1899 by ceding the islands of Eastern Samoa to the United States. Two decades passed before Congress bothered to take note of this action. In February 1929, Congress finally got around to adopting a resolution accepting the islands as of the time they were first ceded. Since assuming responsibility, the United States has governed essentially by fiat from Washington, as provided for in the resolution of February 20, 1929:

Until Congress shall provide for the government of such islands, all civil, judicial, and military power shall be vested in such person or per-

TABLE 2
Governors and Directors of Education of American Samoa, 1950–1980

Governor	Tenure	Director of education	Tenure
Phelps Phelps	Feb. 1951–June 1952	J. R. Trace	1944–51
John C. Elliott	July 1952–Nov. 1952	H. S. Spencer	1951–53
James Arthur Ewing	Nov. 1952–Mar. 1953	L. M. Fort	1953–55
Lawrence M. Judd	Mar. 1953–Aug. 1953	D. A. Rothschild	1955–57
Richard B. Lowe	Oct. 1953–Oct. 1956	M. J. Senter	1957–63
Peter Tali Coleman[a]	Oct. 1956–May 1961	J. C. Wright	1963–65
H. Rex Lee	May 1961–July 1967	John W. Harold	1965–67
Owen S. Aspinall	Aug. 1967–July 1969	Roy D. Cobb	1967–69
John M. Haydon	Aug. 1969–Oct. 1974	Richard Balch[b]	1969–70
Frank C. Mockler[c]	Oct. 1974–Feb. 1975	Milton deMello	1970–73
Earl B. Ruth	Feb. 1975–Sep. 1976	Nikolao Pula[d]	1973–74
Frank Barnett	Oct. 1976–May 1977	Mere Betham	1974–[e]
H. Rex Lee	May 1977–Dec. 1977		
Peter Tali Coleman	Jan. 1978–[e]		

[a]First Samoan to be appointed governor. Also the Territory's first elected governor; he assumed office on Jan. 1, 1978.
[b]Served only four months.
[c]Acting governor. Four other men served in that capacity before 1961, but only briefly, and we have not listed them here.
[d]First Samoan to be appointed director of education.
[e]Still serving as this book went to press.

sons and shall be exercised in such manner as the President of the United States shall direct; and the President shall have power to remove said officers and fill the vacancies so occasioned. (U.S. Congress, 455 Stat. 1253)

In 1950, jurisdiction over the Territory was transferred from the Department of the Navy to the Department of the Interior; and the responsibility for administration, previously held by Navy commandants, usually for a two-year term of duty, now fell to presidential appointees. Few of these civilian governors stayed in office more than two years. From 1950 to Lee's appointment in 1961, there were six governors and four acting governors, or a change in administration on the average of about once a year.

Governor H. Rex Lee was an exception. Not only did he come from a civil service background, but he also arrived with a mandate to make major changes in the situation, as well as with a determination to initiate programs to improve the economic and social condition of the people.

Lee served until 1967. From that time until January 1, 1978, when an elected governor took office, there were five more governors, plus one acting governor (the only man who served long enough in that capacity to be recognized by Interior). The last appointed governor was Lee himself, who was returned to his old post by the Carter administration to help prepare the way for an elected Samoan executive branch. In 1977 the people of American Samoa elected as their first governor Peter Tali Coleman, a Samoan by birth and a man who had previously served in that position as an appointee. Table 2 lists all the governors from 1950 to 1980, along with the directors of education (who changed with almost the same frequency as governors).

In 1905, the Naval governor created a council of 24 Samoans to advise him on the islanders' problems, but their recommendations were subject to the governor's approval; he was free to veto any decision that he considered unwise. The council, called the Fono, initially consisted entirely of matais.

In 1948, the Fono was reorganized into a bicameral legislature.

The senior body, or House of Ali'i, was composed of the 12 matais who held the highest titles as set forth in the Code of American Samoa; they were not elected, but derived their positions from their rank. The junior body, or House of Representatives, was composed of 52 members who were selected in traditional open village meetings to represent all of the major villages or village clusters in the islands, plus two members elected by secret ballot to represent the population groups that had either withdrawn from the matai system or never been part of it.

Under a constitutional revision approved in 1961, the legislature was given additional power, including the power to override the governor's veto of its actions, thereby referring any dispute to the Secretary of the Interior for resolution. At the same time, the structure was changed to provide for a 20-member House of Representatives elected by secret ballot. With this, the *taulele'a* (untitled person) was given a voice in the political affairs of the central government. But in deference to Samoan custom, which still excluded those without titles from participating in local government councils, provision was also made for an 18-member Senate chosen by the country's elite. Thus, these senators, typically the highest-ranking men in their counties who are willing to serve, are selected, directly or indirectly, by the territory's 800-odd titleholders.

In general, the United States has tried to honor and support the traditional Samoan social structure in its administration of the islands. The pattern of political control has changed slowly over the years. From the beginning, the governing of villages and all minor matters have been the responsibility of the matais. An attempt has been made to encourage political self-reliance at the local level, and to develop a system of government fully competent to deal with village (*nu'u*), county (*itumalo*), and district (*falelima*) interests and concerns. But in major political and policy matters, the final decisions have largely come from Washington or its appointees.

By contrast, Western Samoa, which came under the trusteeship of New Zealand after the Second World War, became an independent nation on January 1, 1962. The Western islands, which are more generously endowed with farmland and natural resources and have a population of about 150,000, have tended to look on American Samoa as an indolent, rich cousin, spoiled by the largesse of the United States. In turn, American Samoans have been reluctant to consider independence and even delayed for several years accepting the invitation to elect their own governor. They have also been wary of any proposed union with Western Samoa, partly because the chiefs of that nation outrank their chiefs (and thus have greater authority) and partly because such a union would almost inevitably lead to a weakening of ties with the United States. For these and other reasons, most political observers regard the union of the two Samoas, which many consider a logical step, as being politically impractical.

The Economic Setting

American Samoa's natural resources are few. They consist mainly of its people, a strategic location astride air and sea routes to the South Pacific, an equable tropical climate, and the natural scenic beauty of the islands. The Territory has no known mineral deposits and only a small amount of arable land.

Except for Rose and Swains atolls, the islands are of relatively recent volcanic origin. They are high islands, mountainous and mostly steep. Apart from two small plains, on Ta'u and in the Leone-Tufuna area of Tutuila, the arable land is confined to small patches along the seashore. The soil is rich and productive in the alluvial valleys, but the tuff plains quickly become exhausted if fertilizers are not used. An adequate water supply is a constant problem because of insufficient and inadequate storage facilities. And this in an area in which the annual rainfall exceeds 200 inches!

By far the most important factor in American Samoa's economy is the government itself. Whereas the economy formerly was built around subsistence farming and fishing, with little cash, by 1979 almost half the salaried workers were employed by the territorial government, which operated on a $50,000,000 budget, about 75 percent of which was provided by the United States. Over the years sporadic attempts have been made to trim the government payroll and to emphasize agriculture and industry, but the number of employees and the dollar amount paid to them has steadily grown under the Department of Interior's administration.

Virtually the only industry consists of two tuna canneries, one owned by the Van Camp Sea Food Company (a division of Ralston Purina) and the other by Star-Kist Samoa, Inc. (a division of H. J. Heinz). Together, they accounted in 1974 for an estimated 95 percent of the islands' exports, valued at $83,000,000 (*World in Figures* 1976: 283), and well over half the private sector payroll.

The principal exports, other than canned fish, are copra, cocoa, and handicrafts. The tourist industry has not developed as rapidly as had been hoped, largely because of inadequate air service and a shortage of hotel rooms. A scarcity of safe, sandy beaches, especially given the islands' unpleasantly high humidity, has also proved an obstacle to such development.

Faced with one of the world's fastest growing populations (3.1 percent a year between 1960 and 1970 and 3.4 percent between 1970 and 1974), the government has attempted to encourage agricultural production, but without success. In fact, more and more Samoans have abandoned agriculture over the years as government and other cash-related job opportunities have increased. Taking note of the problem in 1961, the U.S. Senate Committee on Interior and Insular Affairs was moved to comment:

At present, agriculture in this territory is at an all-time low. It has deteriorated over recent years to the point where increasing quantities of food have to be imported in order to make up the deficit. Once self-sufficient in their food supply, the people of American Samoa now require buying power with which to supplement their own production. (Long & Gruening 1961: 57)

Yet in spite of the Interior Department's early and consistent support of the idea of strengthening the agricultural base of the

Samoan economy,* and in spite of the Territory's location in the South Pacific thousands of miles from the mainland, American Samoa continues to be economically dependent on the United States. More than 95 percent of its exports (chiefly canned tuna, as we have seen) go to the United States, and more than 66 percent of its imports come from there. Moreover, with a higher per-capita income and standard of living than the other emerging nations of the Pacific, Samoa does not have any immediate prospect of developing a large export market close to home.

In short, American Samoa has very few of the natural advantages that have so often attracted colonial rule. When Navy ships ceased to burn coal, many decades ago, the islands lost their one military attraction: Pago Pago harbor as a coaling station. American Samoa has no oil, no precious metals, no valuable industrial metals like the nickel in French Caledonia, and too little arable land to build up profitable agricultural exports or even to support its own burgeoning population. Thus the United States, far from reaping economic rewards from the Territory, has been supplying three-fourths of the Samoan budget.

The Educational System

In May 1961, when Governor Lee arrived in Pago Pago with a mandate from President Kennedy to make up for years of American neglect, he found a school "system" that was a shambles, literally in terms of facilities and figuratively in terms of educational standards and results. It was appalling, Lee later recalled, even by comparison with the mainland's ghettos.

All but a few of the 56 elementary schools in the villages were

---

*In 1956 this position was set forth in a statement approved by the Secretary of the Interior: "Economic policy in the territory shall be directed toward creating a sound basic economy that will be (1) suited to the needs and resources of Samoa, (2) will provide adequately for the food and monetary needs of the rapidly increasing population, and (3) will establish a firm foundation for self-government and maintain Samoa for Samoans. The territory's limited land resources and rapidly growing population make it essential that every effort be made to increase agricultural production, industrial development, and tourist trade" (quoted in Long & Gruening 1961: 23).

housed in something less than shanties: one-room Samoan fales, structures with domed, thatched roofs set on wooden poles and with no exterior walls.* Conditions were no better, and in certain seasons were even worse, in the handful of schools located in Western-style buildings, windowless affairs with the look of abandoned army barracks and with tin roofs that often made them hotter and more uncomfortable than the fales. Most of the 4,800 elementary school children brought their own mats and sat on floors of rough stones. The teacher's "chair," if any, was likely to be an old corned-beef crate, and the sum total of classroom equipment usually consisted of a weather-beaten blackboard and a wooden box holding a small supply of paper, pencils, and chalk.

Still more depressing to the new governor was the level of training of the Samoan teachers. Not a single teacher in the elementary schools had a mainland teaching certificate. Furthermore, the few with high school diplomas scored at about the fifth-grade level on academic achievement tests (Gillmore 1977).

Development of the system

Before the United States began its administration of the islands, education was handled primarily by missionaries and churches. The chief purpose of church schools, conducted by Samoan pastors and catechists, was of course religious instruction. But they also succeeded in bringing about a high rate of literacy among Samoans in their own language. The translation of the Bible into Samoan was thus an event of educational, as well as religious, significance.

In 1904, a government school was established on Tutuila near the naval station at Pago Pago, and the teaching of English now became a central focus of education. The school began with 40 students. A second school was opened in the area in 1906; this

*The report of the U.S. Senate Committee on Interior and Insular Affairs (which we cite as Long & Gruening 1961) put the number of schools at 47. However, the figure 56 is cited in the committee's supplemental report (Everly 1961), is supported by most of the official reports, and is the figure we use in this study.

one began with an enrollment of 64. In late 1914, the original government school was moved across the bay to Anua, where a $25,000 schoolhouse was built.

In the period before 1921 there was only one nonsectarian school in the three islands in the Manu'a group. This school, established on Ta'u in 1908, operated off and on until 1915, depending on whether a teacher was available. In that year a hurricane completely destroyed the school building, leaving those islands without a school for the next seven years.

What might be called a public school "system" had its beginning in 1921. On February 12th of that year, a Board of Education was appointed by the governor. Tutuila was divided into 15 school districts, and the Manu'a island into four. Soon after, the Nuuuli public school on Tutuila opened, followed shortly by village schools in other parts of the islands (Sanchez 1955: 80). By June 1922, when this program was completed, there were 19 elementary schools, with 1,567 students and 29 teachers—only five of whom were *palagis* (pahlongees), or foreigners. The estimated total annual expenditure was $9,600. The curriculum consisted of "reading, writing, and arithmetic in the English language" (DOE 1932: 7).

By 1932 five more elementary schools had been established, and the system now had an enrollment of 2,118 students, a teaching staff of 54, and a budget of $20,572. Four schools were added in 1937–38, ten in 1938–39, six in 1941, and one each in 1942 and 1943, making a total of 46 . However, only two of these schools provided education beyond the fourth grade; one offered classes through the eighth grade and the other classes through the fifth.

The Samoan school system was thoroughly disrupted by the war; after 1943, many schools shut down for the duration. But soon after the end of the war, the island administrators began to rebuild school buildings allowed to fall into disrepair or put to military use, and to reconstitute something resembling a school system. By 1951, when the Department of Interior assumed administrative responsibility, there were 46 village elementary

schools, four junior high schools, and one senior high school in
the territory. In addition, there was a vocational training school
for veterans and a one-year post–high school teacher training
institute.

Ten elementary schools were added in the next ten years, together with a combined elementary-secondary school. Supposedly this school (Fia Iloa), which more or less followed a standard stateside curriculum, was for the children of U.S. citizens
living in American Samoa, for whom English was the native language. In practice, however, almost half the enrollment was
Samoan or part-Samoan, with politics and personal influence
playing more than a small part in admissions.

Table 3 shows the growth of the Samoan school system between 1904 and 1980.

TABLE 3
Growth of American Samoa's School System, 1904–1980

Year	Number of schools[a]	Enroll-ment	Number of teachers Total	Samoan	Foreign	Annual budget	Per-pupil expendi-ture
1904	1	40	2	—	2	$ 1,000	$ 25.00
1914	2	144	—	—	—	1,764	12.25
1924	19	1,465	36	—	—	15,196	10.37
1934	19	2,280	50	43	7	19,429	8.52
1944	32	2,054	—	—	—	26,022	12.67
1954	55	5,139	175	170	5	247,186	48.10
1961	57	5,151	284	267	17	404,612	78.55
1964	46	6,653	388	293	95	1,975,507	297.00
1974	31[a]	7,687	460	410	50	8,592,503[b]	941.00[c]
1980	29[a]	8,067	670	566	104	10,082,055[b]	1,041.00[c]

SOURCE: 1904–44, Pedro Sanchez, "Education in American Samoa," Ph.D. dissertation, Stanford University, 1955, p. 82. 1954–61, Samoan Department of Education, annual report, 1962.

NOTE: The dollar amounts have been rounded to the nearest whole number. Some of these figures are at
lower levels than cited in the text. There was a decrease in enrollment between 1922 and 1924 and in the
number of schools and teachers between 1932 and 1934; both decreases were due to natural disasters, in
one case a severe epidemic that swept the islands and in the other a hurricane that leveled many school
buildings.

[a] The lower number of schools in these years reflects consolidations. In 1974 there were 26 elementary
schools, 4 high schools, and 1 special education school; in 1980 the number of elementary schools was
reduced to 24.

[b] Includes expenditures for food services and public libraries.

[c] Excludes expenditures for food services and public libraries.

What the table does not show is the poor quality of the system at the time Governor Lee arrived. He quickly saw that the physical plant was hopelessly inadequate and the teaching staff ill-trained. Not surprisingly, he also soon found that Samoan students lagged far behind their mainland counterparts in their level of achievement.

Elementary education was almost solely a responsibility of the villages. Many of them were isolated. Some were at least connected by footpaths, but for others the only contact with the outside was an occasional visit by a government supply boat. All the islands of the Manu'a group, as well as the north side of the island of Tutuila, were virtually inaccessible during much of the rainy season, which generally coincided with the height of the school year.

Infrequently, when conditions permitted, an inspector from the central administration visited the village schools. However, word of his coming usually preceded him by several hours, giving everyone a chance to "shape up" for the inspection. One of the authors of this report, for example, vividly remembers hiding out in a tapioca patch during an inspector's visit to her school. She was too young to have been in school at the time and was quickly dispatched "to the bush" when news of the inspector's impending visit reached the school.

What passed as a curriculum for these schools was based on a series of hand-me-down mainland textbooks that had been discarded as out-of-date. Samoan children read about snow, railroads, highways, and great cities with tall buildings. All this in a climate where the temperature rarely drops below 75°F, where there is nothing that faintly resembles a railroad, and where an occasional two-story building towers above the native houses. The world of Dick and Jane, in short, had little relevance to the Samoan youngster.

At the secondary level, the one senior high school could accommodate only about one-third of the graduates of the elementary program. As a result, some 300 Samoan youngsters each year were denied a full 12 years of education, something that had been promised to them by one U.S. administration after another and by their own Interior-approved constitution.

Finally, let us put the problem facing the new governor in 1961 in perspective by taking into account several factors that exercised a strong influence on the educational program over the years. The most important was the one we have already discussed: the record growth of the Samoan population. This phenomenal increase alone put a severe strain on the educational system. But it also meant that by the time Lee arrived more than half the young people of the islands were forced to migrate to Hawaii or the mainland in search of jobs. This in turn gave added emphasis to the need for fluency in the English language.

The requirement that English be the language of instruction, and that schools prepare youngsters to fit into an English-speaking economy, thus became even more of a central focus of the educational program. For years the Samoans had been promised, by a succession of governors and directors of education, an educational program that would bring their children up to mainland standards of proficiency in the English language. Yet the reality of the situation was that the average Samoan child only began to use English to any degree in about the third grade, at age nine or ten. Furthermore, he or she used it at most six hours a day; five days a week. Family tradition prohibited anything but Samoan at home, and the language of play, even on school grounds, was mostly Samoan. In brief, the "learning environment" worked in the opposite direction from the educational program. Teachers found they had to spend almost two months of each new school year simply catching up to where the class had been the previous year.

In the face of these overwhelming odds, the promise to bring Samoan performance up to stateside norms would have presented a formidable task for the best-equipped and best-staffed educational system. Given the learning environment in Samoa, it was virtually an impossibility.

The method of instruction was mostly rote learning—students or classes repeating after the teacher the material to be learned—the kind of teaching that a later report (Berry 1965) described as producing students who "can define a past participle but not use one." With inadequately prepared teachers and irrelevant textbooks (or no texts at all), errors in pronunciation and in English usage were simply passed on from one class to the next and from one generation to another.

It must also be recorded that U.S. administration of the islands over the years was consistent not only in its neglect of education but also in its *in*consistency. As we saw in Table 2, directors of education changed with about the same frequency as governors of the islands. Each new governor and each new director of education invariably arrived with "a new set of objectives" and a "reorganization plan," along with, more often than not, harsh words about the inadequacies of the previous administration. Changes introduced by one administration were summarily junked by the next, usually not more than a year or two later. As a result, the system was almost constantly in turmoil, with the only continuity provided by Samoan teachers who went about their daily tasks indifferent to changes at the top. One wise old chief, who had spent a lifetime in the educational system and later became its first Samoan director, was led to try to explain the situation to a visiting group of American educators. "Our educational system, contrary to the systems in Western Samoa and other countries," he said, "has been subjected to so many abrupt changes, so many beginnings all over again, that we have not been able to make as much progress as countries with less experience and less money. Perhaps the most important thing of all," he added, "would be continuity."

Another side of the school system

In retrospect, the school system that Governor Lee inherited appears to have been neglected, backward, and very much in need of change. But that observation is from a Western view-

point, and from outside the school system. It is well to ask how
the old Samoan school system looked from the *inside*.

There is no doubt that the schools were looked on with great
fondness and the teachers were highly regarded by many of the
pupils who attended those fale classrooms. One of the authors
of this book, Mere Betham, remembers the personal interest the
early Samoan teachers took in each student, and the practical
and useful instruction they gave in Samoan arts and crafts. She
writes:

There were times in the school day devoted to Samoan arts and
crafts, like learning to weave mats and to make 'Ava cups [from the
copra-coconut shells], to string shells and flowers into *ulas* [leis], and to
make balls out of coconut leaves, and so forth. A good many of the
finished crafts were sent as Christmas gifts from Samoan schools to
schools in the United States, which in turn would send back stateside
gifts. I recall this being one of the exciting experiences of my early
schooling.

One of my fond memories of earlier schooling is the interest the
teachers took in home-type projects, like taro and banana planting,
vegetable gardening, and similar activities. The teachers would come
on Saturdays to check our projects, and I recall being extremely excited
as I watched a few taro tops sprout. Those teachers who took time to
visit our home projects were a tremendous source of encouragement.

The classes those days were large, at least 30 in a class. More often
than not there would be one teacher for two grade levels. We did a lot
of singing and playing together, and it was taboo to go off by yourself at
any time during the school day. We kept an eye on one another.

The teachers I had *were good*, most of them. Everything was written
on the blackboard. For oral drill, the teachers would read out the
words, the sentences or paragraphs, and we would repeat them until
we got them right. Somehow, there was a sense of challenge in the way
they taught. They kept me so interested in school that I would not miss
a day of it for anything.

Ms. Betham goes on to note that the teacher's wooden chest,
which held all the school's supplies, also "contained the discipline stick." The chest often served as a desk for the teacher,
who had to sit on the floor to use it because there were no
chairs. Her report goes on:

Instead of notebooks, slates were used to write on. Students brought their own. There were many who went without. But that was not a serious concern because a lot of what we had to do in school in those days was committed to memory.

I recall that one of the first things we had to memorize and chant in English was the Lord's Prayer; and then the U.S. National Anthem. Songs like "America," "America the Beautiful," and others followed. English was the mandated language of instruction. However, at the Faife'au [church] schools, everything was taught in our own language, Samoan. We would go to the Faife'au school early in the morning before going to government school. We went back to the Faife'au school again in the afternoon, after government school.

Most of what we were supposed to learn in English in the early years of schooling consisted of English songs and rhymes that we were to memorize well. Formulas to solve basic mathematical problems were also committed to memory. I recall that I took great pride in being able to say my times-tables backwards and forwards, and several measurement tables as well. Later on, the learning of English was basically the rules of grammar. There was not much history or science taught; and whenever there was, it consisted of memorizing data, dates, and events.

School sites changed often in those days, even within the same village. "We must have changed school sites in my village at least four times as I went from first grade to sixth," Ms. Betham says. The village was responsible for providing school fales, and it was usually the fale of the *pulenu'u* (village mayor) that was used. Therefore, when a new pulenu'u was appointed, the school was moved. The village was also responsible for providing a place for the teacher to live.

Roofs of the school fales often leaked when it rained and it rained as often then as now in Samoa. There were times when we would take advantage of those rainy days to play tricks on our teachers . . . or at least we thought we were.

Going to school was looked upon as something we had to do because "it was done." It was not really until in high school that I came to realize that I was in school to prepare for further education somewhere outside of Samoa, to come back at the end of that training to serve and help my country and my people. This concept of "mission" was heavily drilled into our minds at the time by our parents and leaders of Samoa who came to talk to us in high school. It was not until then, as I recall, that the concept of another world outside of Samoa began to take shape clearly; for after all, those Naval officers and sailors who wore white all the time could not have just dropped out of the clouds.

Thus one recollection of the traditional Samoan school as it must have seemed to most other pupils at that time: a warm and happy place, a place where useful skills were learned and useful social customs and behaviors practiced, a school well designed for the kind of culture in which Samoans had lived for centuries until it began to change under the impact of the Western world and of the worldwide movement we call "development."

It was this kind of setting—this degree of contrast between past and present values, between what had been and what was coming to be, between something that had worked well in the past but was no longer adequate and something that had never been tried in this environment but might meet the needs of the future—that Rex Lee, a career civil service officer and not a politician, found when in 1961 he made his first visit as governor to Samoa. And it was against this background that he made his eventual decision to use television in an effort to achieve what 60 years of American educational programs had failed miserably to accomplish.

TWO

The Decision to Use Television

FACED WITH a staggering inventory of critical priorities of every kind on arriving in American Samoa, Governor Lee decided to place a complete overhaul of the educational system at the top of his list. He reasoned that there could be no real progress toward improving the lot of the Samoan people generally without a dramatic expansion of educational opportunities. But the situation called for *immediate* improvement. Most traditional reforms would not produce a significant change for at least a full school generation, or 12 years. Such a delay was unthinkable. It would mean that an entire generation of Samoan youngsters would be unprepared for productive lives in either Samoa or the States.

The governor believed he had an idea, a bold and dramatic one, for accomplishing his purpose. Why not use modern technology, specifically television, to provide the core of instruction and at the same time be the catalyst for a wholesale reorganization of the entire educational system? The idea intrigued him, even though (as he recalled in 1966) it met with a less-than-enthusiastic response from the more traditionally minded Department of Education staff.

Lee was not a total stranger to the use of instructional television. Back home he had observed with considerable interest how his daughter had learned to type via television and then went out and promptly got a job. Encouraged by her experience, Lee himself enrolled in and completed a television course in conversational French.

In discussing the idea with Americans on the staff of the department, Lee found only what he termed "a respectful silence." These mainland experts "felt that there were two alternatives: to pump additional money into the existing program to upgrade the system over a long period of time; or, through local teacher training and improved supervision, to replace all of the Samoan teaching and administrative staff with qualified educators from the mainland" (Lee 1968: 23).

To Lee's mind, these alternatives were the usual and dubious remedies he had heard for failing educational systems. Neither seemed to him acceptable for Samoa. Multiplying the existing inadequacies with more dollars would only lead to more costly programs that would still not meet the current crisis. And importing larger numbers of stateside teachers—no matter how well qualified—would involve replacing a corps of Samoans who had given their best to their work and who were leaders in their communities.

Television, moreover, had an advantage that took on considerable importance as the governor learned more about the situation in Samoa. "I was not only intrigued with what television might do for our children and teachers, but I also was convinced that it would be a useful tool in working with the community as a whole—a community that was grossly undereducated but one that America needed to bring into the 20th century in a hurry," he said. "The possibility of being able to carry adult educational programs to the entire island at once and to convey information to a majority of the people had great appeal" (Lee 1966).

The governor was not deterred by the lack of support from the mainland educational staff. With a vigor and determination that were to characterize his six-year term, he immediately set about getting the appropriate backing for the educational plan that was taking shape in his mind. As he noted later, "Three weeks after I arrived in American Samoa, with the encouragement of my wife and one non-educational staff member, I took the idea to Washington and presented it to Secretary of the Interior Stewart L. Udall. He believed the idea was a unique and

imaginative approach to our problem and worthy of exploration. He gave his immediate and complete support" (Lee 1966).

The Concurring Studies

In a sense the timing could hardly have been more propitious.
There was pressure, both in and outside the government of the
United States, for improving conditions in Samoa. In 1960, the
U.S. Senate Committee on Interior and Insular Affairs had resolved "to conduct a full and complete study and investigation
of conditions in American Samoa for the purpose of determining what should be done to improve economic and other conditions and give the people of American Samoa a greater amount
of self government." Senators Oren E. Long of Hawaii and Ernest Gruening of Alaska had visited the islands in December,
and their report to the committee was published the following
July, shortly before Lee's return to Washington to present his
plan for reorganizing the educational system.

The Long-Gruening report had a great deal to say about the
state of education in Samoa. And a supplemental comprehensive report by Dean Hubert V. Everly of the University of Hawaii
School of Education dealt with the subject in even greater detail.
The senators documented the deficiencies of the system and
called for immediate action to correct 60 years of neglect. "Education in American Samoa," they concluded, "must be attuned
to the needs of an evolving social and political structure and a
developing economy. It must serve a people who only relatively
recently were brought into contact with the demands and benefits of the modern world and later discovered their shortcom-
ings in the role of bridging the gap between the old and the
new" (Long & Gruening 1961: 99).

Their report went on to state: "Improving the quality of education means obtaining more and better trained teachers, improving the curriculum, and providing more adequately for
supplies, equipment, and other teaching aids necessary in raising the standards of instruction. At present the public school
system in American Samoa operates on a virtual shoestring.

Approximately $50 per year per child is allowed for the 5,000 public school children in [56] elementary and in 5 junior high schools in 7 locations" (*ibid.*, p. 100).

In an observation that was later to become relevant to curriculum plans, the committee noted that the Samoan language was heavily used in grades 1–3 in the public schools, with 75 percent of the teaching in Samoan and only 25 percent in English; was used fifty-fifty with English in grades 4–6; and was still used 25 percent of the time in grades 7–9 (junior high school). Only in the one highly selective high school was all instruction in English.

On the basis of this study, the committee recommended that all village elementary schools be consolidated into a much smaller number of better-supported, government-financed schools: "The government of American Samoa should be responsible for constructing permanent type elementary schools as it is for the others in the public school system. . . . The elementary school system would profit very materially by the consolidation of these village schools. Resources which are now diffused among the villages could be brought together under a consolidated system in ways that would increase teaching efficiency and improve the educational program" (*ibid.*, p. 102).

Dean Everly supported the committee's recommendations, pointing out that in most cases villages had been forced to take out loans from the government-financed Bank of American Samoa to build their schools. Once the funds were expended, nearly all the villages had defaulted on these loans, and the bank was no longer willing to make funds available for this purpose. Thus, the government ended up financing the school construction anyway.

Furthermore, the fragmentation of so small a geographical area into tiny village districts was "wasteful and inefficient," Everly declared. "Samoa does not need 56 schools in an area of 76 square miles. A fifth of this number properly housed and staffed would bring about an immediate superior education result" (Everly 1961: 138–39).

Everly observed that the standards of the Samoan schools were the lowest of any territory under the American flag, and that the teachers had gone without a salary increase for a decade. In fact, common laborers in their communities were actually better paid than the teachers were. The annual turnover of teachers was appallingly high, with one out of three leaving the profession each year. And although the Samoan constitution, approved by the Department of the Interior, clearly called for equality of educational opportunity, this was not being provided by the present system.

Dean Everly also faced squarely two other problems that had long plagued the Samoan educational system: whether to prepare students to live in a traditional Samoan society or in a modern Westernized world; and the relative merits of instruction at various grade levels in Samoan as opposed to English. On the question of the schools' overall direction, he had this to say:

> As one reviews the history of Samoa's schools, the conflict of ideas over their appropriate function is striking. Central to the conflict has been the extent to which education was to "Americanize" these Polynesian people. The desire to preserve the "best of Samoan culture" usually has been proclaimed in various policy statements. Nonetheless the determination that the schools should be "patterned after the American schools" and conducted in the English language was an equally dominant policy. The use of American textbooks did little to preserve Samoan culture. On the other hand, the ineptness of native teachers in handling the English language resulted in a low level of learning of the material contained in the "stateside" texts.
>
> It is pointless to urge on these American nationals the advantages of a simpler, more primitive way of life with schools to match. The acculturation process is well advanced and there is no turning back the clock. The examples of Hawaii and Guam are sharply before them. Samoans are well acquainted with both of these areas and have seen what education has accomplished in their Americanization. Education related to the needs of Samoan culture is drawing more and more toward identification with the American way of life. While one may regret such a development from an academic sociologic point of view, it is a fact of life and not a unique one in the Pacific by any means. (Everly 1961: 143–44)

On the question of the appropriate language of instruction, Dean Everly observed that this issue was hardly restricted to American Samoa:

It has been debated in many parts of the Pacific, and differing courses of action taken. The French generally have used their metropolitan language to the exclusion of vernacular languages from the curriculum in territories under their jurisdiction. The British Commonwealth countries have tended to teach English as a second language in dependent areas under their jurisdiction. The Americans in Samoa have fluctuated between these two policies. Had there been adequate books in the vernacular for the entering school pupil, it seems likely that the British policy would have been followed. Lacking these, educators in Samoa have attempted to use American texts in English, but to permit explanation of meanings in the vernacular until better mastery of English is achieved. (*Ibid.*, p. 145)

After an extensive review of the arguments for and against the use of English, particularly in the early grades, Everly concluded that the wisest approach from an educational point of view would be first to achieve literacy in Samoan, then to introduce English as a second language until in the higher grades it could be used almost exclusively:

Beyond the fact that the system does not adequately teach a U.S.-style course of study, it does not give due recognition to the long-stated objective: "to conserve the best of the Samoan culture." To do this adequately, literacy in Samoan is essential. The school is the only agency which can accomplish this. Following the accomplishment of basic literacy in Samoan, English should be introduced gradually until it becomes fully the language of instruction at the junior high school level. Using the aural-oral method, English can be introduced as a subject in the first two years. Beginning writing and reading skills in English should be deferred until the third and fourth years, when the concepts of such intellectual activity will have been established for the Samoan language.

The subject matter of the curriculum (math, science, and social studies) can be introduced gradually in the fifth and sixth years in the second language so that all formal instruction can be in English by the end of the 6-year elementary school period. (*Ibid.*, p. 147)

Everly supported his arguments by pointing out that the increasing emigration of Samoans to Hawaii and other areas of the

United States underscored the importance of the English language for them. The Samoans recognized this, he observed; and the fact that graduates of the elementary and district junior high schools were not generally proficient in English was an important cause of dissatisfaction with the existing school system. For that matter, he added, the Samoan teachers themselves had an inadequate command of the language—a statement that supported Governor Lee's own observations.

Among the other recommendations Everly made were that the free public educational system be extended to all children ages six to sixteen, that opportunities at the high school and vocational educational levels be tripled, and that the central government assume financial responsibility for schools at all levels, including elementary.

The National Association of Educational Broadcasters Enters the Picture

Encouraged by the report of the Senate committee and Everly's supplement to it, and supported by Secretary Udall, Lee returned to Congress with a request for $40,000 for a "feasibility study" to determine if his idea of using television was a valid one. The item was included in the Department of Interior's deficiency appropriation request, which also earmarked funds for the construction of four junior high schools and one senior high school and the construction and furnishing of 18 housing units for educational personnel (FY 1962).

Congressional approval was not long in forthcoming. With $40,000 available and the conviction that he was on the right track, Lee set out to find an organization or group that would give him the answers he needed. He first turned to the U.S. Office of Education, where a staff member provided him with the names of several nonprofit organizations qualified to conduct the kind of study he had in mind. From this list the governor chose the National Association of Educational Broadcasters (NAEB), a leading exponent of the use of radio and television for educational purposes and a Washington-based organization with a national reputation. The NAEB was not only willing but enthusiastic, and preliminary details of a contract were quickly worked out.

Shortly thereafter Lee returned to Samoa, where he promptly called a meeting of the traditional leaders of the island, the high chiefs and high talking chiefs of the villages. Many of them were not entirely certain what a television set was; some were skeptical, others politely respectful. But of one thing all were certain: they wanted a better education for their children and were willing to go along with almost anything that had the potential of achieving that goal.

In the meantime, the NAEB moved quickly into action. Its leaders consulted among themselves and assembled a team to conduct the feasibility study. It consisted of Vernon Bronson, director of research and development for the NAEB, as leader, assisted by William G. Harley, professor of radio-television education at the University of Wisconsin (who later became president of the NAEB); Lawrence H. Shepoiser, superintendent of schools, Wichita, Kansas; and William J. Kessler, professor of electronic engineering at the University of Florida and design engineer of the Florida Educational Television Commission. In addition, the group had the advice of Dr. Lowell D. Holmes, anthropologist and professor of sociology at the University of Wichita.

The NAEB team visited Samoa in late 1961 and rendered its report early in January 1962. Not surprisingly, Bronson and his colleagues found that television was feasible, and strongly recommended making it the core of instruction. More specifically, they recommended making television the major form of instruction for the first six grades and a regular supplementary vehicle for the last six. A television-based system of education, they concluded, provided the most likely means of (1) training Samoan teachers, (2) ensuring quality instruction by topflight stateside teachers for every child in every village, and (3) establishing, after a relatively high initial investment, a low-cost permanent educational facility, complete with a large library of tapes and other visual material. In short, ETV was seen as the fastest, most effective, and in the long run, most economical way of bringing the educational system up to desirable standards.

But the team went a great deal further. It called for a total revamping of the educational program: television was not the major component of the educational system it was proposing; what was being recommended was a new central curriculum, one that was relevant to Samoa and to its customs and people. "The existing instructional program in the elementary schools is in conflict with the mores, needs, and desires of the Samoan people," the NAEB group asserted, agreeing with the governor that nothing short of an all-out crash program was called for under the circumstances (NAEB 1962: 13).

For the most part, the major findings of the Bronson group closely paralleled those of Dean Everly, the Senate committee, and others. Among the deficiencies cited by the NAEB team were:

(1) A lack of clearly established goals for the schools

(2) A poorly defined elementary curriculum

(3) A failure to teach successfully the fundamental skills

(4) An elementary school program that provided no base for effective secondary education

(5) A limited and selective secondary school program

(6) An imprecise secondary curriculum that provided inadequate preparation for college or for effective employment

(7) A method of teaching English based on class drill

(8) A method of instruction emphasizing memorization with little attention given to the development of meaning and understanding

(9) A lack of appropriate instructional materials

(10) No relevant teaching materials in the elementary or secondary schools

(11) Totally inadequate school buildings and facilities

(12) A prevalence of poorly educated and unprepared Samoan teachers

(13) Inadequate supervision of instruction
(14) Ineffective in-service teacher training programs
(15) Unequal learning opportunities among village schools and secondary classrooms

Summing up its evaluation, the Bronson team concluded: "The elementary schools fall far short of teaching the fundamental skills of reading, science, and mathematics which serve as a base for the secondary school in achieving its goals, and the secondary school apparently accepts the child at the level at which it receives him and proceeds with the same materials upon the same base" (p. 13).

None of the instructional materials then in use were suitable for American Samoa, the team reported. Textbooks were cast-offs that had outlived their usefulness in the States, and were so completely concerned with a life unknown to the Samoan children as to have little meaning for basic instruction. Likewise, such audio-visual materials as were available were mostly donations from commercial concerns, and had virtually no relevance to the life and understanding of the Samoan child.

Turning to the subject of the use of English in the curriculum, an issue historically at the root of many of the system's problems, the Bronson team observed: "The children come to school at about seven years of age, and have no previous training in English nor any readiness program of any kind. Yet they are started off with a program of oral English which continues into a reading program on through the elementary grades. Both the oral English and the reading programs are administered by teachers who themselves do not speak English well and comprehend it even less. The result is that the children learn by rote."

Bronson and his colleagues went on to note that in the various villages they had visited no English was spoken after regular school hours. As a matter of fact, it seemed to them that any Samoan youngster who attempted to speak English in an after-school-hours group was likely to be derided by schoolmates and village elders alike. "There is no address by either the parents or the adults [sic] in the village to the students, or the students to the adults in English. Therefore it is obvious that English is being superficially imposed on children who are totally unprepared for it, and without an opportunity to practice it outside their formal situation," they concluded (p. 11). As a result, the scores of the children they tested in the eighth and ninth grades were close to the third-grade level in reading and oral comprehension.

The team made a sweeping series of recommendations to the governor, ranging from the establishment of a "firm educational policy to teach English as a second language while developing literacy and understanding in Samoan" to the reorganization of the school system into elementary schools covering grades 1–8 and high schools covering grades 9–12. The report also recommended that the islands' elementary and junior high schools be consolidated into 20 local school centers (p. 41).

With respect to television, the report recommended that the "new curriculum" should be in the planning for at least a year before the changeover. In the way of equipment and staff, it recommended the construction of a six-channel VHF television station operating through transmitters located atop Mount Alava, Tutuila's second-highest mountain; the establishment of a four-studio production center capable of turning out approximately 200 television lessons each week, complete with lesson guides, worksheets, tests, and materials; and the recruitment of approximately 150 curriculum specialists, engineers, and principals, along with television and research teachers, producers, artists, photographers, and printers.

Transmission from Mount Alava, the report noted, would reach every location on the main island of Tutuila plus the three islands of the Manu'a group. In a theme that also ran through Governor Lee's statements at the time, the team noted that this site would permit service to the schools of Western Samoa, which were assumed to be eager to participate.

Other recommendations of the report called for the development of a pre-school readiness program; the incorporation of the technical-vocational program into the high school; the development of a separate junior college to include the teacher training institute and the nurses' training school; the establishment of a continuing program of in-service teacher training; better recruitment and more careful screening of mainland educational personnel; school buildings with a separate room for each class; and a program of adult education by television with the twofold aim of increasing the general comprehension and use of English and creating a receptive home atmosphere for the in-school program.

Using the Senate committee's figure of an annual expenditure of $50 per pupil, and comparing this with the U.S. mainland average of roughly $487 (U.S. Office of Education figures for 1959–60), the Bronson team recommended an increase to $300 per year. It estimated that its recommendations would add approximately $680,000 per year to the operating cost of the existing system, or an increase of $123 per pupil.

With the children enrolled in the Samoan public schools at the present this [$300 per pupil] would produce an income of $1,650,000 per year. . . . If the present school budget is raised to twice its present amount, to a total of $800,000 per year, and the estimated cost of instructional television, with the additional personnel, would be added to this at the rate of $680,000 per year, this would make a total expenditure of $1,480,000 for public school instruction of 5,500 children in American Samoa. This would leave from the estimated budget $170,000 per year for the replacement of buildings and equipment. (NAEB 1962: 59)

Two persistent themes ran through the NAEB report. The first was that the initial step in any reorganization plan should be the development of a clear set of educational goals, a conclusion based on the premise that the lack of such goals was the principal cause of past failures. In this connection, Bronson and his colleagues observed: "The first significant fact brought to our attention was the lack of a firm policy relative to the goals of education in the Samoan schools." And in another context: "It is our belief that the lack of a firm policy regarding the goals of education has been one of the greatest contributing factors to the poor educational situation. In spite of the unique history of Samoa, and the peculiar interlacing of ideas and customs deriving from eighteenth century island life and twentieth century western life, we believe that *a firm and fruitful educational policy can be spelled out* in such a way that it can be a positive day-to-day guide to the administrators and teachers in the public schools" (pp. 3–4; emphasis added).

Bronson himself was even more explicit when, in a talk to new teachers in 1966, he told his audience, "The first step was to develop an educational policy that would be understood by everyone involved. *Up to this time there has been no such policy*" (emphasis added).

The second principal theme in the report was that only through a "crash" program could the situation be significantly improved. The necessity of such a program was emphasized several times. The team observed, in the introduction to its report, that it had tried to pin down exactly which things were inadequate and which methods inappropriate, and to suggest specific remedies *in terms of a complete rehabilitation of the educational system in a crash program*. And in one of its concluding observations, it noted that in spite of all the system's deficiencies, the members had found "a reservoir of talent, a high rate of intelligence, an eagerness to learn, and a potential motivation for self advancement that makes a crash rehabilitation of the educational system not only possible, but extremely desirable and feasible" (NAEB 1962:12).

Congress Supports the Plan

The completion of the NAEB study was appropriately timed. The Department of the Interior was just then preparing to go before the House of Representatives Appropriations Subcommittee with its budget request for fiscal 1963. Interior approved the program. A budget amendment was added by special letter requesting $2,579,000 for the construction of a six-channel television system in Samoa. The request also included $3,173,750 to begin the construction of 30 consolidated elementary schools, the remodeling of the one existing high school, and the founding of a demonstration school, a dependents' school, and a teacher training college. Funds for the construction and furnishing of living quarters for 53 additional stateside educators were also included in the budget request, along with operating costs anticipating the addition of 44 stateside employees at $347,000 annually, a move intended to upgrade the school system immediately while television facilities were being built.

A receptive Congress met the governor's budget request essentially as submitted, except for $1,000,000 of the amount for television construction. In that category, Congress provided $1,583,000 for the first three channels with the promise of an additional $1,000,000 if the system worked out as expected.

With appropriation hearings proceeding smoothly in Washington, Lee returned to Samoa and called his education officers together to present his plan in detail. It consisted of seven essential elements:

(1) Incorporating the junior high schools into an 8-4 system, with the elementary level covering the first eight grades and the secondary the final four

(2) Lowering the entering age to six years for the first grade

(3) Extending secondary school education to all students of high school age

(4) Constructing 26 consolidated elementary schools (six more than the NAEB had proposed: 20 on Tutuila, four in the Manu'a group, and one each on Aunu'u and Swains Island)

(5) Decentralizing the high school at Utulei by expanding to two other sites, at Leone and Manu'a

(6) Installing educational television in a far-reaching program of instruction for the elementary and adult levels

(7) Including Samoa under the provisions of the National School Lunch Act and the Book Depository Library Act

The NAEB study had emphasized the importance of at least a year's head start on curriculum planning and development before television was introduced into the schools. Accordingly, Lee lost no time in signing a contract with the NAEB for the purpose of setting the wheels in motion. He later was to comment: "As our engineers were climbing mountains, our curriculum people were entering some new educational country. A year before we broadcast our first signal, they were engrossed in devising new rules and methods for teaching. We threw away our old textbooks. In the United States, a child has a basic understanding of English when he enters a classroom. We had to teach English to children who came to us understanding only a few words or phrases" (Lee 1967b).

While the design and construction of the television system was moving ahead, work proceeded on other elements of the program. John Lyon Reid, a well-known San Francisco architect, was commissioned to draw up plans for the 26 consolidated elementary schools and the three high schools called for in Lee's master plan. All were designed in such a way as to blend the traditional Polynesian style with the modern acoustic and visual features that were essential to television teaching. Thus the high roof of the fale became a central architectural feature, along with separate rooms designed especially for television.

At the same time, to verify the findings of the NAEB study, Governor Lee invited Dr. Theodore Reller, dean of the school of education at the University of California-Berkeley, and a team of educators to consider the question of the educational content and fundamental direction of the new system. The other members of the Reller team were Professor Richard Lewis, an audio-visual expert from San Jose State College, and Lawrence H. Shepoiser, a member of the original NAEB team. We have not been able to locate any copies of the Reller team's report, but Lee has told us that it was essentially encouraging to the proposed system being developed under NAEB auspices. With this back-up support, all signals were now "go" for the most far-reaching modification of the Samoan educational system in more than 60 years of U.S. responsibility, and one of the boldest innovations undertaken in education anywhere in the world.

Alternatives to Television

In several of Governor Lee's statements and speeches, and even in the NAEB report recommending education-by-television for Samoa, there are references to the consideration of alternatives. However, so far as we can tell, no careful, detailed cost analyses were made of other possible approaches; nor, apparently, did economic considerations play a significant role in the decision that was made. In fact, John Vaizey, a distinguished British educational economist, has since pointed out (Schramm et al. 1967: 20–21) that a very large amount of training could have been done for the cost of the television system.

Vaizey based this conclusion on the estimated costs of four other approaches that might have been taken. One possibility he considered was the replacement of all Samoan teachers with fully qualified American teachers. This would have achieved the immediate results the governor and his supporters wanted but would have cost on the order of $3,400,000 to $5,000,000 annually for salaries, transportation, new housing, and other expenses. Consequently, such a program would have been more expensive than television. In addition, it would have had the undesirable social effect of displacing several hundred Samoan teachers, many of whom had spent 20 years or more in the system. Vaizey also considered, as a variation of this approach, the hiring, on a stepped-up program of training, of fully qualified Samoan teachers, at an estimated annual cost of between $2,000,000 and $2,800,000. Thus in 1966, the year on which he based his study, an adequately equipped and staffed school system would have cost some $300 per pupil using Samoan teachers and $660 per pupil with stateside teachers.

The second approach he considered would have been less expensive but would not have produced the desired quick results. It involved the development of college-level work in Samoa to train a pool of fully qualified local teachers. Vaizey put the costs of such a project at roughly $600,000 a year for the first ten years, with a continuing annual expenditure of at least $240,000 thereafter.

As a third possibility, Vaizey estimated the costs of upgrading the Samoan teaching staff by instituting an in-service program for the existing teachers and easing the requirement of the U.S. standard for new entrants to the teaching profession. This plan would have delayed still further the achievement of mainland standards; but at $72,000 a year (figured on the basis of 1966 costs), it was the cheapest of the four alternatives studied.

Finally, Vaizey considered the possibility of employing perhaps 100 U.S. teachers, to be placed in key positions throughout the system, parallel with an in-service training program aimed at raising the qualifications of the Samoan teachers to stateside standards.

At the time of this study, the direct annual cost of Samoa's television system was $1,200,000.* For that amount, by Vaizey's reckoning, it would have been possible to hire 120 to 160 additional palagi teachers or, alternatively, to hire fewer outsiders —say 100—and to pay for an extensive program to train Samoan teachers in the States. But then, as he correctly perceived, "when the decision was made among these alternatives, it was made partly on the basis of certain non-economic considerations: (a) the desirability of introducing so many more United States teachers into the Samoan schools; (b) the desirability of a maximum rate of change; (c) the probable impact of television in bringing about change, both in the schools and in the development of the island generally."

One possibility that Vaizey did not discuss was the use of radio either as the direct instructional medium or as a supplement to a much less extensive television system. In fact, there is nothing in the record to indicate that such a program was ever given serious consideration, but it was perhaps worth some

*Note, however, that this is the figure for current outlays and is exclusive of capital charges for depreciation and notional interest of roughly $225,000. The true cost of the system is covered in detail in Chapter Nine.

thought. A radio-based system, it seems to us, would have had distinct advantages. For one thing, such a system would have cost about one-fifth as much as television. This, in general, has been the experience around the world. For another, it would have put far less of a burden on studio teachers than television. In addition, it would have served the central educational goal of teaching English as a second language almost as well as television, providing, as television has, native English-speaking teachers in even the most remote classroom, permitting oral English drill, and so forth. On the other hand, radio would certainly have been less dramatic and therefore less likely to attract attention and excite people, including the members of Congress; and so, in the long run, Congress might have been less willing to appropriate funds for new schools, for electricity for all the islands, for roads, and so on. In addition, school radio broadcasting had a rather poor reputation in the United States in the early 1960's, whereas television looked like a shiny new tool with great potential for in-school instruction and the not insignificant potential of attracting a sizable evening audience.

In Retrospect

Reading this account, one can hardly fail to be impressed by the goodwill and benevolence behind these decisions, by the speed at which the concerned officials were willing to act, and by the boldness of the decisions themselves. Yet the element of speed, in particular, raises uneasy questions. Was enough time given to exploring the alternatives? Was a crash program after all the best solution? Could—and should—more have been done in the way of clarifying goals before the project got under way and in bringing more Samoans into the decision making?

It is easy to look back over 15 years and say that decisions made at the time should have gone another way. Certainly they were made then by people who were aware of the state of the art and deeply concerned about the quality of education in Samoa. Nevertheless, these initial decisions cast their shadow over the entire project. By specifying a crash program they largely determined that most of the teaching would be in English, because there would be too little time either to prepare the necessary study materials in Samoan or to find and prepare many television teachers to teach in Samoan. By hurrying over the problem of goals, they lost a golden opportunity to clarify the ambivalence of the Samoan viewpoint toward education— that it should at one and the same time prepare children to live in the Western world and in the Samoan world, to be at home in an English-speaking modern civilization and to cherish and continue Samoan culture. And in choosing television they selected not only the most dramatic of the available alternatives, but also the most expensive and the one in which educators had the least experience. To make it work they were willing to multiply by six the average annual expenditure per student and to spend more on the physical plant and equipment of the schools than had been spent in the entire history of Samoan public education up to that time. In retrospect we can perhaps question the prudence of the decision, but certainly not its good intentions or its courage. It was a bold experiment indeed.

THREE

Introducing the New System

WORKING against a deadline of the opening of a new school year and faced with obstacles that television engineers had seldom encountered before (including high humidity and torrential rains, rugged jungle-like terrain, and little or no electrical power in outlying areas), the NAEB's engineers achieved what seemed to many the impossible. By October 1964 they had brought into being a project conceived only two years before: a full-fledged television system capable of reaching even the most remote villages of the six islands of American Samoa, along with parts of Western Samoa.

But technically stunning as the feat was, the real significance was the introduction of the medium itself. For the coming of television ushered in a new era into what had been a relatively isolated part of the South Pacific. Looking back, on the occasion of the dedication of the new system several months later, Governor Lee observed: "Some friends have asked me why we wanted to disturb the peace and tranquility of our islands with world news. The concept of a sheltered and primitive Polynesian community, happily enjoying simple pleasures, may not have been too unrealistic early in this century when man traveled the South Seas by sail and steam. The world was simpler then. In our jet-missile-and-satellite age, however, there can be no real sheltered community, not even in the South Seas" (Lee 1966).

King Taufa'ahau Tupou IV of Tonga echoed this theme in his speech at the same dedication: "Our world used to end where the waters of the sea lapped at the sands of our islands. Today events far across the seas affect our daily lives minutes after they happen."

But many were apprehensive about the effects on "Fa'a Samoa," the Samoan way of life. One of these was Brother Herman, a Catholic priest who had spent a lifetime among the Samoan people. Watching the first flicker on the television tube, he commented to one of the American technicians: "At last the palagi has his nails into the heart of the Samoan" (Carroll to Fellows, undated memorandum).

On Monday, October 5, a day after the transmission of the first test signal, channels 2 and 5 began regular broadcast service; channel 4, the last of the initial three channels, began regular service two months later, on December 2. Each channel operated with a visual effective radiated power of approximately 40,000 watts.

As we have noted, the task had not been an easy one. Efforts to get construction materials to the top of the 1,603-foot Mount Alava for the transmission towers had been repeatedly frustrated. First a road had been attempted, but that had to be given up because of the rugged terrain plus frequent heavy flooding. Airlifting the necessary materials and equipment by helicopter was tried next, but strong air currents on top of the mountain forced the abandonment of that idea. Finally, after a number of makeshift devices to get personnel and supplies transported to the site, a 5,100-foot aerial tramway was constructed across Pago Pago harbor.

In the meantime, construction was going ahead on a studio building at Utulei on a site next to the Department of Education and near the high school. In record time for Samoa, a construction crew was completing work on an air-conditioned two-story building containing approximately 16,400 square feet of usable space, plus an annex of approximately 3,100 square feet. Modern even by stateside standards at the time, the building was designed around a two-story-high central core measuring 52 feet by 37 feet, which provided space for a master control room on the first floor with one large office above for producer-directors, studio teachers, research teachers, and writers. The building also housed four studios, each 25 feet by 30 feet and each with its own 7-foot by 11-foot control room. Grouped around the outside of the central area were offices for the various service units: library and viewing room, photographic and art departments, publication department, engineering storage and work space, and offices for the directors of elementary and secondary education, the director of ETV operations, the chief engineer, and the production manager.

When fully operational in 1965, the production facility was equipped with the latest in television hardware, including eight image orthicon cameras; five vidicon cameras, one of them mounted vertically to photograph illustrations; four automatic slide projectors and four 16mm motion picture projectors; four optical multiplexers; ten videotape recorders; four audio consoles with turntables; and five cartridge audio tape recorders. Three and eventually six microwave links were designed to carry signals from the master control room to the transmitter on the mountain.

By then, engineers had solved the other difficult problem involved in the decision to use television, that of bringing electricity to the sites selected for village consolidated schools. Before the decision was made—and indeed many said one of the most important considerations leading to it—electricity had been confined to the Pago Pago bay area. Consequently, the remainder of Tutuila plus the Manu'a islands now had to be electrified.

On still another front, work moved ahead at a steady pace on the first of the 26 village schools. Designed especially for television, the schools nevertheless preserved the fale style, with high shingled roofs and open sides to allow air to circulate freely in the hot, humid Samoan climate. Each building contained two classrooms, back to back, with a blackboard wall forming the partition between them. A 23-inch television set was encased in the opposite wall high enough to be viewed by all students.

To the surprise of those in Washington used to high cost over-

TABLE 4

Expansion of American Samoa's Elementary School System, 1964–1973

School and village	School and village
1964	1966
Alataua-Lau, Nua	Pavaiai, Pavaiai
Leatele, Fagasa	Aua, Aua
Lupelele, Ili'ili	Manulele Tausala, Nu'uuli
Olomoana, Aoa	Matatula, Tula
1965	Faleaso, Faleaso
Mauga-o-Alava, Vatia	Ofu, Ofu
Lauli'i, Lauli'i	Fitiuta, Fitiuta
Pago Pago, Pago Pago	Olosega, Olosega
Aunuufou, Aunu'u	Aasu, Aasu
Leone Midkiff, Leone	Fagamalo, Fagamalo
Masefau, Masefau	1967
Matafao, Fagaalu	Alofau, Alofau
Siliaga, Aoloau	1973
Afono, Afono	Poloa, Poloa
	Swains, Swains Island

NOTE: The village of Fagal'i used television in its fale school from 1964 until 1973, when that school was replaced by Poloa.

runs, the initial three-channel system came in at $1,727,000, an overrun of less than 1 percent, which a pleased Congress permitted to be made up from savings in other government projects in Samoa. In late 1966, the chairman of the House Appropriations Subcommittee and the chairman of the Senate Interior Committee helped to dedicate the system and its first three channels. Shortly thereafter, the $1,000,000 promised for the additional three channels was appropriated.

At the time KVZK-TV went on the air in October 1964, only four consolidated schools were in operation, in the villages of Nua, Ili'ili, Fagasa, and Aoa. Within three years the total had been brought to 24, only two short of the projected 26 (see Table 4). During this period, two new high schools were opened as well, first at Leone and then on Manu'a. A third high school, at Fagaitua, and the last two consolidated schools were brought into the system in the 1970's. All were well equipped to receive television instruction.

Program Production and Scheduling

Channels 2, 4, and 5, the three channels put on the air in 1964, began their broadcast day at various times between 7:30 A.M. and 8:00 A.M. They operated on intermittent schedules with a break between lessons of five to ten minutes until 1:30 in the afternoon. This schedule provided the core of all instruction for the elementary schools. In 1965, the system was extended to the high schools with the addition of three new channels, 8, 10, and 12.

With the exception of activity and study periods, most class hours in the Samoan schools followed a common pattern: a few minutes to prepare the class for the upcoming programs; the telecast itself, which varied in length from 8 to 25 minutes; and a

Classroom and Telecast Schedule, Level 4
(Grades 7 and 8), September 1965

7:30–7:40	Opening exercises
7:40–7:50	Study period
7:50–8:00	Preparing for mathematics
8:00–8:20	Mathematics telecast
8:20–8:45	Follow-up mathematics
8:45–8:50	Preparing for sound drill and oral English
8:50–9:10	Sound drill and oral English telecast
9:10–9:15	Preparing for language arts
9:15–9:35	Language arts telecast
9:35–10:15	Preparing for science (MWF)
	Preparing for hygiene and sanitation (TTh)
10:15–10:35	Science or hygiene and sanitation telecast
10:35–11:00	Follow-up for science or hygiene and sanitation
11:00–11:05	Preparing for physical education
11:05–11:30	Physical education activities (telecast 11:05–11:20 M)
11:30–11:40	Wash hands
11:40–11:45	Preparing for oral English
11:45–12:00	Oral English telecast
12:00–12:30	Lunch
12:30–12:40	Preparing for social studies
12:40–1:00	Social studies telecast (MWF)
	Fa'alogo Ma Aoa, a show-and-tell program (Th)
1:00–1:30	Follow-up for social studies; evaluation and dismissal
1:45–3:00	In-service for teachers, telecast 2:00

TABLE 5

Daily Schedule of Classroom Television in American Samoa, 1966

ELEMENTARY SCHOOL

Level 1 (Grade 1)	Level 2 (Grades 2–4)	Level 3 (Grades 5–7)	Level 4 (Grade 8)
Samoan reading 8:00–8:10	Sound drill and oral English 7:40–8:00	Sound drill and oral English 7:45–8:05	Mathematics 8:00–8:20
Mathematics 8:40–8:55	Language arts 8:15–8:30	Mathematics 8:15–8:35	Sound drill and oral English 8:50–9:10
Our own world 9:50–10:05	Mathematics 9:30–9:45	Language arts 9:15–9:35	Language arts 9:15–9:35
Sound drill and oral English 10:25–10:40	Samoan reading and writing 10:25–10:40	Science (MWF) Hygiene and sanitation (TTh) 10:40–11:00	Science (MWF) Hygiene and sanitation (TTh) 10:15–10:35
Samoan writing 11:35–11:45	Living Samoa 12:00–12:15	Social studies 12:20–12:40	Physical education (M) 11:05–11:20
Play and learn 12:15–12:30	Sound drill and oral English 12:50–1:05	Oral English 1:10–1:25	Oral English 11:45–12:00
Sound drill and oral English 1:00–1:15			Social studies (MWF) Fa'alogo (Th) 12:40–1:00

HIGH SCHOOL

Grade 9	Grade 10	Grade 11	Grade 12
Structural English 7:45–8:10	Structural English 7:45–8:10	English III 7:45–8:10	English IV 9:40–10:05
Geography 8:40–9:05	Geography 8:40–9:05	History 8:40–9:05	Government 10:35–11:00
General mathematics 9:40–10:05	General mathematics 9:40–10:05	Mathematics 12:15–12:40	Mathematics 12:15–12:40
Basic science 11:20–11:45	Basic science 11:20–11:45	Biology 1:10–1:35	Biology 1:10–1:35
Homemaking 12:15–12:40	Homemaking 1:10–1:35		

NOTE: Here as in later tables, school years are referred to by the ending year, i.e. this schedule is for the school year 1965–66.

TABLE 6
Progression from Levels to Grades in American Samoa's Elementary Schools, 1964–1974

Level	Grades in school year ending:[a]									
	1965	1966	1967	1968	1969	1970	1971	1972	1973	1974
1	1st 2d 3d	1st	1st	1st	1st	1st	1st	1st	1st	1st
2	4th 5th 6th	2d 3d 4th	2d	2d	2d	2d	2d	2d	2d	2d
3	7th 8th	5th 6th 7th	3d 4th	3d 4th	3d 4th	3d 4th	3d	3d	3d	3d
4		8th	5th 6th 7th 8th	5th 6th 7th 8th	5th 6th 7th 8th	5th 6th 7th 8th	4th	4th	4th	4th
5							5th 6th	5th	5th	5th
6							7th 8th	6th 7th	6th	6th
7								8th	7th 8th	7th
8										8th

[a] I.e., the year shown as 1965 is the school year 1964–65; the year 1966, the school year 1965–66; etc.

follow-up period for explanation, review, drill, or other class-room activity. The schedule reproduced below both illustrates this pattern and indicates the inflexibility in the instructional program. Table 5 lists the broadcast schedule for all grades in the same period.

Before we go any further, a word about the four-level system of instruction that was adopted for the elementary schools. According to Vernon Bronson, the decision to depart from the traditional organization by grades was taken when "it became apparent that there was little difference in the achievement levels of the children in the first and second grades or those in the third and fourth grades," so that "for the first year at least and perhaps for the second, instead of having eight grades we could have four levels of instruction in the elementary schools" (Bronson 1966: 17). It is worth noting that this decision cut in half the number of programs that had to be produced the first year (still a formidable number, as we shall see later in this chapter). However, it also meant that for the most part television lessons could not be recorded and used a second year because at least half the students in a given level would already have seen the lesson the previous year. Consequently, new material had to be prepared for each level each year. Furthermore, it had to be simple enough for new students entering the level and yet stimulating enough for those in their second year. The assignment was not an easy one.

Acknowledged to be a temporary expedient while the students were improving their English language competency, the level system was gradually modified until the standard eight grades were in effect. Table 6 shows the progression from levels to grades from 1964 to 1975. This progressive shift to grades made possible the recording of lessons to be used again the following year and, therefore, put a somewhat lighter annual burden on the production staff; but it also required a larger number of different programs.

Telecasts were usually longer for higher levels—ranging from 8 to about 15 minutes in the first two levels, 20 in the third and fourth, and 25 in high school. All together they added up to about a third of all class time (see Table 7). The lower grades, even with their shorter class-time telecasts, had many more televised classes and so spent more of their classroom time watching the screen than the other children.

By using six channels and leaving open time between broadcasts, it was possible to fit the television schedule to the preferred hour-long classroom schedule. In the early years, it was also possible, with few exceptions, to serve the same grade level with the same channel all day. Thus, the amount of television required did not strain the technical capacity of the facilities, although it did strain the production capacity of studio teachers and producers.

During the first years of the system, approximately 170 programs were produced locally each week, representing 53.5 hours of air time and some 180 hours of studio time. All programs intended for use in the schools were prerecorded and broadcast from videotape. After the first year, the weekly television schedule was augmented with the use of the videotapes of 51 school programs (mostly language drills) from the preceding year. This represented a weekly output of 221 instructional programs, or about 61.25 hours.

The station also broadcast two to four in-service programs each week, varying in length from 30 minutes to one hour, plus four to six hours of evening programming six nights a week, which normally included six to eight different local programs, totaling approximately three hours. The station was thus responsible for about 88 hours of programming a week, two-thirds of which was new production. Looked at in another framework, the instructional programming alone amounted to more than 6,100 telecasts a year, or about 2,000 hours of air time. In comparison, not even the largest U.S. commercial stations of the day produced local programs at anything like this rate.

This obviously put a severe demand on television teachers and producers-directors. Studio teachers on the average were

TABLE 7

Hours Devoted Weekly to Classroom Television
in American Samoa by Grade Level, 1966

Level or grade	Number of telecasts[a]	Total hours of TV instruction	TV as percentage of class time
Level 1	45	7.55[b]	33%
Level 2	40	7.55	33
Level 3	35	9.20	35
Level 4	35	9.25	35
Grade 9[c]	20	8.20	29
Grade 10[c]	20	8.20	29
Grade 11	20	8.20	29
Grade 12	20	8.20	29

[a]Sound drill and oral English, shown as one program in Table 5, were actually discrete telecasts and are here counted as separate units.
[b]I.e., 7 hours, 55 minutes.
[c]Some ninth and tenth grades took homemaking as an optional broadcast five days a week, raising their television time to 10 hours, 25 minutes, and their percentage to 36.

responsible for between 10 and 15 programs a week, compared with a normal stateside load of around three to five. Some teachers produced up to 20 programs. Producers-directors were assigned to as many as 20 programs a week, with a normal load of 15 to 18. By any standard, it was a backbreaking load indeed. Moreover, apart from the wear and tear on the people involved, that load helped determine the shape of the telecasts: most were in the form of lectures with such visuals as could be quickly made or easily collected. Film clips were rarely used, and production constraints did not permit extensive rehearsals or other such uses of studio time and equipment. Needless to say, there was very little, if any, pretesting and remaking of programs.

Curriculum Planning and Design

We have taken a quick look at program production and class scheduling. What was the educational rationale that under-girded these efforts? The NAEB, in its original report, made a strong case for at least a year of advance planning and teacher training as a prerequisite to the introduction of television, especially on the scale contemplated in Samoa.

But this was not to be. In the rush to get the new system under way, the requirement was brushed aside. Although some planning did take place about a year in advance, the committee charged with the curriculum for the elementary program did not set to work until late in the spring of 1964. Similarly, the curriculum committee for the high school program started its work in the summer of 1965 for classes that were to begin that fall.

Furthermore, these committees faced no ordinary task; they were asked, in effect, to redesign an entire instructional program from the bottom up. The plan initially conceived by the NAEB called for curriculum planning committees made up of American supervisors and studio teachers and the best of the Samoan classroom teachers and supervisors. As it worked out, however, the involvement of classroom teachers was more on paper than in fact. For whatever reasons (time pressures, inadequate qualifications, lack of interest, etc.), classroom teachers were pretty much bypassed in the curriculum planning process. So too were representatives of the churches and local leaders with many years of experience in Samoa and a firsthand knowledge of Samoan culture.

To supplement the work of the general curriculum committees, teams were organized for subjects at each grade level. Each of these teams was supposed to consist of a television teacher, a research teacher, a producer-director, and a representative of the classroom teachers. However, here too the classroom teachers were limited to playing a paper role; in practice their participation could be described as nonexistent.

For guidance and approval, the two general curriculum committees reported to an overall policy group made up of the director of education and his key staff, all principals and vice-principals, and all supervisors. As each of the curriculum committees developed its materials, it referred them to this policy group, which often returned them with suggestions for change.

Each curriculum committee was charged with preparing a set

of guidelines for the content to be covered and the general approaches to be used before setting to work on detailed lesson plans. This assignment reflected another decision of central importance to the program as it developed in the early years: to convene the committees each summer for the specific purpose of totally revising the previous year's guidelines. That decision was based on three premises: that standards would be rising from year to year, that American studio teachers participating in their first curriculum committees would be unfamiliar with Samoan pupils, and that the Samoan teachers, though familiar with their pupils, would be unfamiliar with curriculum planning. Since, with the exception of George Pittman—an English language–teaching expert of the South Pacific Commission, an organization of nations with interests in the area—no curriculum specialists had participated in the initial planning, it was also decided that, for the first few years at least, the curriculum too would have to be reviewed and redone each summer. A consequence of this decision was that telecasts had to be different each school year, and this was another reason why few programs could be saved on tape for later use.

All television lesson plans were prepared in considerable detail, including not only directions for the studio teacher, but also instructions for the Samoan classroom teacher, who was told precisely what to do to prepare for the lesson, what to do during the lesson, and what to do (and what not to do) after the lesson. Thus, although the students spent only about two hours of each school day actually watching the screen, all instruction revolved around the broadcast curriculum.

A comprehensive packet was prepared for each lesson and for each day. It contained course plans and instructions, plus supplemental reading and practice materials produced in the Instructional Learning Center, as the television center was known. These supplementary materials replaced the stateside textbooks that had been discarded. The packet was supposed to be in the hands of each classroom teacher several days before the telecast; but it often arrived days, and in some cases weeks, after the television lesson. Some delays occurred because of missed deadlines by various supporting units, others because of difficulties in reaching many of the remote schools. Whatever the cause, these delays not only frustrated the best intentions of the television teachers and curriculum planners; they also contributed to undermining the system with the classroom teachers who had to improvise under conditions that permitted little flexibility and discouraged innovation. Understandably, many became disenchanted with the entire system and pressed for more local classroom autonomy.

The assignment given to the original curriculum committee was an awesome one. At the first elementary curriculum planning session in early 1964, Bronson, by then fully in charge of the educational transformation and wielding more power than the director of education himself, told the committee that the basic approach to all instruction "must be one of conceptual teaching rather than factual teaching, [one based] upon the development of ideas, understandings, insights, and attitudes, rather than upon factual matter that has a tendency to vary its validity from day to day and from year to year" (Bronson 1966: 14).

In essence, Bronson's instructions were to turn away from the old system of rote learning, which had characterized Samoan education from the days of the missionaries, to an approach more closely associated with Western education theory at that moment: concept learning and the development of reasoning. Such a change, moreover, was to be made in the context of a crash program aimed at producing immediate results. It is little wonder that Governor Lee was to comment of the task:

When it came to people who could build and implement a new curriculum for an entire system, the supply of personnel was very sparse. At that time nowhere in the U.S., or elsewhere in the world, was television being used to provide the core of instruction for an entire school system. There were no texts, no reference material. Our small group of specialists, recruited from widely divergent backgrounds, had to write the text and become the new authorities in this field. (Lee 1968)

In announcing the decision to adopt an instructional television system, Lee and others had emphasized its potential for "saving" (or rehabilitating) Samoan teachers who might otherwise have been dismissed because of inferior qualifications. To this end, Bronson and his colleagues set aside a daily period following the school broadcasts for televised instructions on how to handle the next day's lessons and instituted a formal training program via hour-and-a-half telecasts every Wednesday and Thursday. The after-hours in-service program was intended to be a major element in upgrading the Samoan teaching force. But the example provided by the television teaching itself, as it turned out, was a better means to that end. Indeed, as David Gillmore and other subsequent participants have observed, that example may have had a more profound effect on improving the quality of the classroom teacher's work than any other single element of the program.

Early Policy Changes and Developments

The NAEB team, in its 1962 report, had recommended the following program (the emphasis in all the quoted material in this section is ours):

Oral English can be introduced in the primary grades along with the teaching of Samoan concepts and Samoan reading and writing skills. This would lead naturally into the teaching of reading and writing in English in the third and fourth years and make such activity a great deal more meaningful and realistic to the Samoan children. For these reasons and for many others which have been set forth in previous reports we reiterate that in the formulation of a firm policy by the government *the teaching of English as a second language and not as the prime language should be the base of the policy.* (NAEB 1962: 17)

Yet Bronson, in his instructions to the curriculum committee a little more than a year later, appeared to take quite a different approach, to wit: "Another thing for the Curriculum Committee to consider is the idea of *teaching the Samoan language as a second language,* and stressing the correct use of the Samoan language so that it may be equated with English in the early grades of the

school, and thus enhance the early comprehension and utiliza-
tion of English as a working language." And again: "Language
will be taught in the first grade with concentration, of course, at
this point on oral English. However, a superficial understanding
of the Samoan school system indicates *that the English language
in all of its facets—speaking, reading, writing, and expression—must
be taught in all of the elementary grades, one through eight"* (Bronson
1966: 10). And later, in another speech, he sounded the same
note: "The curriculum planning committee was firm in its conviction that in order to achieve an adequate program of instruction English *would have to be emphasized as the language of instruction"* (*ibid.*, p. 15).

There seems to be some doubt about whether this apparent
change in direction was actually carried out in practice. Many of
those who participated in the early stages of the television project maintain that it was not. The emphasis, they say, was as
originally conceived, with teaching conducted in Samoan in the
first three years (with the exception of oral English), and English introduced as a second language in the fourth.

It is difficult now to be absolutely certain. If any minutes were
kept of curriculum committee meetings, they have been lost.
However, the change, if there was one, appears to have coincided with the arrival in 1964 of George Pittman as a consultant
to the system's planners. A longtime lecturer at Victoria University in Wellington, New Zealand, and a language-teaching spe-
cialist for the South Pacific Commission, Pittman was a strong
advocate of the aural-oral approach to English language instruction. He developed what became known as the Pittman system
for teaching English, a system later modified and known in
Samoa as the Pittman/Tate Method in recognition of the contribution of Gloria Tate, a colleague of Pittman's on the South Pacific Commission and chief author of the syllabus and instruction books.

In essence, the curriculum as developed for the Samoan
school system in 1964–65 made instruction in English—certainly after the third grade—*the core of all instruction* in every

subject. As Bronson put it: "It was then definitely determined that the subject matter had to be geared to language proficiency, and that no vocabulary could be used in instruction that was not familiar to the students at the particular grade level. This simply meant that whatever subject was being taught, the first attention must be given to the understanding and use of the English language" (Bronson 1966: 16).

Tate subsequently stated the requirement in even more specific terms. Writing of the introduction of English in South Pacific cultures, she said: "No subject taught in English can exist in a vacuum, and all relevant aspects of the Curriculum—English reading, written English, and to a great extent other subjects taught in English—should be correlated or co-ordinated with the English syllabus at each stage. Only thus can the English language become an effective vehicle for learning" (Tate 1971: 38).

In effect, what this meant was that no teacher of any subject, at any grade level, could use words or phrases in his or her instruction that had not already been introduced in the English language course at that grade level. It made an already inflexible system still more inflexible and introduced a requirement that many television teachers later were to find seriously inhibiting in their subject areas.

Also, in the initial educational design, daily feedback from the classroom was to be a significant feature of the new system. The theory was advanced by Governor Lee in a 1968 article in *Compact* in these words: "When lessons are not effective, the first assumption is that the instructional program and not the student has failed. Efforts are made to correct the imperfections of the system as they occur, almost on a daily basis. Few methods of instruction anywhere are so subject to modification on the basis of student achievement (or lack of it) as in Samoa."

As part of the plan to achieve feedback, teachers, working with the stateside principals, were asked to evaluate all television programs for each grade or level. Some were reasonably regular in sending in formal evaluation sheets; most were not. With problems of their own in contending with a full teaching day, often without the promised supplemental instructional packets, most teachers and a good many principals contented themselves, after the first month of two, with observing how well the television broadcasts were received, and seldom bothered to comment on the content of the instruction. In any event, the evaluation sheets were only collected when the next week's programming package was delivered to the schools, so that they arrived at the Instructional Learning Center after production was already several weeks beyond the particular segment involved. As a consequence, little immediate change could be made on the basis of the teachers' comments, leading some to conclude that their suggestions were being ignored and not really wanted.

Two types of evaluation sheets were used in the first years of the television program. One was an open-ended form asking for general comments on what things went well and what did not, with respect to both the telecast and the follow-up discussion. The other form was more specific and called for the teacher or principal to check a number of possible responses to materials, the telecast, and the subsequent classroom activities.

The feedback plan also contemplated having the studio teachers visit classrooms on a fairly regular basis. But again the heavy production schedule and the difficulties of transportation put this idea to rest, and the studio teachers were able to make only an occasional visit, usually to a nearby school in the Pago Pago area.

A final development that got an early start was the growth of evening entertainment television. This development, and the accompanying gradual shift of the control of television activities from the Department of Education to the governor's office, will be discussed fully in Chapter Eight. For now, however, we may note that these developments occurred in direct contradiction to the hopes, and the desires, of Governor Lee and his associates.

At the congressional hearings in 1963 at which the television proposal was introduced, Lee was asked by Senator Warren Magnuson if such a move would not "lead to an irresistible demand for entertainment-type programs." He assured the congressional committee that it would not:

Congressman, I am sure there would be some demand for this. On the other hand, I do not think there is the commerce that could support a commercial type of TV. We would plan on trying to show travelogs. We might try also to get a bit of entertainment in the evenings, such as 30 minutes of an old film or something else simply to entertain the people and to keep them interested in TV. This would have to be pretty much of a voluntary proposition. We do not plan on buying this type of service. (FY 1963: 1096)

For reasons that we will cover in Chapter Eight, Samoan television has taken a quite different direction. Instead of a few travelogs and half-hour "old films," the schedule has gradually become dominated by the U.S. networks, complete with commercials, some of which have little or no relevance to American Samoa and others that have had rather spectacular effects on the local sales of U.S.-made goods.

Moreover, once commercial television was introduced, its growth was inexorable, even as educational television was being systematically cut back. And as the audience has grown larger and larger, it has become an increasingly tempting target for political influence and control.

Early Observations of Effectiveness

Time constraints and the pressures of an overwhelming production schedule combined, as we have seen, to prevent any kind of effective evaluation of programs as they were being prepared. There simply was no opportunity to pretest programs before they went on the air, or even to take full account of the occasional comments from classroom teachers, comments that in any event usually arrived too late to alter the course of instruction.

Moreover, the designers of the system were convinced that a truly effective overall evaluation could be made only at the end of a full 12-year cycle. As a result, no baseline data were gathered before the introduction of television and little or no thought was given to making a systematic, methodologically sound evaluation in the early years of frenetic production.

Governor Lee expressed the prevailing mood of the moment when, in an interview for *Saturday Review*, he told the reporter that the "effectiveness of the television idea couldn't really be determined until the present first graders are in high school" (Kaser 1965: 73). Roy Cobb, then director of education, was still of that mind three years later. "If we pursue our course for the full span of 12 years," he told a group of visiting school officials, "those who are skilled in evaluation may have enough data to identify areas of weakness, points of strength—to reduce the variables to a state that will produce reliable, scientific results" (Cobb 1967).

Purely on the basis of observation, however, those responsible for the system, including Lee and many of the dedicated, hard-working education personnel, were pleased with what they saw: average daily school attendance was at an all-time high, children were more attentive than before, and for the first time Samoan parents seemed to be taking an interest in having their children learn English. "The children are not tired of 'looking at television,'" Lee reported in his *Compact* article "but are in fact interacting with the teachers on the television screen as easily as they are with the teacher in the classroom. Samoan teachers are, for the first time, pronouncing English words correctly. Adults as well as children are increasing their use of English and are proud of their advancement in the language" (Lee 1968).

The system's supporters also found encouragement in the results of a spot check Pittman made in April 1966. He tested the fifth- and sixth-grade students of two of the consolidated elementary schools and of one of the village schools still not receiving television. In their grasp of the fundamentals of English, students in the village school scored an average of 33 correct answers out of a possible 82, compared with 63.3 for the students in the two schools served by television.

Soon thereafter, Lee declared in a speech in New York City:

"While it is too early to measure effectively the total result of our educational venture, we believe that our students will soon be getting an education that is equal to that offered by good schools in the United States. We believe that our system has enormous implications for the under-developed countries where the majority of the earth's people labor under the hardships of ignorance" (Lee 1966).

With production and other pressures somewhat eased in the second and third years of operation, the NAEB began negotiating with educators at the University of Pittsburgh and the University of California-Berkeley to design and conduct a long-term study, perhaps lasting over a decade, for the purpose of evaluating the impact of the instructional television program. However, a formal contract was never signed.

In the meantime, the system was receiving a great deal of attention from educators throughout the world, particularly in the developing countries. It was studied, and in general praised, by groups from UNESCO, the World Bank, New Guinea, New Zealand, India, Guam, Western Samoa, Tonga, and the Trust Territories, among others. American visitors were also impressed, as the following sample of comments attests.* Robert Shanks, Superintendent, Burbank (California) Public Schools: "Those kids can speak English, some of them better than pupils in Burbank, and this could not be done as well and as quickly without television. Samoa's educational system is working because like good educational programs it has a plan to achieve certain goals and everyone is working to reach those goals." Dr. Clifford Block, U.S. Agency for International Development: "The major lesson of Samoa is that education can be rapidly reformed in almost every respect through the use of television as the primary source of instruction. This rapid reform, which aspires to the attainment of very high standards, can apparently be accom-

*Except for President Johnson's comments, the following quotes date from around 1967. All the remarks, including his, are quoted in "Education in American Samoa: Observations by Visiting Educators and Other Dignitaries," unpublished manuscript, NAEB files (Jan. 1969, Washington, D.C.).

plished without the usual huge investment of funds, human resources, and time in the training of classroom teachers." Senator
Hiram Fong, of Hawaii: "Now bold steps to advance public education on American Samoa are being taken, including the use of
television for teaching, to do in its schools in a few years what
normally would take a quarter century."

Perhaps the crowning moment came in 1968 when President
Lyndon Johnson visited the islands enroute to Australia and
concluded an inspection of one of the consolidated schools with
the following comment: "Samoan children are learning twice as
fast as they once did, and retaining what they learn. Surely
from among them, one day, will come scientists and writers to
give their talents to Samoa, to America, and to the world." Noting that "one requirement for a good and universal education is
an inexpensive and readily available means of teaching children," the President added: "Unhappily, the world has only a
fraction of the teachers it needs. Samoa has met this problem
through educational television."

In Retrospect

President Johnson's remarks were made toward the end of
what might be seen as the euphoric period of judgment on the
Samoa experiment. Very few hard data on the effect of the
teaching were gathered in those early years, and this was dou-
bly unfortunate because such information might have both prevented overexpectations and sounded danger signals. For danger signals there were, even while the staff was making titanic
efforts to introduce the new system.

Many of the signals were related to the pace of introduction.
In this respect, as we have pointed out, Samoa was quite unlike
Niger, which proceeded one grade at a time, prepared lesson
plans and television programs for that grade, pretested them
and tried them in the classroom for a year, remade such programs as needed remaking, and then moved on to the next
grade. In retrospect it is easy to ask why Samoa did not introduce television at a correspondingly careful pace. The reason

usually given is that such a policy would have violated the honored Samoan cultural norm that all should go forward together: to improve instruction for only one grade at a time would have been seen as unfair to other students. Behind this reason undoubtedly also lies the urgency of the task as seen by officials and planners: it would have been unacceptable to wait 12 years for a completely remodeled school system. And it is easier to say now than it probably was then, that to satisfy those two requirements may have cost more than it was worth.

The cost was paid in effort and quality. The production staff had an enormous burden of producing too much, too fast, for use in a culture imperfectly known, without the advantage of extensive curriculum planning, pretesting, or post-testing. And the staff could only look forward to doing the same thing over, the next year, because it made little sense to save programs of dubious quality, and in any case the level of the audience would change from year to year and thus usually require new programs. The classroom teachers had to move into a kind of teaching with which they were unfamiliar, with a curriculum in which they had very little input, and with, one assumes, a sense of being manipulated by the television teachers. In such a situation, no one—neither the studio teachers nor the producers, the curriculum planners nor the classroom teachers—could do their best. And in retrospect the cost in quality, especially, does indeed seem a very high price to pay.

The inadequate involvement of Samoan teachers, in particular, must have signaled possible dangers. There is no record that classroom teachers were brought into the initial planning. Just as had been the case before television, policy making and administration were kept tightly in the hands of U.S. stateside personnel.

But in 1964 the situation changed fundamentally. Before television the American administrators had been relatively uninvolved in the day-to-day running of the schools. Most of the teachers were isolated in their one-room schools, where they were sovereign and went serenely on their own way, despite frequent changes of directors and official policies. Now, suddenly, the central administration became very active in the affairs of the classrooms. It is difficult to believe that this was accomplished without trauma. The teachers were taken from their small kingdoms and gathered into consolidated schools, where a stateside principal was to supervise them and a stateside teacher was to teach the main part of their courses by television. They were given a lesson plan for each day that told them how to be a "follow-up" teacher, how to get their students ready for the television lesson and how to reinforce afterward what the students were expected to learn from that lesson. Despite the fact that few complaints were heard from the teachers at first, and that there were good things as well as bad ones for them in the new plan, the situation contained the seeds of frustration and dissidence.

The change in policy concerning the language of instruction, if indeed there was a change, also must have cast a shadow over the future of the program. It represented at least a partial move from the British system of teaching English as a second language, with principal instruction in the native language throughout primary school (a system Western Samoa still follows), toward the French system of offering all instruction in the international language. But it was neither the British nor the French approach, for it stopped short of teaching only in English or giving priority to Samoan. Thus it sacrificed the advantage of building on the language base the student knew best without making full use of the chance to teach him or her English. The reasons for the decision seem clear—the classroom teachers' lack of fluency in English, and the lack of Samoan materials and experienced Samoan television teachers. Yet that decision has plagued the system ever since, and even as we write this, experiments with "bilingual" teaching and with the Western Samoan pattern of teaching English as a second language are still in progress or under consideration.

Television also portended trouble for the schools in a broader sense. Wherever television is introduced for the first time, the effect can be traumatic. When it is introduced into the schools before the wider community, as it was in Samoa, then the trauma is concentrated on, though by no means limited to, the school system.

So dramatic is the technology, so demanding both in expertise and in resources, that other changes tend to march to the drumbeat of television. Curriculum and materials, teachers and physical facilities, must be ready when television is. Yet it almost always takes longer to produce satisfactory software than efficient hardware. When hardware gets done first, as in Samoa, the technology usually does not wait for the other elements to catch up. It goes on the air on its own schedule. The year of planning and curriculum study that had been projected for Samoa was foreshortened to a few months, and the station went on the air on schedule with whatever software could be provided to meet *that* timetable.

On the other hand, the introduction of television often opens the door to changes that could not otherwise be brought about. It did in Samoa. Without television as a catalyst, Samoa could never have gotten the amount of money for its schools that the U.S. Congress provided. It could never have replaced its fale school buildings with consolidated schools. The decision to adopt universal rather than selective education did not depend on television, but television and the new school buildings made it easier. After television became an arm of the Department of Education, that department could never be quite the same again. Because television provided both electronics and a need for the studios and the users of their product to keep in close touch, the school system necessarily had to centralize curriculum, planning, and later, testing, and to replace the custom of infrequent contacts with isolated and almost independent schools with daily communication by radio between the department and the new consolidated schools.

The new medium had a far more spectacular effect on the community in general than in El Salvador, where television was known before it was used in the schools, and industrial development was greater. In Samoa, television represented the first introduction of a modern technology on a broad scale. It made necessary the extension of electric service throughout the islands. Electrical appliances of various kinds began to appear, and a service industry began to build up around them. The new schools opened opportunities in building construction. As soon as evening television came into use, it led people to change their living schedules, their social lives, and their tastes in recreation. The "side effects" of school television were thus far broader than the effects in school.

But from the point of view of this book, one of the most dramatic effects of ETV was on the Samoan teachers. That effect we shall look at in the next chapter.

FOUR

Coping with Change

FOR THE poorly trained Samoan teachers, the first years of educational television were something like advanced professional training. This was in part because they were able to watch their students being taught their own subjects in their own classrooms by well-trained American teachers using television. Yet this observational experience had limits. The television teaching was far from the kind of instruction the studio teachers would have conducted in their own classrooms. It was one way, and therefore unable to allow for special student needs or interests. Today, it would probably not even be considered very good ETV. It was stand-up, talking-face television, enriched by some visuals and models, but made in such a hurry that there was no chance for pretesting or remakes or varying the format except on rare occasions. What the classroom teachers had a chance to learn from the studio teachers was a pleasant manner, systematic presentation, the use of visuals and illustrations where possible, and not least, classroom practices that differed from the traditional method of chanting back what the teacher said.

Probably the greatest impact of ETV on the classroom teachers came from seeing daily lesson plans, objectives, outlines, and practice exercises, and being challenged to concentrate on forms of instruction other than lecturing or rote drill. The job of lecturing now belonged to the TV teacher; the classroom teacher was challenged to consider individual differences in his or her classroom, and to bridge the gap between the television presen-

tation and the student. He or she also had to learn how to conduct a varied period of practice in which the activity of the students rather than that of the instructor would be stressed.

To the extent that the first years in a television classroom were
indeed advanced teacher training, then, their main effect was to
expose Samoan teachers to a kind of instruction that was considerably different from what had gone on in the fale schools.
One of the principal objectives of the television system, according to Bronson and others who helped design it, was "to salvage
as many of the Samoan teachers as possible, and to prepare as
many of the younger people as possible to become adequate
teachers." The instructional program, he added, was designed
"with the thought that the Samoan teachers would be learning
along with the children, both in terms of subject-matter content
and of teaching techniques" (Bronson 1966).

Observations over the years by Pittman, Gillmore, and Richard Balch (a consultant to the project and then director of education, 1969–70) seem to support the conclusion that television
teaching did indeed achieve that purpose. In fact, Stuart Cooney, director of tests and measurements for the system from
1970 to 1972, strongly argues that this may have been television's greatest contribution to the Samoan educational system.

If the first effect of being assigned to serve as "follow-up"
teachers to the television lessons was a sense of demotion, and
the second effect an eye-opening introduction to a different kind
of teaching from what they had been used to, a later effect on the
classroom teachers must have been a growing sense of confidence. The classroom teachers saw the limitations of what could
be done on television and the strengths of what they could do
uniquely in the classroom. And along with this awareness of
what the classroom teacher could do that a television teacher
could not, must have arisen a growing sense of impatience.

This was expressed not only by Samoan, but also by some of
the palagi teachers who were assigned to the classroom rather
than the studio. There was *so much* television. One of the palagi

teachers recalls how she felt when she saw that some of her students needed special help with a lesson. Or when they were not yet ready to take up a new topic. Or when they became interested in a project and should have been allowed to turn aside from the schedule and finish the individual experience. But there was never time: there was always the next television program to turn on, following the relentless schedule built centrally rather than in the classroom. "The TV just kept coming!" she said.

While this was happening to the teachers, the pupils also were changing. They were acquiring new skills, a habit of taking a larger part in their own instruction and of speaking out more often, and they began to entertain new ideas of what school might be like.

So by the time television had been in use for two years, and increasingly thereafter, the school system had to deal with a new situation. This is a lesson that any developing country planning to use ETV can learn from the Samoa experience: they can expect that teachers and students will change in a few years of experience with television, and that the system must prepare to adapt to such changes.

Yet in the case of Samoa there were special difficulties in the way of making substantial changes. For one thing, new TV teachers and principals kept arriving on two-year contracts. Educational administrators in Samoa found that this term was either too short or too long. It was too long for teachers who could not fit into the unfamiliar demands of the Samoa system. It was too short when teachers could accommodate and contribute valuable service, for it took a half year to learn the situation, and a half year at the end to get ready to leave. But this constant inflow made it necessary to indoctrinate new teachers into an ongoing system rather than using them to restructure the system.

Moreover, the decision to begin with a complete elementary school curriculum by television in the first year of the project, and to add a complete high school curriculum in the second year, laid such an enormous burden of production on the studio and TV teachers that there was no time left for any substantial review of, and changes in, the television and its relation to the classroom. There was no opportunity, as there might have been if television had been introduced one grade at a time, to try out different ways of using the medium to fit Samoan needs, to revise the system where necessary, and to get one grade going well before moving on to the next one. There was no pretesting, and the feedback questionnaires were general enough and came in late enough that they contributed little to the operation. At the height of production, 182 live programs were being produced and broadcast each week. The four studios were in use from early morning to late night. Some teachers had as many as 20 programs to prepare and record per week, as well as lesson plans and practice materials to get ready and circulate. Obviously this frenetic pace of production, in which every program had to be live and little lead time was possible, left little opportunity to sit back and consider whether changes in the classroom might require some fundamental changes in the television. And even when the load was cut to five to ten programs per week for teachers—twice as many for producers—that was still a crowded schedule.

Furthermore, some features of the blueprint led to rigidity in the operation. For example, the choice of the Pittman/Tate system of language teaching required that *all* instruction in *all* subjects adhere strictly to the vocabulary and concepts being developed in the television English classes. As a consequence, science teachers found themselves restricted in their explanations and discussions to words and sentences being used at the time in a particular level of English instruction. Another result was that school libraries were disapproved because they might introduce students to a vocabulary not consistent with the Pittman/Tate plan of development.

Thus, ironically, a system that itself had begun as a bold innovation in teaching now found itself discouraging innovation. As

Samoan teachers learned from the new system, they began to ask for more flexibility and more responsibility in their own classrooms. This request was often answered, not with encouragement or helpful guidance, but with a hardening of the central administration's position against deviation from the centrally planned instruction. One of the authors of this book, who participated in the television project from its beginning, firmly believes that if there had been any considerable degree of flexibility, any willingness to recognize the improvements television had brought about in classroom teaching and to encourage greater responsibility in the classroom, the project would still be thriving.

The architect of the revised educational system, Vernon Bronson, was in the United States, and came to Samoa only a few times a year. If he had been able to spend more time observing the system, it is entirely possible that he might have found ways to accommodate to changing conditions. But everything was against substantial accommodation. Rather, the force of the plan that had been made and the conditions under which it was being administered led the administrators to want to defend it against attack and change rather than to change it. One director of education expressed this attitude frankly. "If you were interviewing a cross-section of the educators who have served here for the past four years, but for various reasons have returned to the United States, you would likely hear the terms 'dogmatic' and 'autocratic' used frequently. . . . We are dogmatic and autocratic in the sense that we believe we have isolated our problems, defined our objectives, and selected the ways and means for accomplishing our goals." "We are unwilling," he added, "to allow even qualified, well-intentioned persons to entice us to stray from the pathway that leads to our objectives." Period. (Cobb, 1967.)

Samoan teachers still tell the story of how they found it difficult to conduct discussion sessions and practice periods when several hundred students watched the same television program in one large room at Leone school. They sought to remedy the difficulty by using bookcases to divide the room so that the teachers could "follow up" the television by discussion and supervised practice with 30 or 40 students each. The chief consultant and planner came on one of his visits to Samoa and angrily ordered the bookcases instantly removed because this was a deviation from the "Stoddard Plan," one of the doctrinal foundations of the Samoa blueprint, which specified that in a large school large numbers of students should watch the television lessons together.

Complaints began to be heard, some loudly, some in the soft way that Samoans usually complain. First from the teachers, then from the students, and increasingly from Samoan leaders in the community. Some of these problems were aired publicly, and many of them in the councils of the schools and the community. It was in this setting that Milton deMello, who became the director of education in 1970, decided to act.

An experienced administrator, deMello first arranged, under the school system's contract with the University of Hawaii, for the appointment of 25 "task forces" covering all areas of operation from TV manpower to community college faculty development. Staffed mostly by University of Hawaii faculty and in some cases composed of only a single consultant, the task forces reported during 1970, 1971, and 1973. Among the other areas covered were English language curriculum, elementary mathematics, elementary science, mathematics, social studies, bilingual education, English language arts, the redesign of the patterns of use of instructional television, English as a second language, testing and evaluation, health education, and business education.

An advocate of individualized instruction and team teaching, deMello asked each of the task forces where appropriate to recommend ways of strengthening the educational program along those lines. At the same time, in 1972, he appointed a commission composed of classroom teachers, television teachers, and administrators to advise him what to do about TV. While all this was happening, certain other developments were occurring that changed the situation in which television had been operating.

The Buildup of Opposition to ETV

When the idea of using television was first brought up, Governor Lee noted that he found no enthusiasm among the personnel of the Department of Education or among those stateside teachers then serving in Samoa. Their first reaction, as we have seen, was respectful silence. Later, during the feasibility study for educational television, not one member of the department spoke in favor of the proposal, according to Lee.

The director of education at the time, M. J. Senter, left in 1963 and was replaced by J. C. Wright, a former superintendent of education for the state of Iowa and a man considered more favorable to the idea of television. In fact, in a speech in 1964 Wright commented: "What I like to tell these skeptics . . . is this: 'Whatever we are doing now cannot help but be better than what we are replacing.' If you come right down to it, the bulk of skepticism is based on the fact that nothing like this has ever been done before. If Mr. Edison and Mr. Bell and men like them had felt that way, you know where we would all be today."

But Wright eventually soured on the television idea and left after his two-year contract was up. His replacement, John W. Harold, who served for the next two years, seems from the record not to have taken a stand for or against the project. Not so, however, his successor Roy D. Cobb, a former Kentucky high school principal and one of the first NAEB contract employees to come to Samoa, as principal of Nua consolidated elementary school. Appointed to the top post in 1967, Cobb immediately distanced himself from the conservative members of the educational establishment, most of whom "would have prevented its [ETV's] birth by abortion if they could, or would have insisted on a mercy killing after birth because of hopeless deformities recognizable in the system. Failing in this, they would have

pled for enough major surgery to reduce the system to an ane-
mic audio-visual tool" (Cobb 1967).

During most of the early controversy revolving around the introduction of television and its use in the school system, Samoan teachers and school officials had remained relatively si-
lent. However, two of the authors of this book vividly remember
going for a moonlight walk during their first visit to Samoa in
1966 and being accosted by a stately looking Samoan who wanted
them to know that the people of Samoa were strongly opposed to
television. He turned out to be the brother of the high chief who
later became the first Samoan director of education.

In the buildup of forces that later led to the destruction of the
instructional system as conceived by Governor Lee and the
NAEB, three additional factors need to be considered. The first
of these, which we have been discussing, was the assumption
that it would be possible to persuade stateside educators then in
Samoa to adapt to the new program and therefore to assume
supportive roles in its implementation. This did not happen,
and it was a bitter disappointment, as subsequently noted by
Bronson:

In the beginning, when we attempted to organize a total staff for the
educational system, we thought it would be possible to salvage some of
the American administrative and secondary teaching personnel that
had been temporarily employed on the island. However, the first year's
experience proved that this was a false hope because all of these people
seemed to have been well grounded in traditional systems and were extremely reluctant to adapt to any kind of a new system. As a matter of
fact, in many instances they openly opposed the new system and created considerable dissension. (Bronson 1966)

Bronson went on to identify what he termed two kinds of
"human failure in the early days of the system": the inability
of people to adapt to a new methodology and a new concept of
professional work; and their inability to adjust to isolated island
living. One of the main sources of this problem of "human
failure" was an early decision to hire some 40 stateside teachers
with a view to improving the quality of education even while

the television system was being constructed. These teachers were all personally interviewed by Bronson and were on temporary contracts, with the expectation that the best of them would be retained when the system was operational. Most of the group declined to, or failed to, make the adjustment to television and were subsequently replaced—but only after they had created a fairly well-organized opposition to the new system.

The third decision that added to the buildup of forces opposing television was the decision to continue Fia Iloa, the "superior" stateside school, and not to use television in any of its classes. Supposedly for dependents of U.S. personnel serving in Samoa plus Samoan youngsters who had had at least part of their education in mainland schools, the school was made up of approximately one-half Samoans, with political pull and personal influence apparently playing a considerable role in admission.

Governor Lee argued the case for retaining the school on the grounds that it maintained the standards required for children to return to stateside schools or go on to stateside colleges. Fia Iloa school, he noted, was not only for the children of stateside personnel, but also "for the exceptional Samoan student with verbal and written fluency in the English language, and for any student whose educational achievement is comparable to stateside academic standards" (Lee 1967a). Television was not introduced into the school, according to the governor and the NAEB, because television's basic purpose was to improve competency in the English language, an ability that those in Fia Iloa had already demonstrated. Whatever the reasons, in practical terms, exempting this school from the use of television created an impression among Samoans that television instruction was somehow second best—not good enough for the stateside "quality" school, but good enough for the regular public schools in Samoa.

Added to the normal problems of operating schools of differing standards, this suspicion of the quality of the televised teaching created a formidable burden for the system to bear. Dean Everly had earlier warned against any such practice when he wrote, "Operating schools of greatly differing standards and personnel for Samoans and Americans is a dubious policy and one which has created difficulties on Guam in the past" (Everly 1961: 151). But his advice went unheeded.

Changes in the Top Command

Lee resigned his position and left the islands in 1967, having served longer than any other appointed governor. He was succeeded by Owen Aspinall, the son of Congressman Wayne Aspinall of Colorado, who headed the House Interior and Insular Affairs Committee. It was a little kept secret that Lee, under whom Aspinall had served as lieutenant governor, had tried to prevent the appointment. In turn, once inaugurated, Aspinall began quietly to downplay Lee's accomplishments and to undermine and dismantle some of the projects he had started. In this respect, Aspinall was little different from previous governors, each of whom came in, according to one longtime observer of the Samoan scene, "with his own hobby horse, intent on destroying those of his predecessors."

One of Aspinall's first targets was Lee's pride and joy: the educational television system. Almost immediately, the NAEB and top Department of Education officials began to get pressure from the governor's office to discontinue some practices, substantially modify others, cut back the hours of TV instruction, change focus, and even purchase European television receivers not tested under tropical conditions.

Aspinall also brought in an outside study team, from the University of Southern California, with instructions to evaluate the system without talking to any of the top-level stateside personnel in responsible positions. Presumably this action was based on the conviction that the views of those in charge would be so biased as to be valueless. Nevertheless, the tactic not only cut the team off from the most knowledgeable sources of information, but also created deep morale problems in the system.

The USC team's visit was followed by a trip by Aspinall to Los Angeles, where he and university officials discussed the possibility of USC's taking up the consulting contract when the

NAEB's contract expired in 1969. In this visit, and in the actions leading up to it, the governor worked in close collaboration with the head of the U.S. Office of Education's regional office in San Francisco.

Largely as a result of these activities, the NAEB's James Fellows, who had taken over for the ailing Vernon Bronson, was sent to Samoa to assess the situation and to make a decision on the future of that organization's participation. He arrived in Samoa while Aspinall was in Los Angeles and spent the time until the governor's return talking to teachers and key administrators of the educational system.

As a result of these consultations, and after conferring by telephone with his colleagues in Washington, Fellows drafted a letter for the signature of NAEB president William G. Harley announcing the association's intention to terminate its service on completion of the current contract. Dated February 17, 1969, the letter was delivered to Aspinall the following day, on his return from the States.

In essence, the letter reviewed the history of the television idea and its implementation by NAEB and stateside educational personnel assigned to the project; cited instances of lack of support or grudging support from the governor; brought up his trip to Los Angeles reportedly for the purpose of negotiating a new contract with USC; pointed out the damaging effect this apparent lack of confidence was having on staff morale; and concluded by notifying the governor that the NAEB had decided to withdraw as outside consultants for the system. Specifically, the letter charged: "Since assuming office in the summer of 1967, your public statements to the contrary notwithstanding, it has been clear that the Governor's tolerance of the NAEB and the main officials in the Department of Education was grudging and impatient. All conversations between the NAEB and the Governor of American Samoa have illustrated a major failure to understand the central characteristics and needs of the educational system, and an unwillingness to support it" (Harley 1969).

According to NAEB reports, when Aspinall was presented

with the letter, he was initially upset by the association's with-
drawal but later attempted to follow through on the proposed
contract with USC. By October 19, these negotiations were far
enough along that the *San Francisco Examiner* could carry a dis-
patch from Pago Pago headlined "ETV Loses Out in Pago Pago
to USC Group."

In the end, for reasons not entirely clear in the record, USC
failed to gain the approval of Department of Interior officials in
Washington, and the contract was finally let to the University of
Hawaii, which had a long record of teaching English and other
subjects to pupils with a Polynesian cultural background. Eventually, that contract too was allowed to lapse, in late 1971, and
the system operated from that time forward with only occasional education and technical, chiefly commercial, consultants
brought in from Hawaii and the mainland.

Aspinall did not remain long in office. He was succeeded in
August by John M. Haydon, a Seattle advertising executive, appointed by President Richard Nixon. Like his predecessors,
Haydon had his own pet projects and could see little worth saving in any of the previous administration's efforts. On December 11, before he had hardly settled down in Samoa, the new
governor was quoted in the *Honolulu Advertiser* as pronouncing
the instructional television system an "utter and complete failure." Although Haydon subsequently denied that he had been
correctly quoted, he repeated the charge in testimony before a
congressional committee on March 1, 1970, terming teaching by
television an "absolute failure" (*Honolulu Star-Bulletin*, March 4,
1970). In any event, by then word had gotten around: the top
boss considered the system a failure and wanted it discarded.

Director Cobb and his wife, Millie, two of the stalwarts of the
television group, resigned and left the island in 1969, as did
many of the other key officials of the system. Cobb was succeeded by University of Hawaii Vice-President Richard Balch,
who was appointed by Haydon and summarily dismissed by
him four months later. The system then struggled along without

a director of education until the fall of 1970, when Milton de-Mello, principal of one of Hawaii's public high schools, deputy director of education for the Windward area of Oahu, and former football coach, was named to the post. DeMello was no stranger to the problems of the Samoan school system, having earlier served for two months as a consultant under the University of Hawaii contract. He found a system in complete chaos and set about trying to restore some semblance of harmony and order. It was under deMello, as we shall see later, that most of the cutbacks in the television system took place.

Redrawing the Blueprint

Governor Haydon's criticisms of the system had been given impetus by the findings of Wolf Management Services, an organization commissioned by the U.S. Department of Commerce to recommend an economic development program for American Samoa. The Wolf report, issued in 1969, not only criticized the educational system for its failure to relate its programs to Samoa's current and potential manpower needs, but specifically questioned the effectiveness of television as a teaching tool.

In 1970 a team organized by the University of Hawaii under its consulting contract with the department of education—five persons, all with considerable experience with the Samoan educational system—visited the territory and documented inadequacies in the program as measured against its own stated goals and objectives. Somewhat later, a sixth consultant also visited Samoa and added his findings to the report. Among the team's major findings was that opposition to television, by both teachers and students, had become a problem of serious proportions in the high schools, although there still was general acceptance at the elementary level, particularly in the early grades. The report further noted that vocational education, in spite of clearly demonstrated needs, had been neglected in the preoccupation with improving the Samoan students' English language competency. Thus there were on the one hand large numbers of Samoan young people unable to find gainful employment at home, and on the other, a severe shortage of skilled technicians, ranging from refrigeration servicemen to auto mechanics.

At about the same time as this report came out, another one, with far-reaching implications, was issued by the assistant director of education for secondary instruction and the television instruction supervisor for the secondary division proposing that substantial changes be made in the high school program beginning with the 1970–71 school year. The most important of the proposed changes called for a significant reduction in the number of hours of television instruction and the immediate addition of up to 40 new stateside teachers, mostly of English, to replace television in the classroom. Quick to deny that they were recommending the elimination of television instruction at the high school level, the authors nevertheless stated that their purpose was "to investigate the feasibility of converting the secondary education program of instruction from the present system whereby maximum use of television is made to a comprehensive type program which will make use of Samoan classroom teachers who are college graduates, where possible, and qualified stateside classroom teachers." Elsewhere in the report, they stated that "television may be continued *on a very limited basis for enrichment*" (DOE 1970: 3; emphasis ours).

These recommendations were debated at some length in the educational system and engaged the attention of the Samoan legislature (Fono) as well. The opposition came primarily from the elementary division and studio teachers, the support from Samoan high school principals and the Fono. Most of the program, including the hiring of 24 new secondary classroom teachers, was implemented in the fall of 1970. Carefully worded denials to the contrary, the instructional television system conceived by Governor Lee and carried out by the NAEB and its associates was in the process of being dismantled.

Responding to demands from the Fono, teachers, educational staff, and parents, deMello appointed a task force in October 1971 to review the status of television and to make recommendations concerning its future. The task force was made up of a selected cross section of ETV personnel, teachers, and administrators, and it had the advantage of the first extensive survey of opinion in the history of Samoan education.

New Data on Students and Teachers

A change in attitude toward research on the Samoan project had become evident in the early 1970's, and one of the first useful results of the change was a survey in 1972 of teachers' and students' opinion of television. This survey was conducted by Lloyd Clark, the school system's ETV coordinator. He gave the questionnaire to 243 teachers and administrators at all levels of the system, to 1,915 students in the upper elementary grades, and to 1,624 high school students. As might be expected, the returns were near 100 percent. When the responses were tabulated and the report became available on June 1, 1972, the members of deMello's new commission, the school administrators and teachers, and a number of other people looking over their shoulders, found themselves considering some stunning results, as shown in Tables 8 and 9.

Thus in 1972, the eighth year of television in Samoa, the me-

TABLE 8

Teachers' Attitudes Toward Educational Television in American Samoa, 1972

(*Percent*)

Survey item and response	Grades 1–4	Grades 5–8	High school
Generally speaking, how well do you think children have learned from the television lessons presented this year?			
Good or excellent	86%	81%	38%
Television is used too much.			
Agree or Strongly agree	55	60	70
Television is used in the wrong way.			
Agree or Strongly agree	22	27	46

SOURCE: Lloyd Clark, "Results of Instructional Television Survey," memorandum to Milton deMello, director of education, American Samoa, Pago Pago, June 1, 1972, pp. 3, 6–7, 10.

TABLE 9

Students' Attitudes Toward Educational Television in American Samoa, 1972

(*Percent*)

Survey item and response	Grades 5–8	High school
I can learn better when we have/don't have a television lesson.		
Have	56%	24%
Do you want to have television lessons in school next year?		
Yes	54	23
How many television lessons do you want in mathematics each week?		
Five	49	9
How many television lessons do you want in science each week?		
Five	37	7
None	11	39

SOURCE: Same as Table 8, pp. 1–2.

dium was still relatively well accepted in the elementary grades, but strongly criticized in the secondary schools. The higher the grade, the less favorable the response to ETV. But even in grades 1–4, where the usefulness of television was hardly challenged by anyone, more than half of the teachers and administrators felt that teachers should have the right to decide where and when to use it.

As part of the survey, teachers and administrators were asked their preference among four different ways of using television in the classes. These were:

Plan A. TV should *present and develop* the main parts of the course [in other words, television should be used about the same way as it had been used between 1964 and 1972].

Plan B. TV should only *introduce* basic skills, concepts, and information, with the development left up to the classroom teacher [meaning less use of television].

Plan C. TV should be used only to *add enrichment* to a course; it should *not* introduce basic skills, concepts, and information [this meant not only reducing the amount of television, but also fundamentally changing the concept that had governed its use until then].

Plan D. TV should *not be used at all* in the particular subject [teachers and administrators were asked to answer this for each of the four subjects].

Still another alternative was presented: if the respondents did not like any of the plans, they could suggest something else. Very few took advantage of the opportunity to do so. The results are shown in Table 10.

The difference between the responses of the elementary and the high school personnel was clear. Whereas well over half the elementary teachers and administrators wanted to keep television as it was, and almost 90 percent would have been satisfied to keep it unchanged or divested of some of its job, the high school teachers and administrators were divided almost evenly

TABLE 10

Teachers' and Administrators' Preferences Among Four Proposed Ways of Using Television (Plans A–D) in American Samoa, 1972

(Percent)

Subject and grade levels of administrators and teachers	Prefer TV to be used in this subject:			
	As at present (A)	For introduction only (B)	For enrichment only (C)	Not at all (D)
Language arts:				
Elementary school[a]	58.1%	26.9%	7.3%	5.4%[b]
Mathematics:				
Elementary school	58.1	26.7	7.4	6.6
High school	18.4	28.6	24.4	28.6
Social studies:				
Elementary school	55.6	27.4	8.5	7.3
High school	24.5	22.4	42.9	6.1
Science:				
Elementary school	57.6	30.3	6.6	4.3
High school	22.4	32.7	20.4	20.4

SOURCE: Same as Table 8, pp. 4, 8–9.
[a] Language arts not offered in high school.
[b] Not all the rows add to 100 percent. The discrepancy is due to the teachers (fewer than 5 percent in each case) who did not express an opinion on the use of television for a particular subject.

among the four plans in two of their three subjects. Fewer than
one out of four wanted to keep television as it was (but then,
except for mathematics, fewer than one out of four wanted to
get rid of it). Mathematics drew the highest proportion of totally
negative responses (Plan D) and social studies the highest proportion in the second-most-negative category, i.e., limiting its
purpose to enrichment (Plan C). But it is worth noting that over
the entire sample of 243 teachers and administrators, only 24 on
average (9 percent) voted to dispense with television entirely. In
other words, as of 1972 the teaching corps of American Samoa
did not want to get rid of television in the schools. Large numbers of them, particularly in the high schools, simply wanted
less television and a different kind of television.

The Task Force Reports, the Director Responds

The task force appointed by Director deMello essentially recommended giving teachers control of the television in their
classrooms and leaving television to do what it could do best in
the Samoa situation. They called for a thorough review of the
nature and place of television in the school system and bluntly
rejected the original blueprint: "We no longer view 'teaching
done by means of TV' as the 'core of all instruction in the system' and no longer consider that the sole purpose of classroom
activities is to reinforce TV instructions. Nor can we continue to
operate on the basis that 'planning for each lesson at the Instructional Resources Center is total.'" Following this line of
thought, they said that "TV should continue to be used as one
of several instructional tools, but its role in providing the core of
instruction should be diminished," and that "consequently, the
number of telecasts in most instructional programs should be
reduced, with TV used when it provides the best means of effective learning" (quoted in deMello 1973: 9).

The director considered their recommendations against an increasingly stormy background. The Fia Iloa situation was becoming more and more irritating, with pressure from the U.S.

Department of Health, Education and Welfare to end the elite school, balanced against louder complaints from the Samoan community, some segments of which wanted to retain Fia Iloa for their own children. There were severe financial pressures as well. Contrary to expectations, the cost of television had not decreased over the years, nor had it reduced the cost of education as a whole. Indeed, it was the pressure to reduce costs that had led to the cutback of television in 1971. In 1972, however, the director realized that if he was going to find money anywhere to buy books and other instructional tools for the classrooms, he had no pocket to find it in except the television budget. Consequently, rather than choosing to review in a basic way the educational function of television, which would have required extensive replanning and the hiring of expert personnel, he chose to accentuate the parts of his task force's recommendations that dealt with reducing television where it was least valued.

DeMello's response, in March 1973, was a definite vote on the side of the task force. Henceforth teachers, pupils, principals, and supervisors would participate in course planning, and they would be aided by subject-matter specialists when funds permitted. Their plans would guide studio teams. If possible the load on studio teachers would be cut in the hope that this would raise the quality of the programs. Television would be used less for the instruction of students and more for the instruction of classroom teachers.

The decisive and instantly applicable part of his decision, however, decreed an even sharper reduction than his task force had recommended in the amount of television offered to classrooms. Television was to be eliminated in the high schools except for occasional special programs and instructional films broadcast at the request of teachers. Science on television had already been dropped from the seventh and eighth grade curriculum in 1972; now televised language arts were likewise to be dropped for those grades. Social studies and science telecasts were to be scheduled not oftener than once a week for first- and second-graders. The cutbacks in studio personnel were correspondingly sharp: the number of stateside personnel fell from approximately 125 to 25, the number of Samoan personnel in comparable proportion.

DeMello completed his contract in 1973, and this dismantled system was inherited by Chief Nikolao Pula, the first Samoan to hold the post of director of education, a well-loved, dedicated man who had nearly 40 years experience in the system. In 1974 Chief Pula died and was succeeded by his associate director, Mere Betham, another Samoan with extensive experience in the Samoan school system both before and after television (including a stint as principal of Samoana High School).

Chief Pula and Ms. Betham both made further reductions in the use of television in 1974. The impact of these changes can be seen in Table 11, which shows the number of hours of ETV per week to which students were exposed in 1965, when the new system was fully operative in all 12 grades; in 1972 when the amount of live programming was sharply cut back; and in 1975, when the full effect of the task force report and the deMello decisions had become apparent.

The figures for 1972 and 1975 represent the *maximum* number of program hours. By no means all students saw this much television, because teachers by then had the option of not using it.

TABLE 11
*Students' Average Weekly Exposure to Classroom
Television in American Samoa, 1965, 1972, and 1975*
(*Hours and minutes*)

Grade level	1965	1972	1975
Grades 1–4	7.55	6.03	5.23
Grades 5–8	6.58	4.53	3.18
High school	8.20	1.25	0

NOTE: Until 1974 the elementary school students were assigned to classes by levels, which could incorporate more than one grade (see Table 6). For the sake of comparison with 1975, when a full eight-grade system was in effect, we have converted the 1965 and 1972 figures to grades according to the number of years the students had been in school.

But since some teachers gave students the choice of watching programs like "Sesame Street" and "The Electric Company" during school time, these figures probably permit a fair enough average for comparison with the 1965 averages.

After 1975 no TV production personnel were under the supervision of the Department of Education, and little or no ETV production went on. The programs in use were mostly reruns.

In Retrospect

In 1976 the magazine *Direct*, published by the French Agency for Cultural and Technical Cooperation, wrote a requiem for the world's most ambitious attempt to use modern technology to bring about a rapid and explosive upgrading of an entire educational system. The article, an informed and generally sympathetic review of the experiment, concluded: "If the balance sheet of the television operation of American Samoa is far from being negative, still the impartial observer cannot fail to find it strange that an instrument with such important possibilities and not negligible effectiveness suddenly has its rules radically changed and its place at the heart of the educational world taken away."

The chief reason for what happened, *Direct* said, was "in effect the lack of deep integration of the system of television teaching into the whole of the Samoan educational system. . . . The television operation of American Samoa has done badly at winning the confidence of the traditional education teachers and administrators." And, as a result, the decisions of 1972 and 1973 "altered educational television from an academic to an out-of-school instrument."

Although we do not argue with these general conclusions, as far as they go, we are disinclined to ascribe the changes in Samoan ETV to any one cause. Their effect was cumulative. Among them, we would put special emphasis on the changes that took place *after* the introduction of television.

Television almost inevitably comes in with high hopes. The technology is dramatic. If it is brought in from the outside, as it was brought to Samoa and most of the other developing countries where it has been introduced in a massive way, it comes with the implied promise that sophisticated technology can work educational miracles as it has wrought other miracles. It provides an excuse to make other changes of importance—for example, to build modern consolidated schools in American Samoa—and these too tend to build the expectation of what television can accomplish with education in the classrooms. Therefore, it is almost inevitable that hopes for ETV are likely to be too high and to lose some of their sheen with a little experience.

But another fact of major importance emerges from Samoa's experience: that a school system does not stand still when ETV is introduced. Television brings change of many kinds. One of the most important in this case was in the Samoan teacher corps, both in their abilities and in their confidence in those abilities. Apparently, there were also changes in the expectations of the students. We shall see in the next chapter that these changes took place chiefly in the upper six grades of the school system. Throughout the system, however, they represented a profound change in the climate within which television was designed to serve Samoa, and in the needs and challenges it had to meet.

We believe that this sort of anticipation must be built into the blueprint for every large ETV project, especially in a developing country: after a few years, it must expect to be playing a new ball game. The teachers will be different, the students will be different, the community's expectations will be different. The entire instructional system, including but not limited to television, had better make allowances for what is likely to happen and prepare to accommodate it.

What took place in Samoa in 1971–74 was not a rejection of educational television. It was a rejection of a certain way of using it, in a certain part of the school system. There was too much of it; it was given too much to do; it was probably less well produced than it might have been if allowed more time and introduced more slowly; and it no longer fit comfortably into the upper grades of the school system. If those changes and new requirements had been perceived early enough in the history of the project, and if the situation had allowed for a review of what television was doing and needed to do, the events of the 1970's might not have occurred, and television might still be a useful tool of learning in the Samoan high schools.

FIVE

Teachers' and Students' Attitudes Toward Television

AS WE HAVE SEEN, there were no opinion surveys in the early years of Samoan educational television when they would have helped most.* However, four such surveys were conducted between 1972 and 1976, and these are one of the few time-series measurements of teacher and student opinions ever made during a major ETV project. They contribute to our scant store of knowledge of what factors cause such opinions to vary and change with time. More important for this book, they illuminate some of Samoa's experience with television: how the attitudes toward it must have developed, where the opposition to and support of ETV were centered, and what effect on attitudes the great cutback of television had.

Three clear trends stand out in the data.

How Opinions Vary by Grade Level

The higher the grade, the less favorable the attitude toward ETV. This was the case in 1972 and held true through 1976. It held for both teachers and students. In 1972, for example, students from level 5 (then corresponding to grade 5) through

---

*In order not to complicate this chapter, "attitude" and "opinion" are used interchangeably in most cases. There is, however, a technical distinction. Attitudes are in what psychologists call the "black box": that is, they are states of mind, and are thought of as tendencies to respond favorably or unfavorably toward a certain stimulus. They cannot be measured directly, only inferred from behavior. The kind of pertinent behavior we can measure most easily is opinion—that is, what an individual says about his own perceptions of the attitudes he holds. When we cite figures on "attitudes" in this volume we are usually talking about "opinion" measurements.

grade 12 (high school seniors) were asked to respond to two items: *I can learn better when we have/don't have a television lesson,* and *Do you want to have television lessons in school next year?* The answers to these two survey items are shown in Table 12.

Each of these levels represented such a large number of students (the smallest was 344) that a difference of only a few percentage points between means would be statistically significant. We can therefore say with some confidence that as a Samoan student moved through the upper grades and into high school, his or her evaluation of ETV became less favorable.

Opinions expressed by teachers follow much the same pattern, as we have already seen in Table 8. Is this a general pattern for both teachers and students wherever television is used in a major way for instruction, or is it unique in Samoa? About the only comparison we can make is with Hagerstown, Maryland, which, in 1966, at approximately the same stage in its television project as Samoa was in 1972, also conducted a system-wide opinion survey. The Hagerstown survey asked two questions that differed only slightly in wording from those used in Samoa: *How much have the television lessons helped you in your work,* and *With television do students have a richer experience* (Hagerstown), *learn more* (Samoa)? The results are shown in Table 13.

TABLE 12

Grade Level as a Variable in American Samoa Students'
Attitudes Toward Educational Television, 1972

(Percent agreeing)

Grade level	Learn better with ETV	Want ETV next year
Grade 5[a]	70.6%	66.0%
Grades 6, 7[b]	50.8	48.5
Grade 8[c]	46.4	48.4
Grade 9	29.6	25.6
Grade 10	19.7	20.5
Grade 11	21.3	24.8
Grade 12	23.5	21.8

SOURCE: Same as Table 8, pp. 1–2.
[a] Level 5.   [b] Level 6.   [c] Level 7.

TABLE 13

Comparison of Teachers' Assessment of Educational
Television, by Grade Level, in Hagerstown, 1965, and
American Samoa, 1972

(*Percent agreeing*)

Grade level	TV lessons have helped	Learn more with ETV[a]
Hagerstown		
Grades 1–4	77%	94%
Grades 5–6	81	88
Grades 7–9	63	81
Grades 10–12	41	66
American Samoa		
Grades 1–4	77	86
Grades 5–8	63	81
Grades 9–12	29	38

SOURCE: Hagerstown, International Research Associates, Inc., "Attitudes Toward Instructional Television," August 1965. Samoa, same as Table 8.

NOTE: Agreement in the Hagerstown responses is considered "much" and
"some" in help, "much" and "some" richer experience. For the Samoa responses it is defined as "very much" and "quite a lot of" help, "strongly agree"
and "agree" on learning more from ETV.

[a] The Hagerstown and Samoa items represented in this column were not exactly the same. The Hagerstown teachers were asked whether students have a
richer experience with a television class, the Samoa teachers, whether students
learn more when there is a television class.

As we see, the same decline appears, although it is steeper in
American Samoa, where troubles were more evident. Similarly,
in Hagerstown as in Samoa, students' assessment of ETV were
less favorable in junior high than elementary school, and less
favorable in senior than in junior high school. It would be helpful to have other system-wide studies of this kind so that one
could speak with more confidence about how general the pattern is, and the extent to which it is a necessary concomitant of
ETV.

How Attitudes Toward ETV Change Over Time

There is apparently a negative relationship, if the evidence
from Samoa is representative, between favorable opinions of
ETV and the amount of experience with it. We can follow fifth-

grade classes in Samoa from 1972 through 1976, during which time the 1972 fifth grade became the sixth grade in 1973, the seventh in 1974, and so forth. During that time the degree of enthusiasm for ETV does not vary markedly from year to year on the same grade level, and, if anything, seems to increase. Thus, 70 percent of fifth-grade students in 1972 said they learned better when they had a television class, and 75 percent gave the same answer in 1976; 66 percent of the fifth grade in 1972 said they wanted to have television next year, 69 percent in 1973, and 68 percent in 1974, and 79 percent in 1976. But the 1972 fifth graders, 66 percent of whom expressed themselves in favor of having television next year, voted only 59 percent in favor when surveyed two years later; the fifth-grade class that was 69 percent in favor of continuing television in 1973 was only 25 percent in favor of it by the time the class reached the eighth grade in 1976. A similar trend appears in answers to the statement *I learn better when we have/don't have a television lesson.* The 1972 fifth-grade class was 7 percentage points less favorable two years later, and the 1973 fifth-grade class dropped off 37 percentage points by the time it reached the eighth grade. Thus, for these students, the longer the experience with ETV and the higher the grade level at which it was used, the greater the antipathy toward it. See Table 14.

The question we would like to be able to answer is how much of the declining enthusiasm for ETV in Samoa has been due to the grade level and how much to the amount of experience. Our figures do not allow us to make that comparison. We know only that there is little change on the same grade level during the years when we have comparable figures from Samoa, but that there is a very sharp change in opinion from level to level.

Some supporting evidence comes also from the El Salvador ETV project, 1968 to 1973, reported in Hornik et al. 1973, and Mayo et al. 1976. The researchers in charge of the El Salvador project obtained opinion data covering four years, 1969–72. These results, like those from Samoa, showed very sharp declines in favorable attitudes toward in-school television, on the

TABLE 14

American Samoa Students' Changing Attitudes Toward
Educational Television Over Time and by Grade Level, 1972–1976

(*Percent agreeing*)

CAN LEARN BETTER WITH TELEVISION LESSON

Grade or level	1972	1973	1974	1976
5	70%	67%	65%	75%
6	51	70	60	66
7	46	47	63	49
8	—	—	43	30

WANT TO HAVE TELEVISION CLASSES NEXT YEAR

Grade or level	1972	1973	1974	1976
5	66%	69%	68%	79%
6	49	59	60	64
7	48	44	59	52
8	—	—	40	25

SOURCES: Lloyd Clark, "Results of Instructional Television Survey," memorandum to Milton deMello, director of education, American Samoa, Pago Pago, June 1, 1972, p. 2; Instructional Television Division, Department of Education, Attitude Surveys, 1973, 2: 1, 10, and 1974, pp. 48, 51; Marilyn Barry, "ITV Attitude Survey," report to the director of education, American Samoa, Pago Pago, 1976, p. 18 (mimeo.).
NOTE: During these years the Samoa schools were completing their transition from a system of levels to a system of eight grades. In 1972 and 1973 there was no eighth level. Level 6 in 1972 comprised grades 6 and 7, and level 7 was grade 8. In 1973 level 7 comprised grades 7 and 8.

part of both students and teachers, as four years passed and as students moved through the El Salvador middle school (corresponding to Samoa's grades 7–9). Students showed sharp declines in favorableness with higher grade levels during the two years in which the Salvador researchers were able to measure their respondents very carefully on identical items (1971–72). Teachers showed correspondingly sharp declines over four years of time. Table 15 shows the kinds of changes that took place in teacher opinions, and the figure on p. 98 the changes in student opinions.

In one sense the most striking set of results from the El Salvador project is the chart of student perceptions of what their teachers thought of ETV. Actually the students perceived their teachers as less favorable than the teachers themselves said they were. Between 1969 and 1972, the teachers' assessments of television in the classroom fell steadily but not very sharply. For example, between 1969 and 1972, the percentage of teachers who agreed that "students learn more by television than by teaching without it" declined only from 73 percent to 56 percent, and in the two years during which student attitudes were reported, it fell only from 59 percent to 56 percent. In those two years, however, the students' perception of their teachers' attitudes showed a decline of more than 25 percentage points.

It is not entirely surprising that students should think of their teachers as less favorable to ETV than they really were. Again and again, observers of instructional television have noted how a teacher's attitude toward television affects the students' attitudes. If the teacher appears to look forward to the broadcast and to watch it with interest, the students are likely to do the same. If the teacher grumbles and greets the broadcast with

TABLE 15

El Salvador Teachers' Changing Attitudes Toward Educational Television, 1969–1972

(*Percent agreeing*)

Year	Students learn more with ETV	Class discipline harder with ETV	Students can't ask questions in ETV class
1969	73%	17%	36%
1970	70	14	39
1971	59	24	65
1972	56	26	69

SOURCE: John K. Mayo, Robert C. Hornik, and Emile G. McAnany, *Educational Reform with Television: The El Salvador Experience* (Stanford, Calif., 1976), pp. 124–25, 188–89.

NOTE: The questions asked in El Salvador were almost exactly the same as those asked Samoan teachers: "Students learn more with ETV than without"; "It is more difficult to maintain classroom discipline when using ETV"; and "There is a serious obstacle to learning by ETV because students cannot ask questions until the program has ended." To each of these there were five alternative responses: Completely agree, agree, undecided, disagree, completely disagree. The percentages here represent the response "agree" or "completely agree."

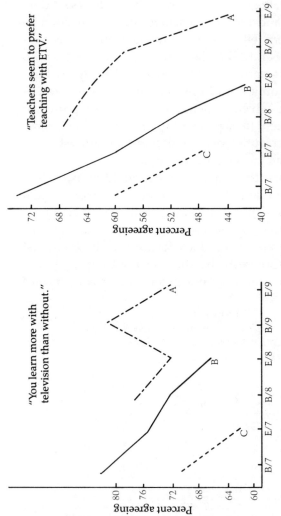

Students' attitudes toward educational television in El Salvador, 1970–1972. These data are for three separate cohorts of seventh-, eighth-, and ninth-grade students during the school years 1970–71 and 1971–72. Students' opinions were measured at the beginning and end of each school year. In the figures above, B stands for beginning and E for end. Thus the students who were beginning the eighth grade in 1970–71 were surveyed four times before they passed beyond the ninth grade at the end of 1971–72. Students who were beginning the seventh grade in 1970–71 were also measured four times during the two years. Students who were beginning the seventh grade in 1971–72 could only be measured twice. These are the three cohorts, identified on the charts, respectively, as A, B, and C. Figures adapted from John K. Mayo, Robert C. Hornik, and Emile G. McAnany, *Educational Reform with Television: The El Salvador Experience* (Stanford, Calif., 1976), p. 88.

some such statement as "Well, I guess we have to stop what we are doing and turn on the television again," then the students too are likely to consider ETV an intrusion.

We must be cautious in comparing the opinion results from El Salvador with those in Samoa. The surveys in El Salvador were made during the first four years of the project, which were stormy years in the school system for reasons only partly attributable to television, whereas the Samoa series did not begin until the project was in its eighth year, by which time some rather special actions had been taken to deal with the teachers' objections. Therefore, though the span of years is nearly the same in the two cases, one would expect a sharper downturn in the El Salvador data than in the Samoan. Furthermore, early in the Samoan series ETV was withdrawn from the high schools, thereby removing the most unfavorable teachers from the opinion sample. Among the remaining teachers, opinions of ETV actually became slightly more favorable between 1973 and 1976. So the two situations are not wholly comparable, but the El Salvador studies help us to reconstruct what must have happened in the early days of the Samoan project, and we shall return to that topic.

Relationship Between Teachers' Views of ETV and Their Level of Education

It is reasonable to assume that teachers and students will be more favorable to ETV if they feel a need for it. This suggests one of the reasons why teachers of the more advanced students are less enchanted with in-school television than their colleagues in the lower grades. High school and junior high school teachers typically have more professional training than elementary school teachers, and might therefore feel less need of television in their classrooms, in fact might be rather insulted if another teacher is sent in, electronically, to help them. To test this, we analyzed the 1976 Samoa opinion survey data by the level of the teachers' education, and did indeed find that favorable attitudes toward

Table 16

Educational Preparation as a Variable in American Samoa Elementary Teachers' Opinions of Educational Television, 1976

(*Percent*)

Level of education	Agree or strongly agree	Disagree or strongly disagree	No answer
High school	30%	59%	11%
High school + less than AA degree	24	64	12
AA degree	32	50	17
AA degree + 30 hours	36	48	15
AA degree + 45 hours	23	62	15
Four-year college degree	48	31	21
Average for all teachers	31%	53%	16%

SOURCE: Compiled from raw figures obtained in 1976 opinion survey, available in Samoa Department of Education; and from data in Marilyn Barry, "ITV Attitude Survey," report to the director of education, American Samoa, Pago Pago 1976 (mimeo.).

television go down as education goes up. Table 16 shows the answers to the question *Do you think television is used too much in our schools?* as given by teachers with different amounts of education.

The same trend, though not in every case so sharply marked, is found in the teachers' responses to such items as *Television is used the wrong way in our system, Lesson material is generally good,* and *Television doesn't leave the classroom teacher enough freedom.* All these show a trend toward less favorable attitudes with more education. The one exception to the trend is the case of the eight teachers who were graduated from the community two-year college and earned an additional 45 hours of advanced credit. We do not fully understand why they are more favorable toward ETV than the others.

Of course, merely discovering that more highly educated teachers are less likely to welcome television into their classrooms is not sufficient guidance for educational broadcasters. A more basic question is whether they resent *any* intrusion into their classrooms, or whether they would welcome *some* kind of television but not other kinds. We are inclined to believe that the kind and amount of television and the degree of participation permitted to the teacher in deciding on the content of the television are the decisive points. To be sure, that still leaves the question of what kind of ETV a school system like American Samoa's must design and produce to meet the varied needs and tastes of a varied teacher corps, many with only high school education, a few with college degrees, and a very few with doctorates. At any rate, this finding helps us to understand why impatience and dissatisfaction appeared first among the high school teachers of American Samoa, spread into the upper grades, and were little heard of below grade 7.

Relationship Between Teachers' Views of ETV and the Location of Their Schools

Just as the more highly educated teachers in Samoa presumably felt less need than others for assistance from television, so also certain schools must have felt less need for it than others did. For example, a school in the capital city of Pago Pago, where a great deal of information circulates and many visitors come, must have felt less need for school television than a remote school on the north shore of Tutuila, accessible only by boat. We tested this assumption by comparing the opinions of teachers in the schools of the Pago Pago area with those of the teachers in the schools of the remote parts of Tutuila and the Manu'a islands. The differences were striking, as Table 17 shows.

Teachers are more grateful for ETV if they feel more need for it. This is not a startling discovery, and like the finding about the portent to ETV of a teacher's educational level, it may raise more problems than it solves. For instance, can the same program schedule meet the very different needs of a capital city school and a remote school? The problem of how to cater to individual and classroom differences has long been a classical one for instructional television, and will probably remain so for a while longer.

TABLE 17

Location of Schools as a Variable in American Samoa Elementary Teachers'
Opinions of Educational Television, 1976

(*Percent agreeing*)

Survey item	Pago Pago area	Remote areas
TV classes are not as good as last year.	22%	16%
Students can learn better with television in class.	55	65
Television classes do not give students enough time to ask questions.	41	36
I like classes with television better than classes with no television.	34	43
I want to have television classes in school next year.	55	66

SOURCE: See Table 16.

In Retrospect

From these 1972–76 Samoan data, and especially with the help of the Salvadorean data on opinions during the early years of a project, we can at least make an attempt to reconstruct the path by which attitudes toward ETV changed in the schools of American Samoa.

The project undoubtedly began with high hopes and anticipation. This is the testimony of those who were on hand at the start, and what one would expect from the example of El Salvador. The teachers apparently felt some uneasiness because their situation had changed so suddenly, but if there was opposition, except from the group of palagi teachers, it was not recorded. For the students it was a great adventure, as the introduction of television always is. When impatience and dissatisfaction began to appear, after about two years, they appeared first in the high schools, where the teachers had more education, were more resentful about invasions of their classrooms, and felt little need to share their responsibility with a television teacher. They began among teachers who, because they had received the equivalent of an advanced two-year course in pedagogy from watching skilled teachers teach their own subjects and working with lesson plans made out by experts, were far different from the sort of teachers they had been in 1964. If the dissatisfaction had been caught at that point, it might have been taken care of. But it was not, and therefore it spread to the students, who are always quick to reflect the viewpoints they detect in their teachers. And it spread from the high schools into the grades immediately below, where the teachers and needs are much the same as in the high schools.

What might have been done, two or three years into the project, about that situation, as we see it now with 20-20 hindsight? Perhaps it would have been well to give the dissatisfied teachers responsibility for a larger proportion of their class time. They might have been brought in to help in planning the kind of television they felt they needed, and especially to help devise more flexible uses of television to fit the individual and classroom differences with which they had to work. What if the amount of television had been reduced in the upper grades at that time? In 1972, many teachers said they no longer wanted instruction by television to be "the core of all instruction." Was this because they objected to television teaching as a method, or did they simply object to the amount of it? Did it mean they would have been grateful for a change in the kind of television teaching, or did they want only the addition of some alternative sources of knowledge and study—books and radio or other media, perhaps—and the chance to choose some of these alternatives rather than having all their time prescribed for them and all their authority centered in one talking electronic head?

One implication of the Samoa experience is that if attitudes toward television are going to change as time passes and as teachers acquire new skills, then television too must be ready to change. Educators and ETV broadcasters must be more alert to the changing needs of teachers than was the case in Samoa, and be prepared to meet these changing needs more quickly than

Samoa did. Efficient feedback from the classroom, frequent visits to the classes, opinion studies (six years earlier) would have
repaid their cost many times over.

There is very little in the data to encourage anyone to think
that what happened in the early 1970's was a rejection of television per se. It was not that, not even in the high schools. Rather
it was a rejection, by parts of the school system, of a way of
using television, or perhaps of too much television. Even among
high school teachers and administrators in 1972, only about
one-fourth were willing to recommend that television be discontinued in high school classes. In the elementary schools,
ETV had, and continues to have, strong support. Even in the
first years of the 1970's, if the school administration had been
willing to review and revise the goals of television and the way
it was being used, ETV might not have been lost to the high
schools, live production might not have come to an end, and
Samoa might have shown the way to other users, who also must
face the problem of maintaining flexibility with an essentially inflexible system.

In Hagerstown and El Salvador, we have found the same generalization supported—that teachers and pupils are less favorable to ETV in high school than they are in elementary school,
less favorable in the upper grades than in the lower ones. This is
where the infection began in Samoa and where the closest attention must be paid. But does television *have* to be less acceptable in the higher grades? How much of that is due to the fact
that teenagers like to talk rather than listen, like to take a more
active part in their own education? To the fact that high school
teachers have more pride in their education and are more inclined to resent having someone teach for them? To what extent
are these obstacles insuperable? What if a different concept of
television is applied to the high schools? Is it reasonable to believe that core teaching by TV, or at least any large proportion of
core teaching, is not the kind of help that a well-trained teacher
in the higher grades of a school system needs or will accept?
Perhaps a few well-made programs, on topics where the teach-

ers indicate they feel the need of help or illustration, might be a better formula for those levels. And low-priced videotape recorders, when they become widely available, may solve some of the problems of inflexibility of schedule. In other words, we are not convinced that it is necessary to give up television as a tool of instruction in high school and junior high merely because those grades have a distinctly different set of needs from the lower grades.

The question arises, however, whether it is really feasible to give such a large responsibility, throughout a school system, to the television teacher as Samoa did. Certainly, that kind of use recommends itself strongly where children do not have schools, where adults are studying at home or in informal groups, or where schools lack experts in certain subjects. But even an institution like the British Open University, with its heavy emphasis on home study, thinks of itself, not as a "university of the air," but rather as an educational system in which reading and correspondence materials, television, radio, and optional tutorials play allied roles. It would be a very brave educator today who would prescribe core teaching by television for an entire school system, and an even braver one who would install it without trying it out cautiously, bit by bit, and standing always ready to make adaptations or alterations.

Anything we say about the change of attitudes toward ETV in the early years of the project must necessarily be based on a certain amount of assumption and conjecture: the first hard evidence on opinions we have is from 1972. And we know very little about opinions concerning television in the high schools since 1972, because opinion surveys disappeared from the high schools when television did. But this we can say with confidence: that in the elementary grades the opinion of ETV has been generally rising since 1972. The proportion of elementary teachers and principals who feel that "television is used the wrong way in our schools" was never higher than 25 percent in the elementary schools, and by 1976 had fallen to 10 percent. From a high of 38 percent in 1972, agreement that "students are just plain bored with television" fell to 31 percent in 1976; and agreement that "television does not allow classroom teachers enough freedom to use their own ideas in teaching" from 55 percent to 40 percent. Some 90 percent of elementary teachers in 1976 said that "television is very helpful in teaching oral English." The use of television for teaching language arts was similarly endorsed by 76 percent, for mathematics by 72 percent, for social studies by 71 percent, and for science by 51 percent. The significance of these 1976 figures is that at the time they were recorded, no ETV was available to the elementary teachers except aging reruns. Only 50 percent of the teachers had access to social studies on TV, only 14 percent to science. Despite this, three times as many teachers as could get science telecasts, half again as many as could get social science telecasts, still remembered them as "very helpful."

Therefore, whether or not the decision to liquidate ETV in the high schools and to cut back severely on elementary school television and the production of new programs, whether or not that was the right decision at the time, it has clearly reduced opposition to ETV in parts of the system where television is still used.

SIX

How Much Did the Students Learn?

WHAT WAS the level of performance in the Samoan schools before television? The chief evidence available from 1964 or earlier is anecdotal and deals almost wholly with the standard of English language used in the schools. Some visitors to the schools in the early 1960's left rather spicy comments. Governor Lee himself, soon after he took office, had to call for interpreters so that he could talk in English with teachers who were supposedly teaching a curriculum in English. George Pittman described the kind of English he heard in the schools in 1964 as a "tense-less, article-less, often plural-less pidgin English incapable of carrying any precise message" (Pittman 1969).

Bryson Wallace, a linguist who visited American Samoa during the 1963–64 school year, while preparations were under way for the new system, described the problems—and the results—of the English language teaching program:

> The greatest handicap is the shortage of trained elementary school teachers. Samoan teachers staff the 47 public elementary and seven junior high schools, but only one has a college degree. Most are graduates of the public high school which started in 1946 or the new Mormon high school; others are graduates of the two-year teacher-training school. Although all of these institutions are staffed by Stateside teachers, they have produced elementary-school teachers who have an appallingly low ability to speak English and practically no ability to teach it. In a recent interview with one of his elementary teachers, the director of education had to call in an interpreter in order to communicate with the teacher. These are the teachers who are responsible for initiating the English program in the first grade and continuing it until the

children enter the all-English-speaking high school between the age of 15 and 19. . . .

In effect, the elementary system is its own worst enemy, because its feebleness has crippled the high schools which produce most of the teacher candidates. . . . The teacher problem has been compounded by a shortage of teaching materials suitable for both the teachers and the students. In the elementary schools, most of the English teaching materials have been elementary texts designed for use in the U.S. schools, and English-as-a-foreign-language texts designed for use by well trained, highly skilled language teachers. The program's results are painfully evident in the matriculating high-school students.

Until 1962, only a small percentage of junior-high graduates were accepted by the high school on the basis of an entrance examination written in English. But when universal high-school education began that year, the number of students suddenly jumped from 300 in 1961, to 800 in 1962, and to 1,200 in 1963. This further complicated the school's already difficult English-teaching situation.

Early in the summer of 1963, 533 junior-high graduates were given the Science Research Associates, Inc. (SRA) High School Placement Tests in four areas, in order to classify them in groups before they entered high school. The tests were typical aptitude and achievement examinations written in English. The group's composite scores ranged in grade placement from 3.9 [i.e. three years, nine months] to 11.5. The median for the group was 5.8, and only 21 out of the entire group scored 9.0 or better. (Many of those in the higher range had attended school in the United States at one time or had other unusual advantages.) It might be concluded, then, that the average matriculating Samoan in high school has the reading ability of a typical Stateside sixth-grader, but observation reveals that he can only speak a handful of coherent English phrases and sentences. In many instances the high-school teacher faces an insurmountable task in teaching this student remedial English because the student has been learning poor structure and pronunciation habits from elementary and junior-high teachers for the preceding nine years. (Wallace 1964: 168–69)

It is too bad that the observational evidence deals almost wholly with the language question; students must have done much better, for example, in arithmetic. But any observer visiting the schools today describes the standard of English far differently from the way it was evaluated in 1964. So far as those early observations constitute a baseline, therefore, they indicate an impressive growth in competence since ETV began.

The Pre-Television Studies

Like many large educational projects initiated before the recent emphasis on "accountability," Samoa ETV did not include a
baseline study against which to measure the progress of its students. In some ways this is extraordinary, because there are records of standardized achievement tests having been given in
American Samoa as early as 1931. A Stanford achievement test
battery was given to teachers and teacher-candidates in December 1931 and again in December 1932, and to all public school
students in May 1935.* All ninth-graders were given another
Stanford test battery in 1954. These old test results, of course,
should not be compared with recent ones, not only because the
tests and the norms are different, but also because little information survives about the students or the relation of the tests to
their curricula. Furthermore, before the 1960's public education
in American Samoa was selective rather than universal, and the
school population was therefore different. We have put some of
these old test records in Appendix A for historical interest, but
they give us very little basis for comparing what happened after
television with what happened before.

It is interesting to note that the teachers and teacher-candidates in 1931–32 averaged 5.7 in educational level on the Stanford battery. They did best in arithmetical computation (8.1),
worst in paragraph meaning, i.e. reading (4.6). The students
tested in 1935 scored at first-grade level at age ten and a half,
and the level achieved had worked up to only about the fourth
grade for those who were seventeen and a half. This performance was not as poor as it sounds, however, because the test
was in English, and English in the schools must have been
pretty bad in the 1930's.

Ninth-graders did about as well on a Stanford achievement
test in 1954 as the teachers and teacher-candidates in 1932. Their
average grade level on the whole battery was 5.6, and they did

*In this chapter and throughout, unless otherwise stated, the grades and
classes we discuss do not include the private schools.

very well in arithmetical computation (8.0), although not at all well on paragraph meaning (4.3). But these were students who had been specially selected for the ninth grade on the basis of their superior performance; about two-thirds of the elementary-school students were not allowed to go on to high school until 1962, when secondary education was opened to all children of high school age.

Another set of pre-television tests is particularly tantalizing because it might have provided some baseline for later performance. Parts of the Stanford achievement tests were given to ninth-grade students in 1962, 1963, and 1964. Unfortunately, some handwritten records and a few hand tabulations of median scores are the only surviving data on these tests to be found in the Samoan Department of Education (though one of the authors of this book can recall having used the scores for placement purposes in those years). We have worked with these surviving tabulations and have found it possible in some cases to figure means and standard deviations, but for most of the tests the N's are unknown and even the form and level of the tests can only be guessed at. Therefore, they are of no use as a baseline, and their chief usefulness is to give us an idea of how performance must have been affected by the opening of the high schools to all students in those years.

Here is a series of these ninth-grade test medians, apparently copied from the official records that have disappeared. The figures are grade-equivalents.

Year	Reading	Arithmetical computation	Language arts
1962	5.4	7.4	6.7
1963	5.2	6.3	5.8
1964	4.9	6.7	5.7

These data indicate that test performance dropped, on the average, by one-half to one academic year as more students were admitted into the schools.

The earlier tests also furnish a bit of incidental information,

TABLE 18

Stanford Achievement Test Scores of Amercan Samoa Teachers and Students, 1932, 1935, 1954, and 1970

Year	Group tested and size (if known)	Reading	Spelling	Ratio	Mathe-matical reasoning	Compu-tation	Ratio
1932	Teachers, teacher-candidates	—	—	—	6.7	8.1	1.21
1935	Grades 4–12 (N = 532)	—	—	—	38.1	47.0	1.23
1954	Grade 9 (N = 227)	4.5	7.1	1.58	6.7	8.0	1.19
1970	Grade 9 (N = 495)	5.4	7.8	1.44	6.5	8.4	1.29

SOURCE: 1931–32, 1935, Mark M. Sutherland, "A Study of Teacher Training in American Samoa," M.A. thesis, University of Hawaii, 1971, pp. 104, 133. 1954, 1970, Department of Education files, Pago Pago.

NOTE: In this table and in the others that follow, scores are for public schools only, unless it is specifically stated that private schools are included. The scores for 1935 are raw scores, the others grade equivalents.

although certainly no baseline on which to evaluate later performance. Since 1970, when standardized tests were first given regularly in American Samoa schools, Samoa students have done relatively better with tests of rote learning than tests of reasoning skills. For example, the ratio of their scores in spelling to their scores in reading, and their scores in arithmetical computation to their scores in mathematical reasoning, are comparatively higher than corresponding ratios among mainland students. This phenomenon is not unique to Samoa; it is found also in the tests of disadvantaged U.S. students, and in the student populations of many developing countries. The early tests, some of them administered more than 30 years before television, show that the phenomenon is not unique to post-television Samoa either: as we see in Table 18, precisely the same trend can be found as early as 1931, and again in 1954. Thus there is every reason to believe that the phenomenon is related to something in the Samoan students' situation and culture, rather than to the reliance on television teaching.

A Surprising Set of Scores

Although Samoa entered on its bold experiment without a
test-score baseline, and the architects of the project resisted testing, several small-scale measurements were in fact made during
the first six years. One of these, conducted about the middle of
the school year 1966–67, after television had been in the high
schools for more than a year and in most of the elementary
schools for more than two years, provides a remarkable insight
into the problems that the new system had to face as it moved
into the Samoan schools. This was the Gates Reading Survey,
which was administered to all students in grades 5–12 and to all
elementary teachers. The Gates Survey has been widely used in
the United States and at that time had become sufficiently standardized that the publishers were willing to translate scores into
grade equivalents. The results are shown in Table 19.

What does it mean when an entire system reads at about the
same level? For this is what the scores say—that all classes read

TABLE 19
*Gates Reading Survey Scores of American Samoa
Students in Grades 5–12 and Elementary Teachers, 1967*
(Grade equivalents)

Group tested and size	Vocabulary	Comprehension
Grades 5–6 (N = 960)	4.3	4.3
Grades 7–8 (N = 260)	4.7	4.8
Grade 9 (N = 565)	3.9	4.0
Grade 10 (N = 316)	4.2	4.3
Grade 11 (N = 254)	4.4	4.8
Elementary teachers (N = 237)	5.4	5.8

SOURCE: "Results of Testing, Gates Reading Survey, 1967," Department of Education files, Pago Pago.

at about the fourth-grade level, and that the teachers were only about a year ahead of them. Obviously, it might mean that the test was inappropriate, but the officials of the Department of Education clearly did not think so when they selected it. Or it might mean there was an error in the way the test was administered, but the error would have had to be a massive one indeed to yield so consistent a result across all the grades. Could it mean rather that the schools were operating under a ceiling of accomplishment set in large measure by the ability of the teachers? If so, we might see this as an inheritance from the pre-1964 system, a problem that would be difficult to overcome, and one that would affect all other scores, since instruction and testing were to be in English. Or, finally, do these scores reflect to some degree the emphasis on oral English as opposed to reading, and the leveling effect of everyone's having to move through the Tate syllabus that controlled the level of English to be used in all classes? Whatever the causes, this is an extraordinary set of results, which illustrates the problems that educational reform in American Samoa had to face, and suggests one of the reasons why swift changes could hardly be expected.

What to Substitute for a Baseline

Small studies, most of them intended to measure English language skills, were conducted beginning early in the history of the ETV project. Pittman himself apparently was responsible for a test of oral English administered to the seventh grade in 1964, and the test was repeated four years later. See Table 20. We have absolutely no other information on these results. In fact, we have no reason to think that such a test was given in 1964, and rather suspect that it was in 1965—that is, toward the end of the 1964–65 school year. We do not know how the schools were sampled or exactly what the test consisted of. Nevertheless, if it is justifiable to speak of significance in regard to these tests, the 1968 scores were significantly higher than the 1964 scores.

To provide some sort of baseline in the early years, the authorities usually administered the same test at the same grade

How Much Did the Students Learn?

level to students who had been exposed to a different number of years of television. Thus, for example, when B. Thomas Harwood came to Samoa in 1966 to serve as the first supervisor of tests and measurements, he applied statistical treatment to the data from a test of oral English (also apparently devised by Pittman) that had been administered near the end of the 1965–66 school year. That test covered students from three schools in which television had been available for two years, one school that had been exposed to it for a single year, and three others that had not yet introduced television. The raw figures are shown in Table 21.

Harwood's statistical analysis of these data credited television with some impressive gains. His F ratio, obtained by an analysis of variance, was 108, which is highly significant, and he calculated that the difference in number of years of TV experience accounted for 55 percent of the total variance. But later, in 1967, when he attempted to replicate these findings in tests at three schools, with 30 students each, he could not do it. In fact, the results were exactly opposite. "These results were so surprising," Harwood reported, "that I could hardly put any credence in them. I suggest that the results were due to examiner variance, rather than student variance, although there are other possible explanations" (Harwood 1968).

In the hope of resolving the issue, Harwood then devised a new test of oral English and administered it to randomly se-

TABLE 20
Oral English Scores of American Samoa Students in Grade 7, 1964 and 1968

	1964			1968		
School	N	Mean score	Standard deviation	N	Mean score	Standard deviation
Aua	42	12.096	3.869	34	14.441	3.395
Lauli'i	26	13.192	3.970	14	18.786	5.423
Leone	62	14.887	4.209	53	12.566	4.306
Pago Pago	64	12.734	3.981	44	15.023	5.232

SOURCE: B. Thomas Harwood, memorandum to George Pittman, language consultant, June 11, 1968, Department of Education files, Pago Pago.

TABLE 21
Oral English Scores of American Samoa Students
in Grade 7 by Years of Experience with
Educational Television, 1966

School and size of group	Years of ETV	Mean score
Aua (*N* = 20)	2	70
Ili'ili (*N* = 58)	2	64
Nua (*N* = 58)	2	65
Matafao (*N* = 29)	1	57
Asu (*N* = 10)	0	39
Faga'itua (*N* = 26)	0	34
Fagamalo (*N* = 7)	0	43

SOURCE: Same as Table 20.

lected students at four different age levels in seven schools where the years of ETV use varied from none to three. The results are shown in Tables 22 and 23.

All the differences were highly significant.* The interaction between age and years of ETV was weaker than might have been expected, leading Harwood to question whether the oral English program was designed to encourage smooth and consistent improvement. He was also disturbed by the fact that the students with only two years of TV experience had done slightly better than those with three years' experience. He speculated that the administration of the test was the factor in the relatively poor performance of the three-year schools. Moreover, it appeared that the students at Aunu'u (which had TV for two years) had been coached before taking the test. "These students were so outstanding," he noted, "it is difficult to believe that they were not coached or selected for their excellence. The school principal was not there to assist with the sampling" (Harwood 1968).† Nevertheless, Harwood was prepared to conclude, on

*See analysis of variance, Appendix A, Table A.12.
†This question, we may note, has been raised in connection with other tests given in the Samoan system; it is often difficult, after the fact, to distinguish between excellent teaching and skillful coaching.

the basis of his study, that older children, as expected, spoke better English than younger children, and that more exposure to ETV and the new oral English program contributed to that improvement.

In January 1969, and again in January 1970, another test of oral English based on the Tate syllabus was administered to large samples of students in grades 3 and 4. These two tests made it possible to compare the performance of two grades, and also of the same grades in consecutive years. Note that in Table 24, which shows the results, the number of students, and therefore the samples, were not exactly the same. But though that reduces the importance of the findings, the figures are at least interesting.

These results indicate that students did better in oral English

TABLE 22
Oral English Scores of American Samoa Students
by Age, 1968

Age	Number of students	Mean score
7	18	18.333
9	24	33.042
11	24	55.375
13	24	66.583

SOURCE: Same as Table 20.

TABLE 23
Oral English Scores of American Samoa Students
by Years of Experience with Educational
Television, 1968

Years of ETV	Number of students	Mean score
0	18	29.222
1	18	45.222
2	18	68.944
3	18	66.583

SOURCE: Same as Table 20.
NOTE: Results do not include seven-year-old children.

TABLE 24

Oral English Scores of American Samoa Students in
Grades 3 and 4, 1969 and 1970

(*Percent*)

	Grade 3		Grade 4	
Response category	1969 (*N* = 832)	1970 (*N* = 459)	1969 (*N* = 631)	1970 (*N* = 476)
A	49.6%	55.0%	61.2%	72.2%
B	13.6	14.4	11.9	11.5
C	6.5	11.9	6.7	3.7
D	30.3	11.5	20.3	11.9

SOURCE: Department of Education files, Pago Pago.
NOTE: Response categories are as follows:
A, complete and correct sentence using the desired grammatical feature.
B, complete and correct sentence, but without using the desired grammatical feature.
C, incomplete or incorrect sentence, but correctly using the desired grammatical feature.
D, any other response or no response.

when they had one more year in school under the new program, and supposedly were a year older. This is not a great finding. More interesting is the finding that both grades were doing dramatically better in oral English in 1970 than in 1969 and that the improvement carried across the years, with a drop in the only completely wrong response, *D*, from 30.3 percent for the third-graders of 1969 to 11.9 percent for the same class in 1970. To be sure, we do not know how much faith to put in the sampling, but we do know that special efforts were made to obtain reliability in the administration of the test. And in the absence of a baseline with which to compare performance before and after ETV, findings like these were about all the school system could depend on to tell whether the new program was working or not.

The Swains Island Study

One study took a different direction in its search for a baseline. In 1972, the senior member of the oral English staff in the Department of Education and several members of the teaching staff under the guidance of the senior author of this book, studied the only public school in American Samoa that had never had television. This school was the one on Swains Island, too far to the north of Tutuila for decent television reception. The school was small, as it is today, with six grades and 28 students at the time of the study. The school was so isolated from the main islands that communication to and from the Department of Education in Pago Pago, and the movement of teaching materials to the school, were very slow. But the Department of Education supplied the teacher, much of the same curriculum had been introduced as on the other islands, and the teaching was supposed to be in English (at least as much of it as was done in English by the Tutuila schools before the advent of television). How similar this school was to the typical pre-television schools we cannot say with confidence, but this at least we can say: that it was closer to those schools than anything else in the Territory.

The 20 students in Swains school who were beyond the first grade were tested on their ability to understand spoken English, and their ability to read English. The tests had been developed by the Department of Education, using the Tate syllabus and some of the Tate testing materials, and had been tried out in numerous other places and situations. They were felt to represent a fair test of the English-language competence of students in the first six grades.

Fifteen of the 20 students had received all their education on Swains Island; the other five had spent varying amounts of time on Tutuila, with parents or other relatives, and while there had attended schools operating under the new system. Let us accordingly divide the students into two groups, calling the five educated elsewhere the A group and the others the B group, and look at their performance separately.

Only three of the 15 students in Group B could make any oral response whatsoever in English, although that was supposed to be the chief language of their instruction. On the other hand, all the students in Group A could speak some English, and those who had been in the new schools for several years could speak it pretty well. Only nine students in Group B scored higher in the understanding of spoken English than they could have scored purely by guessing, and only five scored above the guessing level in reading.

The second- and third-graders in Group B ($N = 5$) could do very little with the test. The mean scores of the other ten students in the group were as follows: understanding of spoken English (maximum score 50), 18.5; English reading (maximum 32), 4.9; responses in English (3 students of 10; maximum score 114), 10.

To put these scores in perspective, two small elementary schools on Tutuila were given the same test. One of these was in Asu village, which is nearly as isolated as Swains Island but is nevertheless close enough to have received television for five years. The other was in Lauli'i, a somewhat larger village and not so isolated as Asu, but still not in one of the population centers of the island. Asu had only four grades; the students in grades 2, 3, and 4 were tested. Lauli'i, like Swains, had six grades; students in grades 3 and 6 were tested. The results are shown in Table 25, with the Swains scores repeated for comparison.

As we see, the students in the two television schools scored

TABLE 25
Oral English and Reading Scores of American Samoa Students in Schools With and Without Television, 1972

Group tested and size	Understanding of spoken word	Speaking	Reading
Asu school (TV)			
Grades 2–3 ($N = 5$)	24.2	41.8	8.3
Grade 4 ($N = 8$)	32.4	61.1	10.6
Lauli'i school (TV)			
Grade 3 ($N = 14$)	32.6	69.6	12.0
Grade 6 ($N = 15$)	42.1	102.7	21.9
Swains school (no TV)			
Grades 4–6 ($N = 10$)	18.5	10.0[a]	4.9

SOURCE: Wilbur Schramm, memorandum to Milton deMello, director of education, Dec. 27, 1972, Department of Education files, Pago Pago.
NOTE: Maximum possible scores: Understanding of spoken word, 50; Speaking, 114; Reading, 32.
[a] Mean for the only three students who could make a spoken response in English.

How Much Did the Students Learn?

TABLE 26

Comparative Scores in Oral English and Reading of Swains
Island Students With and Without Educational
Television Experience, 1972

Group tested and size	Years of ETV	Understand- ing of spoken word	Speaking	Reading
Individual scores in Group A (N = 5)				
Grade 3	1	29	9	4
Grade 3	1	25	19	5
Grade 4	2	31	14	9
Grade 5	3	25	44	10
Grade 6	4	39	97	17
Mean scores of Group B Grades 4–6 (N = 10)[b]	0	18.5	10.0[c]	4.9

SOURCE: Same as Table 25.

NOTE: Maximum possible scores: Understanding of spoken word, 50; Speaking, 114; Reading 32.

[a] All ETV experience was gained in the Tutuila schools.

[b] These students had spent all their school time on Swains, where up until that time there had been no ETV.

[c] Mean for the only three students who could make a spoken response in English.

markedly higher than the students in the non-television school. However, still more interesting is the performance of the five members of the Swains Island school's Group A. Their scores, with the Group B scores again shown for comparison, appear in Table 26.

Small as the sample is, it is clear that, with one exception, the children who had been exposed to the new system had gained year by year in their command of English, as they were expected to do, whereas those who had never been exposed to the new system and its television had learned very little.

The importance of these findings should not be overemphasized. We really do not know to what extent the Swains Island school represents the pre-1964 schools. The absence of television was not the only difference between the test school and the schools on Tutuila; the island's isolation effectively cut the people off from many of the developments in other parts of Samoa.

But the results can hardly leave us in doubt that what happened in 1964 must have helped to bring about a noteworthy, even a spectacular, difference in the quality of English used in all of the elementary television schools of American Samoa. And English was regarded as the key to the successful growth of the system.

Some Later Tests

The reader will recall that the scores in the Gates Reading Survey conducted in 1966–67 were undifferentiated between grades (Table 19). Assuming that the new system was developing as expected, we should find a great deal of differentiation, in later years, between students at different levels of schooling. We cannot verify this with later Gates figures, but we do have the results from Stanford and SRA tests given in 1971 and 1972, and both indicate that some differentiation was indeed taking place, albeit very slowly.

The Stanford test was used for grades 3–6 and tested students in both word meaning and paragraph meaning. The results are shown in Table 27. The SRA test was given to all students in grades 7 and 8 in one year only, 1971. Unlike the Stanford test, it examines the students' skill in the single broad category of reading. Furthermore, because of the difference in the scoring of the tests, one should not expect a smooth fit to the results of the

TABLE 27

Stanford Achievement Test Scores of American Samoa
Students in Grades 3–6, 1971 and 1972

(*Grade equivalents*)

Group tested	Word meaning 1971	Word meaning 1972	Paragraph meaning 1971	Paragraph meaning 1972	Group size 1971	Group size 1972
Grade 3	1.8	2.1	1.7	2.0	860	767
Grade 4	2.2	2.6	2.1	2.3	815	855
Grade 5	2.6	2.6	2.7	2.7	705	724
Grade 6	2.8	3.0	3.0	3.2	581	664

SOURCE: Department of Education files, Pago Pago.

TABLE 28
SRA Achievement Test Scores in Reading of American
Samoa High School Students, Elementary Teachers,
and High School Teachers, 1972
(Grade equivalents)

Group tested and size	Reading
Students	
Grade 9 (N = 624)	4.3
Grade 10 (N = 512)	4.8
Grade 11 (N = 405)	5.5
Grade 12 (N = 343)	5.8
Teachers	
Elementary (N = 209)	5.9
High school (N = 52)	7.7

SOURCE: Science Research Associates, "Report on American Samoa Test Results," 1972, Department of Education files, Pago Pago.

Stanford test. But here is what the SRA had to tell us about the seventh and eighth grades in 1971:

Group tested and size	Reading score
Grade 7 (N = 399)	4.3
Grade 8 (N = 530)	4.6

We also have SRA scores on reading for all high school students and all teachers in 1972; see Table 28. All these data seem to say that by the early 1970's a process of differentiation between grade levels was going on. It looks as though high school students in 1972 were reading a bit better than in 1967. There is not much evidence of change in the scores of the elementary teachers. But our 1966–67 table offers us still another insight into the difficulties that were faced in trying to make any swift improvement in the Samoan system.

The Time Series Scores

In 1970, the Department of Education began to give standardized achievement tests on a regular basis. In 1971 and 1972, these were given to all students in grades 5–12. There was a break in the testing in 1973, and thereafter the tests were given annually only to grades 8 and 12. Thus the series of eighth- and twelfth-grade scores are the only two that cover the entire period 1970–79, although so many of the data are missing from the twelfth-grade results in 1970 and 1971 that we have decided to omit those years from our consideration.

The eighth-grade scores in Table 29 and the twelfth-grade scores that follow in Table 30 are stated in "growth scores." *

The most obvious feature of Table 29, and undoubtedly its most disappointing aspect to the Samoan Department of Education, is the lack of gain in the course of nine years. Scores in language arts moved up a bit, but scores in mathematics and science moved down, and the variation in the other scores is well within the limits one would expect from a time series of tests given to a large number of students. Why is there no greater change? That is something we shall talk about in a later chapter.

The twelfth-grade scores give us a somewhat different picture. Here we see a steady and substantial, if not spectacular, improvement in every subject except science: a gain of more than a year in reading and two years in social studies for the high school senior of 1979 over his or her counterpart of 1972; a gain of about half a year in language arts and mathematics. Indeed, we ought to ask ourselves whether we should, in fact, expect anything more dramatic. School systems are notoriously resistant to change. And then we should consider, too, the general downward trend in college entrance and other scores on

*Science Research Associates (1972: 68ff) explains why "growth scores" were developed as an alternative to grade-equivalent scores. Whereas the grade-equivalent scores may change meaning every time a test is re-standardized, the growth score does not, and therefore growth scores can be more easily compared across tests and years. SRA feels also that growth scores are less easily misinterpreted than grade equivalents. And the results of applying statistical tests to grade equivalent scores are less likely to be valid than applications to growth scores. For any given test and year, growth scores can be translated into grade equivalents, if desired. But in a case like that of Samoa, growth scores have the further advantage of not drawing attention to a comparison of grade equivalents between Samoa and the mainland when, because of cultural differences, this comparison may be misleading.

TABLE 29

SRA Achievement Test Scores of American Samoa Students in
Grade 8, 1970–1979

(*Growth scores*)

Year	Reading	Language arts	Mathe-matics	Social studies	Science	N
1970	241	248	356	267	263	483
1971	240	257	352	268	258	530
1972	243	273	316	259	271	418
1974	244	279	338	261	269	470
1975	252	284	340	275	262	718
1976	236	280	328	272	257	733
1977	239	276	319	269	253	653
1979	241	275	320	265	254	601

SOURCE: Science Research Associates, annual reports on American Samoa test results, 1970–72, 1974–79, Department of Education files, Pago Pago.
NOTE: SRA tests were not given in 1973. 1978 scores are excluded from this summary because irregularities in the administration of the test cast doubt on the results.

TABLE 30

SRA Achievement Test Scores of American Samoa Students in
Grade 12, 1972–1979

(*Growth scores*)

Year	Reading	Language arts	Mathe-matics	Social studies	Science	N
1972	289	331	364	325	311	343
1974	307	342	368	356	306	361
1975	303	340	372	349	303	430
1976	311	336	364	360	303	307
1977	312	342	374	359	398	373
1979	317	343	378	365	310	376

SOURCE: Same as Table 29.
NOTE: On the omission of 1973 and 1978 scores, see note to Table 29.

the mainland since 1970 and at least recognize the American Samoan performance as a healthy exception to the national trend.

Another way to measure performance in the high schools is to compare the scores of these seniors of 1979 with the 1975 performance of the same class as eighth-graders. (Of course, the population was not identical; since 1975 there had been some dropouts and some entrants. But we have no reason to think there was a systematic shift in the kind of students.) Between 1975 and 1979 we should expect students to gain the equivalent of about four grades as measured by standardized tests. They actually gained:

> 3.9 grades in social studies
> 3.3 grades in science
> 3.0 grades in language arts
> 2.9 grades in reading
> 1.6 grades in mathematics

Thus, except in mathematics, Samoan high school students are gaining at the rate we would expect of a mainland high school student. Teachers ascribe the lower grades in mathematics to the thinness of the high school curriculum in that subject, and the fact that comparatively few students take advantage of the courses that are available.

Another set of test results is worth citing in connection with these results, namely, the scores on TOEFL (Test of English as a Foreign Language) examinations given to all seniors in 1976, 1977, and 1978. These results, shown in Table 31, indicate that in those characteristics of the English language that are likely to be of the most benefit to the Samoan student who plans to work or study in an English-speaking culture, substantial gains are being registered. Each of the four high schools showed year-by-year gains on these tests.

TABLE 31

English as a Foreign Language (TOEFL) Test Scores of American Samoa Students in Grade 12, 1976–1978

Year	Mean	Range	Number of students above percentile:		
			75th	50th	25th
1976	385	290–638	12	13	19
1977	396	297–653	15	20	21
1978	414	303–647	22	35	46

SOURCE: TOEFL reports for 1976–78, Department of Education files, Pago Pago.

In Retrospect

The trend in twelfth-grade scores over the period 1972–79 and other evidence of yearly gains in the high schools are encouraging. But the eighth-grade scores have not shown much improvement since 1970, and this makes us even more regretful that no standardized tests were given at regular intervals during the first half dozen years of the project. For with those results we could tell, first, whether the gains were really as substantial in that early period as observers thought they were, and if so, then perhaps why the curve flattened out in the 1970's. All the other tests suggest that performance in the elementary grades was improving in the earlier years of the project. If tests had been given regularly it should have been possible to catch any signs of a slowdown when they first appeared. As it is, we must remain puzzled about the meaning of the eighth-grade scores after the project was well under way, although rather pleased by the scores from the twelfth grade.

The results we have described in this chapter lead in retrospect to questions rather than conclusions. How do we interpret the scores we have available? We should not forget that Samoan scores are still substantially lower than mainland scores for students of the same age or grade. By the end of the 1970's the Samoan students were making progress, in the twelfth grade at least, toward catching up with national norms, but still had a considerable way to go. How do we explain this gap? That is a question to which we now turn.

SEVEN

How Should We Evaluate This Performance?

HOW ONE READS the foregoing tables will determine how encouraging or discouraging one finds the evidence. The dream of a Samoa ETV project, as it was dreamed in 1964, was that a massive infusion of instruction by television would stimulate a lagging school system to perform at the level of an average, preferably an outstanding, mainland school system. In 1979 that dream had not been realized. At the least we might hope for a steady rise, from 1964 on, in academic performance by the students. We have just seen such a rise in the twelfth-grade scores after 1972, but no corresponding rise in the eighth-grade results. We return therefore to a question about which we can only guess: what happened to performance during the first six years of the project, for which we have no time series of test scores?

If there was no more improvement in the elementary schools between 1964 and 1970 than between 1970 and 1979, that would be discouraging indeed. But we doubt whether that is the case. The observations of people who knew the schools well belie it. Such tests as were given belie it. There is every reason, at least, to think that the standard of English usage improved notably during those years, and this must almost necessarily have been reflected in courses in reading and social studies that depend so much on facility with the language. If one can assume that much, then one can read the tables somewhat more encouragingly. Which is to say, they represent a school system that began low (as measured by standardized tests) and operated under difficulties that almost necessarily depress performance. The fact that the schools were able to show some rather impressive gains after 1972 in the twelfth grade (during a period when scores on the mainland and particularly scores of twelfth-grade students taking college entrance examinations were consistently dropping)—this makes the tables we have presented seem rather less discouraging.

The Absolute Level of Samoan Scores

Samoan students performed, not at the level of the wealthy suburban communities of Scarsdale, New York, or Palo Alto, California, but rather at about the level of disadvantaged groups in the crowded cities of Detroit, Chicago, and Los Angeles— southern Blacks, Puerto Ricans, Mexican Americans, Native Americans, and the like. We shall have more to say later about why this might be the case. But here let us record simply that when Samoan test scores in terms of grade equivalents are compared with the scores of mainland disadvantaged groups (see Coleman et al. 1966), it is evident that the Samoan students scored a little lower than these groups in reading, a little higher in mathematics.

It is rather hard to compare Samoan test scores with the scores of students in other countries, but the Samoan performance on tests seems much like that of other developing countries where students are taught in languages foreign to them. Donald Leton, of the University of Hawaii, who has considered various school systems where the language of instruction is a second language—Ireland, the Philippines, India, and other countries in Southeast Asia and Africa—has found that the average eighth-grade student is about three years behind in academic achievement (Leton 1971: 112ff). This is about where the Samoan students have been, and it is worth noting that their scores were obtained in a system where education is available to everyone, rather than in the selective kind of system more commonly found in developing countries. In the years 1973–76, a monumental study in nine volumes, comparing school performance in six subjects in 16 countries, was released by the International Association for the Evaluation of Educational Achievement. The students in the three developing countries in that sample—India, Iran, and Chile—were estimated (like the Samoan students) to be several grades behind the average student in the more fully developed countries, including Sweden, France, Japan, and the United States. Viewed in that perspective, the evidence available suggests that perhaps the Samoan school children accomplished about as much as we ought to expect of them.

This reading would satisfy no one who has been an interested observer of the Samoan project, and in particular would fail to satisfy those who invested money and years of dedicated effort in trying to demonstrate in Samoa that modern educational technology could bring about a quick and spectacular improvement. And it should be pointed out, quite rightly, that the time series we have presented relate to the last nine years of a 15-year project in which the more spectacular changes may very well have occurred in the first half-dozen years. It should be noted also that ETV, the chief technology of the new system, was cut back by about two-thirds near the beginning of the series, and that by the end of the nine years it had been taken entirely out of the high schools, much reduced in parts of the elementary schools, and had its live production curtailed almost to zero. Therefore, the original plan for the Samoa project became less and less applicable to the actual workings of the system as the time series moved from 1970 to 1979.

But let us suggest another way to look at the quality of performance in the Samoa schools.

The Rate of Gain in Samoan Schools

Think of education as an investment, as indeed it is. We invest money in operating and equipping schools and in sending children to them. Students invest their time and effort. For our investments we expect a return. If we invest $10,000 at 6 percent, we expect $600 at the end of the year. The return we expect from education cannot be that simply calculated: much of it may not become evident until years later, and it is difficult to put a money value on ability to think well, solve problems, or get along with other people, to all of which education is expected to make some contribution. But one very simple way to make some partial estimate of return is to measure a student's academic achievement year by year.

Each year a child brings to school a certain amount of knowledge and skill. At the end of the year he has acquired a certain additional amount. Unlike a bank or a bond, this rate of return will not be the same every year. During the early years of school, when a child has relatively little knowledge, he will gain more in proportion to what he brought than he will gain 10 years later, when he starts with more. That is, in third grade we might expect the rate of gain to be 20–25 percent, in high school perhaps 10 percent. Standardized tests are made, therefore, not with a fixed percentage of gain, but rather with the supposition that a student, on the average, will gain one academic year (as compared with the average of a very large population of students) in every school year. The *amount* of return will be the same each year, but the *rate* will decrease the farther one goes in school. When we talk about standardized tests in Samoa, we usually talk in absolute terms: a student "gained six-tenths of a grade equivalent this year," or a student "is an academic year behind the norm for his grade."

Suppose now we consider the rate of gain. It is easy to approximate the rate of gain expected on the standardized tests. For example, if a student takes one of the standardized tests in the seventh month of his third year, and one year later scores exactly one grade equivalent higher, then his rate of gain could be estimated as about 1 divided by 3.7, or 27 percent. But if his test score in the seventh month of his eleventh year is one grade equivalent higher than it was in the seventh month of his tenth year, then the gain would be about 1 divided by 10.7, or only 9 percent. This presumes that the rate of gain depends somewhat on how much a student brings with him, and that the efficiency of a school can be estimated not only in terms of absolute grade-equivalent scores, but also, and perhaps more justifiably, in terms of the rate of gain compared with what the students started with.

We have calculated these rates of gain from standardized test scores in Samoa for the years 1971 and 1972, which was the only time when tests were given throughout the school system, from third to twelfth grade. For those years it is therefore possible to calculate the average gain of the *same class* in the following year. In Table 32 we have put the actual percentages of gain of the Samoan students side by side with the percentages expected in the standardized tests.

Bear in mind that these figures are only rough approximations to students' actual gains. But this table presents a somewhat different picture of the average performance of Samoan students. It does not deny that they still started each year low,

TABLE 32

Expected Rates of Gain on Standardized Tests and Actual Rates of American Samoa Students, 1971–1972

(*Percent*)

Between grades	Expected rate	Samoan rate
Elementary school		
3 and 4	27%	37%
4 and 5	21	30
5 and 6	18	15
6 and 7	15	11
7 and 8	13	9
Combined annual average	19%	20%
High school		
8 and 9	11	7
9 and 10	10	3
10 and 11	9	11
11 and 12	9	8
Combined annual average	10%	7%
Overall average annual gain	14.8%	14.6%

and ended each year low in terms of mainland norms. But the rate of gain, based on the previous level of achievement, is overall almost exactly the same in the Samoan school system and in a mainland system that operates at the middle of the distribution—that is, the norm.

The table, moreover, has an impressive face validity. It shows that in the first school years the Samoan student acquired knowledge very rapidly because he brought relatively little with him. He was getting acquainted with a new language of which he knew little or nothing. He was learning elementary skills of arithmetic, which he had little occasion to practice before he came to school. Therefore, at first the rate of gain was even higher than would be expected of mainland children: they come to school *already* knowing the language of instruction, and have less to learn. However, at about the fifth grade, when children have to master the higher cognitive skills of abstract thinking, reasoning, and problem-solving, the Samoan student's gains fell off, for reasons that we shall discuss a little later in this chapter. Furthermore, it is also apparent that something happened to the rates of gain as the student prepared to make the transition from elementary to high school. This may reflect the change in tests, from Stanford to SRA. It may also be related to the cutback in television that was made rather suddenly in 1971. The lower gains in high school may also be related to the elimination of television as a teaching tool, but that cannot be proved or disproved from the evidence at hand. Moreover, the 1979 twelfth-grade scores show greater gains in high school than in 1971 and 1972. But the interesting point remains that, regardless of these changes in the system, the average overall rate of gain in Samoa was about the same as the rate in a mainland school, if that school operates precisely on the expected norm of one academic year gained per school year.

The table has face validity from another perspective, too. If a person invests $3,000 for a year at 6 percent in one account, and $5,000 at the same rate in another account, one investment is just as efficient as the other, but the totals in the two accounts will be farther apart at the end of the year than they were at the beginning of the year. If the investor lets his money accumulate for 12 years, as we do in a school system, then the totals will be considerably farther apart than they were at the beginning. This is precisely what the standardized scores on a system like Samoa's report: a student who starts a school year with a third-grade achievement level will gain less, in absolute terms, than a student who starts with a fifth-grade achievement, although the rate of gain may be the same. This is what the studies tell us happens to disadvantaged students. They bring less with them to build on, and as a result they fall farther and farther behind what we call the norms, which is simply the expected performance of students in mainland schools who came in with no comparable disadvantage.

Why Is the Performance Not Better?

This is clearly what happened in Samoa, and yet the explanation will not make any observer of the Samoan system happy. The implied hope of the Samoa ETV project was that with the aid of television and a new system of teaching, students might break out of this pattern, and they too might gain an academic year per school year, rather than falling farther behind mainland norms each year.

There is nothing in the genetic inheritance of Samoan children that kept them from making that kind of progress. As a matter of fact, they did make it—in Fia Iloa, the school that was established primarily to cater to the needs of the children of American citizens in Samoa but whose student body, by 1970, was about half Samoan. The example of Fia Iloa scores presented in Table 33 show a school operating almost exactly on mainland norms. Yet it is only fair to point out that all the Samoan students admitted to Fia Iloa already had a good speaking knowledge of English and some of them a reading knowledge, and they came from homes where the skills they had to learn in

TABLE 33
Stanford Achievement Test Scores of Fia Iloa Students
in Grades 1–4, 1971
(Grade equivalents)

Grade tested	Word meaning	Paragraph meaning	Spelling	Arithmetic computation	Arithmetic concepts
Grade 1	2.0	2.1	1.9	2.1	
Grade 2	2.9	2.9	3.0	2.8	
Grade 3	3.8	4.0	4.1	3.8	4.0
Grade 4	4.6	4.9	5.1	5.1	4.9

SOURCE: Department of Education files, Pago Pago.

school were practiced and reinforced. In other words, they brought more achievement with them on which to build their school experience.

In any case, we are clearly not dealing with a situation that is immutable or inexplicable, but rather with something that relates to children's experience in school and out. Five explanations of this relationship have been suggested oftener than others. We do not believe any one of them is sufficient. We doubt whether there is any single cause in a child's experience that accounts for his school performance. Each of these suggested influences, and perhaps others, may contribute to the records we have been examining, and it probably will never be possible to say how much each one of them has contributed, although we have our own guesses about that. Here are the most common explanations for the increasing gap between the Samoan performance and the mainland norms.

The standardized tests explain the gap

The tests were in English, an unfamiliar language to most Samoans entering school, and one in which they had less competence than mainland students throughout their school careers. This handicap, however, should have diminished as the students moved through elementary school. The "Study of Unmet Educational Needs in American Samoa" (Thomas et al. 1974–

76), conducted under contract with the University of California at Santa Barbara, tried to find out something about that handicap by giving a mathematics test in both English and Samoan versions to students in different grades. Up until about grade 5, students did better with the Samoan version; after that, they actually preferred to use the English version, doubtless because they had learned the technical vocabulary in that language. We gave several tests in English to ninth-year students in Western Samoa (where the basic teaching for the first seven years is in the Samoan language), and found that they handled the tests easily and well. The chief differences, if any, between the American and Western Samoa performances on these tests had to do with the fact that the Western Samoa students at that level and that time were a selected group, whereas the American Samoa students were not. But in any case it would seem that by the eighth grade (as noted, after 1972 system-wide standardized testing was dropped for all lower grades), students who have had eight years in a school system where English is the language of instruction should not be greatly handicapped in taking a test in English.

Another consideration is that the SRA standardized tests used in the upper grades were made to fit a mainland culture, curriculum, and environment, rather than Samoan ones. Teachers in Samoa have noted a few test items that may have puzzled some Samoan students: for example, an item referring to railroad trains, which have never been seen in Samoa; and another asking what kinds of clothes are appropriate for various temperatures, when the Samoan child has rarely experienced a temperature below 75° F, and would have only the vaguest idea what to wear at 32° or even 50°. But such items are few and become fewer at higher academic levels as the tests begin to concentrate on general matters rather than specifics.

The fit to the Samoan curriculum raises a more serious question. Educators in Samoa tried conscientiously to tailor a curriculum to the local culture, even though the television teaching was derived almost wholly from mainland experience and the system was guided in early years almost wholly by mainland educators. Nevertheless, the content of courses in the public schools of Samoa had to be less extensive and the course offerings less rich than in typical mainland schools. There had to be greater concentration on the basic skills of a new language, and consequently less time could be devoted to science, social studies, history, literature, and foreign language (except English). Even though the SRA tests are directed mostly at general aspects of learning rather than details to be remembered, still there almost has to be a relationship between what the students derived from the curriculum available to them and what they did with a test made on the assumption of a more extensive curriculum.

A technical problem about the tests may also have something to do with the Samoan scores. There was a wide range of ability in the schools of Samoa. In choosing a standardized test, therefore, it was not always possible to select a form and level of test that would be neither too difficult for the weakest students nor too easy to keep the best students from showing their full ability. Since there were likely to be more students in the lower parts of the achievement distribution, they became the principal consideration in determining the choice of test, and the best students probably got the worst of the deal. The good students do seem to have some problem of "ceiling effect"—that is, the tests did not always give them a chance to show up at their best, and they could probably have made a relatively better score with a more difficult form of test. This was not a major contributor to overall scores, but it must have had some effect.

The turmoil in the islands explains the gap

We have tried to suggest in earlier chapters that the story of the Samoa ETV project was not exactly a smooth or peaceful one. The project began in a great hurry, with little time to bring the Samoan teachers into the planning at an early stage. The experience of being demoted to the level of follow-up teachers must have been shocking to some Samoan teachers. Because of the design and the timing of the project, for a number of years there had to be more attention to producing an almost impossibly large number of programs than to trying out and perfecting these programs. A rising current of dissatisfaction and tension grew up among both teachers and students, and this was not recognized as early as it might have been. The leadership of the Department of Education (director of education) changed five times in the first 10 years of the project. Five different men sat in the governor's chair from the inception of the project until 1977 and a sixth took office in 1978, each with somewhat different ideas of what had been done and what should be done. In the sixth year of television the professional organization that had been responsible for the design and operation of the project withdrew; in the seventh year television was sharply cut back; and in the ninth year it was removed wholly from the secondary schools and reduced further in the elementary grades. Throughout this whole period there were political problems, of which the bitter controversy over the Fia Iloa school in the early 1970's was an example, and in 1976 the Samoan director of education was suspended by fiat of the acting governor, and then soon reinstated. This is far from a placid or uneventful history, and if it were not reflected to some extent in school performance we should be greatly surprised.

Schools are sensitive organisms, reluctant to change even under the best of circumstances. The history of turmoil surrounding the ETV project provided an unfavorable climate for the swift and broad educational change that was envisaged. The architects of the Samoa project would have liked to see their plan given a full 12 years—a school generation—to prove itself, without trouble or turmoil or fundamental change. But innovation takes place in life, not merely on paper. If a plan becomes a political lightning rod, or draws opposition from within the school system, these are part of the conditions with which those in control must deal, and change therefore has to be a part of plan-

ning and administration. But the amount of turmoil and opposition with which the administrators of the Samoa project had to
deal presented them an especially severe challenge.

The students' background and environment explain the gap

We have noted that the pattern of test scores in Samoa could
be interpreted, at least in part, in terms of what preparation for
learning the students brought with them.

In a notable review of findings regarding children's learning
in school, Alex Inkeles points to the importance for a child's development of a stimulating early environment, particularly in the
home, and claims that it is therefore totally unfair to compare the
test performance of students from developing countries like India, Iran, and Chile with the performance of students in more
fully developed countries like Sweden, France, Japan, and the
United States. In these more developed countries, he notes, "a
mere 5% or 6% of the students lived in a home containing fewer
than 10 books." In this and other ways, students in such developing countries, he feels, are greatly "disadvantaged" in comparison to those in developed countries (Inkeles 1977: 173).

If we use the word disadvantaged to refer to the Samoan students we studied, we do so with no intention to disparage either
the Samoan culture or the Samoan home life, for which we
could hardly be expected to feel anything except admiration and
affection. However, we wonder how many of those students
lived in homes where there were more than 10 books! In this
particular, they compared poorly even with the disadvantaged
groups on the American mainland. In another respect, also,
they were far more disadvantaged than the children of Iran or
Chile, and more like, say, the Spanish-speaking groups of the
mainland. For the children of the developing countries named
by Inkeles come to school already speaking fluently the language of instruction, some of them even beginning to read it.
Like the Mexican-American students, few of the Samoan students came to school speaking much English, but in this respect

they were even at a disadvantage compared with the mainland groups, who are at least surrounded by a culture that speaks English all the time, reads English, and writes English. Therefore, English is a tool of great value to residents of the mainland, and if they learn it they can use it to advantage.

The Samoan children live in a culture where most people do not speak primarily the language of the schools. The children used English a great deal of the time for five hours a day, five days a week, in school, but they played in Samoan, interacted with their friends in Samoan. When they came home at the end of the school day they were not encouraged to practice their English. Their parents continued to speak the native language that was precious to them because it helped to preserve the culture. There was little opportunity for homework, little opportunity to practice their new language skill as a major tool of living. Their situation was quite different from that of the students living in a bilingual area like Eastern Canada, where *both* languages are used as tools of the culture. Samoans who shift to speaking English in Samoa are taking a step out of their culture into another one. What has been said about the language applies also to the other home and environmental stimulation that, on the mainland and in countries like Japan, Sweden, and France, would contribute to preparation for school. In other words, Samoan children, despite all their admirable qualities and the happy setting in which they live, are at a disadvantage when their school performance is measured against the norms of a country like the United States.

Few studies have tried to measure what a child brings with him to the first grade of school. It is to James Coleman's credit that he tried with his large sample to do this. Even with the primitive measures one has to use for such a test, he found that Black children came into the first grade scoring two-thirds of a standard deviation below the norm, and Puerto Rican children a little less than half a standard deviation below (Coleman et al. 1966: 44ff). Thereafter they fell farther behind—about a standard deviation within a few years. This translated into two or more years below the norm at the end of the sixth grade, three or more in the ninth, four or more in the twelfth. If these students had no English reading material at home, or if their parents continued to use mostly a language other than English, their scores fell still farther behind.

The Stanford University studies of the El Salvador project found that students' home backgrounds had more influence on test grades than either the school setting (e.g. teacher training, money spent on the school, facilities and equipment) or the community (e.g. isolation, presence of higher schools, employment, amount of business, cultural institutions), although all three played an important role. As Table 34 indicates, the school had a slightly greater influence as the students moved beyond the seventh grade, and their background slightly less influence. Perhaps the most important feature of the table, however, is how strongly the El Salvador students' background continued to relate to their academic performance. Even after nine years of school, background was still the chief correlate with test scores.

We think that if correlations of this kind existed for Samoa, they would probably look much like the El Salvador table. That is, the school, the community, and the home and family background would all prove to be related to the student's academic performance, but the background would be a dominant factor in

TABLE 34

Average Correlation Between Cognitive Skills Index and Background, School, and Community Variables for El Salvador Students in Grades 7–9, 1970–1972

Cognitive skills index	Background	School	Community
Grade 7	.725	.366	.442
Grade 8	.639	.487	.549
Grade 9	.652	.471	.420

SOURCE: Robert C. Hornik et al., "Television and Educational Reform in El Salvador: Final Report" (Stanford, Calif., Aug. 1973), p. 153.

the early years and would continue through the school years to be a better predictor of the student's record in achievement tests than either of the others.

The language of instruction explains the gap

We have already pointed out that the Samoan child's unfamiliarity with English when he came to school and the lack of reinforcement at home for practicing English probably made it harder for him to score well on achievement tests. However, there is another aspect of the problem of using English as a second language of instruction that is even more disturbing.

In connection with some of the pre-television tests we noted that there was a consistent difference in those tests between the Samoan students' performance on memory skills and their performance on higher cognitive skills. That is, for example, they invariably scored higher on spelling than on reading, higher on arithmetical computation than on mathematical reasoning. The 1979 scores, 25 years after the first really comparable evidence, showed the same relationship, almost unchanged: spelling scores were still significantly higher than reading, computation higher than reasoning and concepts.

A member of one of the University of Hawaii's task forces, in a memorandum to the director of education proposing some research in the Samoa schools, spoke of those long-continuing differences:

It is well known and demonstrated in the results of the standardized achievement battery, that Samoan students show relatively high achievement in memory-based curricula. Their relatively high scores in arithmetical computation is a manifestation of associative memory. Their lower scores in mathematical concepts and in reading comprehension indicate a lack or an underdevelopment of cognitive abilities such as comprehension and reasoning. Their educational experiences, and perhaps also their parents' educational experiences, can be characterized as rote-learning, and emphasizing imative-repetitive responses. . . . Samoan high school students [appear to be] relatively low in critical thinking, i.e., the ability to make evaluative judgments of information. (Hawaii 1972: 6)

In observing Samoan children aged three to five in pre-school classes, the memo writer felt they showed normal perceptual abilities, attentional control, response to both verbal and non-verbal cues, excellent ability to shift attention and modify action, and abilities to count and enumerate—in other words, the sort of development one would expect to find in normally intelligent children of pre-school age. The deficiencies in learning higher cognitive skills most probably can be traced to something that happened during the school years. What was it?

As we noted earlier, in Table 32, it is evident from the 1971–72 data on the Samoan students' rates of gain that the children started fast but hit some obstacle by the time they reached fifth grade that led to a notable slump in their achievement scores thereafter. Let us see if we can zero in on the obstacle.

Some observers have questioned whether the skill levels of the elementary school teachers, especially their skill in using English, might have had a kind of ceiling effect on the performance of their students. The rather startling table presented in the preceding chapter, which showed the average elementary school teacher in 1972 reading at just under sixth-grade level (Table 28), lends some credence to that suggestion. It would be surprising if any large proportion of students would rise above the level of their teachers in elementary school.

There is another possible explanation, however, which also has to do with the level of language skill. A child must be able to use the language of instruction easily, efficiently, naturally, before he can take on the more difficult challenges of education. Therefore, despite the Samoan children's early gains, language was a major problem from the first day of school. It caused less trouble in the first years because much of the class work was in Samoan, and furthermore a great deal of learning time was necessarily devoted to memory tasks—vocabulary, spelling, computation. The harder intellectual tasks enter slowly into school experience.

These first years of school are precious times in a child's development. His life space is just filling up. He is interested in everything. His mind is fresh; he is capable of seeing new patterns that in a few years he will discard as "childish." At this age he is a natural poet and a natural explorer. A six-year-old child can call a lampshade "a skirt for the light," and be completely unaware that he is creating a poetic image. A seven-year-old can be captivated by the smallest event and is able to accept the most unexpected relationships. All this time the unfilled little minds are filling up, laying the basis for the concept formation, reasoning, and critical thinking that lie ahead.

Now what happened in Samoan classrooms as the child moved through these precious years toward the middle of elementary school? Once past the first orientation to schooling, he attended classes conducted largely in English, working in a foreign language of which he had only a rudimentary command, talking a kind of foreign baby talk with teachers who had only a little more command of English than he had. In that situation it is obviously easier to practice the memory skills, to drill on spelling or subtraction or the simple language forms that come early in the Tate syllabus. But it is dreadfully hard to leap from that stage to the stage of reasoning, critical thinking, and problem-solving—to the kinds of abstraction that form an increasingly large part of the educational experience throughout the remainder of schooling.

Visitors and members of the school system have been troubled by the thought that the choice of language of instruction is perhaps a moral problem as well as a professional one. Do we have the right to take away from children the kinds of intellectual experiences they might be enjoying in the first four or five years of school if their command of the language of instruction were adequate to the demands on them? Is it fair to use these formative years, on which so much of the child's future intellectual development depends, largely for rote-learning, and neglect the more demanding and subtle growth that can only be accomplished with a language one really commands? In other words, did the use of English as a language of instruction, by slowing up the mastery of higher cognitive skills, almost doom

Samoan children to the situation that we and other scholars have described as a characteristic of disadvantaged students everywhere—to begin below their more fortunate peers, and to fall farther behind the farther they go in their schooling?

The obvious alternative is to teach in Samoan. But there is nothing obvious about whether that decision should have been made. It would certainly have run into opposition from parents who were eager to have their children know English well enough to work or study on the mainland or in Hawaii, if necessary, and to interact with English-speaking people. It would have made it necessary to create teaching materials in Samoan. It would have made it almost impossible to borrow short-term teachers from elsewhere, except for English language teaching, because so few people in advanced countries speak Samoan.

It was not a decision to be made quickly and arbitrarily. But might it not have been worth experimenting with? Even as the ETV project moved forward, Western Samoa was teaching most of the first seven grades in Samoan, all the while emphasizing courses in English as a second language. Only at the end of seven years did English become the chief language of instruction. By that time the students who survived and entered intermediate school could handle English quite adequately. And they had the advantage of being introduced to the higher cognitive skills, to history and literature, and to abstract thinking in a language with which they were thoroughly at home.

We feel that this kind of arrangement was and is worth study and perhaps experimentation. It worked in Western Samoa with a selective school system; could it be made to work in a system of universal educational opportunity? At least until 1979, no better suggestion has been made in American Samoa to ease the transition to higher mental skills and escape the straitjacket of depressed achievement scores.

The cutback in television explains the gap

We are hesitant about making this suggestion because it sounds a bit like special pleading for a cause in which we might have developed a special interest by studying it. Furthermore, there is the fact, previously noted, that the twelfth-grade students gained steadily in SRA scores through the 1970's, even though television disappeared from the high schools in the early years of the decade. But television must have been more important to the elementary schools than to the high schools. Teachers must have depended on it more, because they had less professional training than the high school teachers. If elementary teachers continued to use English at sixth-grade level, as the SRA tests indicated in 1972, the only way for elementary school students to get better language models would be from television. It is also worth noting that the only subjects where eighth-grade students notably performed more poorly between 1970 and 1979 were those in which ETV was completely eliminated from the elementary grades—science and mathematics. Oral English, language arts, and social studies continued to be taught with the aid of television; SRA scores rose in language arts between 1970 and 1979, and held about even in reading and social studies. But in science they fell 4 percentage points, and in mathematics 10 points. Furthermore, without denying the impressive gains made in the secondary schools after television was all but deleted, we must also observe that this happened at a time when better trained teachers were returning from overseas, and a special Title I project made possible more emphasis on English. Therefore, the cutback in television is a hypothesis to be considered along with the others.

In Retrospect

There is nothing in this evidence to say television succeeded or failed, except that it did not accomplish the expected miracle. The case is blurred. It is not television itself that is on trial, but rather the way television was used. The home background of the children is not on trial but is obviously a factor of importance. The language of instruction is a factor of uncertain, but potentially great, importance. Whether the Samoan students' performance on tests was good or bad is a relative matter. And we are sadly handicapped in trying to adjudicate it by the scarcity of test data from the years that would tell us most about the effect of the television curriculum—the first half-dozen years of the project.

What stands out, in retrospect, is that ETV is not a miracle drug for a school system. On the other hand, there is reason to believe that ETV will help an educational system, any system, at any stage of development, if it is used skillfully to meet the special needs of that system. There is little doubt that it helped in Samoa, even though it may not always have been used in the best way at all times for the best purposes. It certainly helped to accomplish things not directly measurable in terms of student performance—for example, getting the money to build consolidated schools, encouraging the building of electric power lines throughout the islands, establishing efficient communication links between the remote schools and the Department of Education, and ultimately creating a workable program of testing in the schools. Beyond those indirect contributions, there can be little doubt that it contributed greatly to raising the standard of English in the schools. The observers are unanimously convinced of this, almost all the tests say so, and the improvement of English has helped to improve the learning of other subjects that depend so heavily on the language for textbooks and discussion.

When one begins to talk about ETV in Samoa, one soon finds oneself talking about the system of education itself. Systems with different goals, operating with different educational strategies, at different levels of development, have different needs for television. In a sense, television must be regarded as the follower rather than the mover of the system. If TV is used skillfully, as we have said, it can help almost any system, but the major result depends on the system, not the technology.

In the early chapters we emphasized the importance of the way television was planned and used. We talked about the way it was decided on and introduced, the frantic speed at which it was required to begin and at which it was supposed to develop, the lack of success in coping with the change that accompanied it.

All these and other aspects of television's use must be considered when we try to explain how well or how badly it did. But having described some of these problems, we now find ourselves returning to the basic strategy of the system. On one hand, the need for Samoan young people to learn English was widely perceived and agreed on. On the other hand, Samoan young people came from an extraordinarily infertile background for mastering English quickly. Given those conflicting circumstances, was the strategy of instruction built around television the best one that could have been chosen? Would television have been of help if it had been used in support of a school system in which the principal language was Samoan until the young learners had mastered the higher cognitive skills? Suppose that the original plan of English as a second language in the elementary grades had been maintained. Would the result have been more satisfactory? It is impossible to say what might have been. But the opportunity for experimentation with a different language strategy *always* exists.

EIGHT

The Impact of Television on the Home Audience

A REPORT on television in American Samoa would be incomplete without a discussion of television outside the school system. The French magazine *Direct*, in its requiem for ETV in American Samoa, remarked that "what remained [was] an out-of-school service." This is not far from the truth. In 1979, a school service that had once produced 6,000 programs a year, was producing only one series of programs, 40 minutes of oral English. By contrast, an out-of-school service that once offered only 28 hours a week on a single channel, was filling three channels every day from late afternoon until late evening. The balance of education and entertainment had been reversed.

Even at the outset, plans for Samoan television included service to home viewers in addition to the schools. Just as television was counted on to bring expert teaching, native English speakers, and visual aids to the classrooms, so it was expected to bring information on health, agriculture, and public affairs, news of the world, and children's entertainment to viewers at home. School television began with a rush, and in the early years absorbed most of the talent and resources. In Appendix D we have reproduced a week's schedule of home television from the spring of 1966, the second year of television in Samoa and the first when all levels of the schools were being served. There was very little time then for locally produced programming: news was read off the wire, the government aired a few information programs, and there was a weekly 45-minute English lesson. Therefore, most of the evening programs were mainland products: "The Mickey Mouse Club" for the children; popular adult shows like "Cheyenne," "Hawaiian Eye," and "Bonanza"; Disney movies for the general audience. These proved a great attraction, and the sales of television sets boomed. One of the early regular viewers was reported to be the head of state of Western Samoa, for the signal could easily be received in many parts of that country.

As the popularity of the evening service increased and more and more people bought sets, it was the imported programs that grew in number and the commercial network programs that drew the audience. The series of sample evening schedules reproduced in Appendix D will supply some detail of the expansion from 1966 to 1977. By 1967 two channels were needed in the evening. "Cheyenne" and "Bonanza" remained on the schedule, and were joined by programs like "McHale's Navy," the Rosemary Clooney and Garry Moore shows, "I Love Lucy," and ABC's "Wide World of Sports." National Educational Television—the predecessor of the Public Broadcasting Service—was represented by programs like "The Friendly Giant." And there was a regular news program in Samoan.

By 1968 "Misteroger's Neighborhood," the perennially popular children's program from NET/PBS was available in Samoa, and by 1970 such NET features as "The Forsyte Saga" (borrowed from the British Broadcasting Corporation) were being shown. Yet all the evidence available from those years indicates that the audience-pleasers in Samoa were the same mass entertainment programs that were leading the mainland ratings.

By 1972 home programming began at 4:30 P.M. on the two channels and continued until 10:00 or a little later. The station was then offering the chief PBS programs, including "Sesame Street," "The Electric Company," and "Misterogers" for the children and "The Advocates" for adults. But nearly five hours of programs from the American networks were also being telecast. These included "The Flintstones," "The Three Stooges," and "The Wonderful World of Disney" for the children, and for the adults (in theory but for everyone except the youngest children in practice), programs like "Star Trek," "Mission Impossible," "Bonanza," "Perry Mason," "I Love Lucy," "Boxing from the Olympic," and three movies a week. This pattern was followed until 1977: children's programs in the late afternoon, then one channel devoted chiefly to PBS shows, the other to commercial network shows. The schedules on both channels were punctuated occasionally by local newscasts and some programming in Samoan. The evening program was cut back to one channel in 1974, but was restored to two channels the next year and expanded to three in 1977.

In short, despite Governor Lee's vision of an evening service consisting of an occasional travel film or an old movie, the three channels on the air in 1979 (reduced from the initial six) provided a weekly total of 174 hours of network programming from the mainland. One of the three channels was devoted almost exclusively to the PBS product, with 63 hours of programs a week. Another carried a weekly schedule of 77 hours of NBC shows and the third 34 hours from the ABC network. During fiscal 1978 the station originated only about 14 hours of local programming a week.

So marked has been the change from the late 1960's, in fact, that one of the NAEB team members who helped establish the system was led to comment, on revisiting Samoa in 1976, that "if the official status of the station is 'educational' its climate is commercial." Even to the extent, he went on to say, that the station manager referred to one of the channels as "an NBC affiliate" (Gillmore 1977).

It is important to note that the expanded evening network entertainment services did not come about overnight. It was a gradual process, but one that once set in motion was seemingly irreversible. At first, ABC's nightly news was recorded, unofficially, off the air in Hawaii and shown without commercials, along with a few syndicated shows like "I Love Lucy," which were purchased directly from independent distributors. However, to satisfy a growing demand for entertainment shows, the three U.S. networks were approached about making available some of their more popular programs. Only two, NBC and later ABC, showed any interest; CBS chose not to participate. Contracts were then signed with both networks, which among other things prohibited the station from deleting material of any sort. This meant that all programs from those two sources would include commercials, whether relevant to Samoa or not.

Until 1979, at least, the station had not received any revenue from this advertising, although it proved to be a bonanza to local merchants in Western Samoa, as well as in American Samoa. Almost all could recount numerous examples of goods that sat on store shelves for years until commercial television came along, or of a sudden demand for a product that had never been heard of in Samoa until it was advertised on the air.*

To be fair, we should emphasize that the swing to mass-entertainment television did not result from commercial or advertising pressure. From the start, television in Samoa was conceived as a government-financed, nonprofit, and noncommercial entertainment. Samoan merchants benefited from the introduction of advertising, as did the companies that make the products, but the pressure for more entertainment shows came from the Samoan people themselves.

Budget and personnel figures, as much as anything else, reveal the station's increased reliance on imported network programming. In 1968 the budget for direct operating costs was $1,200,000 plus an estimated $225,000 for depreciation and notional interest, and there were 77 staff members, almost all palagis. By 1978–79 operating costs had dwindled to $528,000 (of which $98,517, or roughly 19 percent, came from the Department

*Indeed, Barry Siegel of the *Los Angeles Times*, who visited Samoa in early 1979, reported that the firm of S. V. Mackenzie in Apia, Western Samoa, for 57 years agents for many American products, had found business so good that it was tearing down its current store and replacing it with a modern five-story supermarket with a parking lot. The store, Siegel said, reported sharply increased sales of heavily advertised brand-name items: soft drinks, mouthwashes, potato chips, and so forth. Siegel quoted Vernon Mackenzie, the owner, as saying: "Pepto Bismol never sold here before at all. Now it sells like hotcakes. Also things like Bufferin, Nytol, and Sominex. And the great thing is, we don't have to pay for the advertising" (Siegel 1979).

of Education for instructional TV), and there were 35 employees, all but five of them Samoan. This was the last budget fund-
ed out of the U.S. government's appropriation for the islands.
For fiscal 1979–80, at least, the territorial government supplied
the funding from local tax revenues.

It is not surprising that a shift in power and the locus of decision making took place simultaneously with these changes. By
1979 the station was no longer organizationally a part of the Department of Education. Instead, the station manager, a profes-
sionally trained broadcaster, reported directly to the governor's
office. And as with the shift from a largely educational television operation to an essentially commercial one, this change took
place in steps. Lee's successor, Governor Aspinall (1967–69),
moved immediately on the departure of the NAEB to have the
station manager report to his office, although the formal organization chart still showed a direct line to the director of education. The next governor, Haydon (1969–74), tightened the reins
of the governor's office over the station and its day-to-day operations. (On one occasion, he even scaled a protective fence and
threw a switch that took off the air a program he considered
offensive.)

In 1976 and 1977, Governors Ruth and Barnett completed the
reorganization process, cutting the budget almost in half, reducing the number of channels in use from six to three, and
bringing about the dismissal of much of the staff. In the process,
control of the station, together with its budget and administration, was formally removed from the Department of Education
to a new office reporting directly to the governor.

Initially, when the evening network entertainment shows
were introduced, the station officials attempted to involve Samoans in program decisions (what programs to use, at what
times, and so forth) through an informal advisory committee
composed of several of the islands' most respected and knowledgeable leaders. But the committee functioned only briefly and
thereafter, though Samoan members of the program staff occa-

sionally had a say in the program decision, it was the station manager, a professional broadcaster brought in from the U.S. mainland, who had the final word on which programs would be seen in Samoa and when.

The Viewing Audience

In late 1976 station KVZK-TV commissioned an audience survey that provides a great deal of information both about the home audience for television and the distribution and use of that medium and others in American Samoa. The survey sample ($N = 702$) was designed to be proportional to the population 15 years of age or over in five principal areas of American Samoa. The interviewers, who were Samoans, used a questionnaire that asked about access to television and the use of other media; inquired whether the respondents viewed each of the programs that occurred every weekday (e.g. news and daytime serials); took respondents through a week's program schedule, inquiring whether they had actually watched each of the programs; and asked a series of preference questions concerning types of programs. Nothing was asked about out-of-school viewing of school programs, although in response to a question about whether the person interviewed ever watched television before 3:00 P.M., the startling answer from 20 percent was that they did so *almost every day*: there was nothing on the air weekdays before that hour except school television.

The answers on media behavior add up to a degree of mass-media activity in American Samoa that Margaret Mead, remembering her year in Manu'a, would assuredly have found startling. If this sample had any validity, there would have been about 3,800 television sets in the Territory at that point, or just over one for every eight people. (Informal estimates say that there were at least that many sets in Western Samoa as well.) Thirty-seven percent of the respondents said they watched color television; and 93 percent said they had ready access to television, which is not surprising considering the close family relationships and the open Samoan fales. Answers to the question "How many people were watching with you the last time you watched TV" averaged out to 7.88 viewers per set per program! Even assuming that this figure was inflated by as much as 100 percent, it would still be astonishing by Hawaii and mainland standards. The corresponding figure for Hawaii is just over two viewers.

In respect to other media, 90 percent of the respondents had a radio in their family; 46 percent reportedly listened to it every day, and 35 percent a few times a week. Most listened to the local commercial station; only 1 percent said they listened to short wave. In the way of newspaper reading, 48 percent said they read the *Samoa News* (published in Pago Pago) every week, and 35 percent once in a while. Thirty-two percent read the government's mimeographed news bulletin every day, and 37 percent a few times a week. Regrettably, no questions were asked about movie attendance.

Television preferences turned out to be not greatly different from the preferences of Hawaiian and mainland viewers. The NBC channel got most of the audience. (ABC had not yet come in.) The channel carrying PBS did about as well as PBS stations in the States, considering that at this point it had to compete against only one other channel. In the survey week, about 21 percent of the respondents watched the PBS children's programs—"Sesame Street," "The Electric Company," "Misterogers," and "Zoom"—which is high compared with the mainland but about at the median point for Samoa. Fourteen percent watched "Washington Week in Review" (the only PBS public affairs program to draw a significant audience), 16 percent "The Way It Was" (sports), 13 percent "The Golden Age of Hollywood" (movies), and 11 percent a yoga lesson. "Evening at the Symphony" drew 6 percent, "Masterpiece Theatre" (*Madame Bovary*) 4 percent, and "The Adams Chronicles" 3 percent (or about 20 out of 700 viewers).

But the viewing of the NBC channel was really quite remark-

TABLE 35
Top Ten Programs in Samoa During Survey Week, December 1976

Total sample (N = 702)	Percent watching	15–19 age subsample (N = 60)	Percent watching
Police Woman	87%	Police Woman	92%
Sanford and Son	83	Sanford and Son	92
Beauty and the Beast	80	Beauty and the Beast	85
Wonderful World of Disney	74	Wonderful World of Disney	80
Baa Baa Black Sheep	70	NBC Midnight Special	77
Van Dyke and Company	69	Van Dyke and Company	75
Little House on the Prairie	68	Police Story	75
NBC Best Seller: "Once an Eagle"	67	NBC Sunday Night Mystery Movie	70
Police Story	67	Little House on the Prairie	70
NBC Sunday Night Mystery Movie	65	NBC Big Event: "The Moneychangers"	67

able, as the list of the Samoan "Top 10" in Table 35 illustrates.*
A full 87 percent of the people sampled not only watched television at one given hour, an unheard-of-audience on the mainland, but watched the same show. And even if we were to deflate this by 50 percent, a viewership of 43 would still be remarkable. As we see, this remarkable showing was made by the crime drama "Police Woman." The favorite sports program was NFL football (44 percent), though "Boxing from the Olympic" ran a close second (36 percent). The U.S. daytime game shows and serials were shown in the early evening and had a far wider viewership than in the States: "The Wheel of Fortune" (51 percent), "Hollywood Squares" (46 percent), "Days of Our Lives" (39 percent), "Another World" (28 percent). But the audiences they attracted, as in the States, were predominantly female and young.

*These figures are percentages of the sample interviewed who reported they had watched the program during the survey week. This kind of "rating" is not comparable with television ratings in Hawaii and the mainland, which represent percentages of homes reached by a given program. Obviously many Samoans were viewing the very popular programs elsewhere than in their own homes.

The interest in news? Very high. Fifty-four percent of the respondents said they viewed "News in Samoan" almost every day, 49 percent "News in English," and 34 percent "NBC Nightly News." Twenty-two percent watched NBC's "Meet the Press," as compared with the 14 percent for PBS's "Washington Week in Review" and 5 percent for its "Agronsky and Company."

The general pattern of viewing one deduces from the survey is that in Samoa most viewers (in December 1976) turned on the commercial network channel and left it on. When they broke out of this pattern, it was usually for Samoan programs, and the most-watched of these was the news in Samoan. The three most-watched programs on the PBS channel were all in the Samoan language. The viewers of Samoan programs, as might be expected, tended to be older than those who watched the English programs, and the difference was especially notable among the fifty and over age group.

The Teenage Audience

Because our principal concern was with the Samoan young people, we obtained and analyzed the responses of the 60 respondents in the survey sample who were between fifteen and nineteen years old.

Who were these 60 young people? They had, on the average, more education than the older people in the sample. Apparently about a third of them were still in high school, and some were in vocational training or community college. About one out of four was no longer in school of any kind. All except two lived in homes that had television: 15 (one out of four) had two sets at home, and one of them had three sets. Twenty-nine of the 60 (48 percent) had color television. All except two owned radios, and 31 (52 percent) reported that they listened to radio every day. They made somewhat more use of radio than the total sample (only 46 percent of whom listened every day) and considerably less use of newspapers (22 percent vs. 41 percent). The best estimate we can make from the data is that the average teenager spent about one hour a week reading the news, at least twice that much time viewing or listening to it, and from 12 to 20 times as much total time on television and radio as on newspapers.

As we saw in the "Top Ten" table (Table 35), the teenagers' tastes in television programs were much like those of the general population, but they watched those shows in still greater numbers. This was true consistently down the list, with an average increase in the size of the group watching of 6 percent for five of the six top programs. The teenagers tended to concentrate on favorite programs, but were somewhat under the general population's average in watching the low-ranking programs.

We might call their taste in television lower-middlebrow: little of social significance in their favorite programs, but a great deal of violence, adventure, and escape from the real-life problems of American Samoa. They did *not* go for the kind of highbrow programming represented on the PBS channel. The typical PBS program attracted only two or three of these 60 teenagers (3–5 percent). The programs they liked on PBS tended to be as similar as possible to the ones they liked on the NBC channel— movies, plays, and action. But not the PBS showcase programs. "The Adams Chronicles" attracted not a single viewer during the survey week from among the teenagers. Nor did "Masterpiece Theatre" or the poetry program "Anyone for Tennyson." "Washington Week in Review" had one viewer out of 60; "Evening at the Symphony" had two. And so it went.

On the other hand, their attention to news programs was slightly higher than the total sample, and their attention to NBC news considerably higher (42 percent vs. 34 percent). The proportion of the young people watching NBC programs like "The Wheel of Fortune," "Hollywood Squares," "Days of Our Lives," and "Another World" (which, as noted, were shown on the mainland mostly in the daytime but in Samoa in early evening) was consistently higher than the sample as a whole. On the Sunday of the survey week, NFL football featured a doubleheader: Buffalo vs. Miami, and New England vs. Tampa Bay. These games drew 52 percent of the teenagers, compared with 44 percent of the total sample. But boxing and wrestling drew fewer of the teenagers than of their elders. And the 52 percent for a professional football doubleheader, compared with 92 percent for a crime drama, suggests that perhaps the Samoan teenagers like their violence in fiction more than on the athletic field.

To sum up, we can say that in 1976 Samoan teenagers watched a great deal of home television, and overwhelmingly the kind of show that Americans on the mainland were watching on the commercial networks. Television dominated their media time, and American commercial television dominated that. It bathed them in American entertainment, American news, American behavior, and the values depicted in dramatic programs and by favorite entertainers. Thus, if exposure to television from another culture has any substantial effect on young people's values, role concepts, and social behavior in a traditional culture, some of that effect ought to be visible in American Samoa.

The Effect of Home Television

Measuring the effect of television out of school, of course, is a different problem from measuring the effect of in-school television. There are no curricula outlining the content to be mastered, no lesson plans with specific objectives on which to base questions. The audience is not in classrooms five hours a day, five days a week, to be observed and to provide feedback. The "classroom" for home television is all of American Samoa and a considerable part of Western Samoa.

What kinds of effects can one look for in the big classroom of home television? Perhaps the most obvious ones are *time* effects. We know that viewers were spending, on the average, several hours a day with television. What activities was it replacing? Not school homework, probably, because not much homework was assigned, and most Samoan houses are not designed efficiently for home study. Did television replace reading? In most Samoan homes there was not a great deal of reading anyway, and well-educated persons for whom reading is important are not likely to be distracted from it. So the chief time changes, we would suppose, would have come in family and community activities. What activities of that kind were being replaced by the time now consumed by the tube? Family conversation? Village talk? Social events, like the singing, dancing, and feasting traditionally associated with the South Pacific? It would be interesting to know this in detail, but we do know at least that two or three hours a day that were formerly devoted to other pursuits were now devoted to television, and that a considerable part of people's daily schedule perforce was revised.

There were certainly also *knowledge* effects, out of school as well as in school. News of events in the distant world, descriptions of how people live in other cultures and countries, a new gallery of persons and events—these passed every day before the television viewers in Samoa. Therefore, television must have been doing something to restructure their world views, focusing their attention on events they would otherwise not have been aware of and establishing in their minds a new galaxy of "very important persons" with which to compare their matais and their other leaders.

Television was also furnishing *models for behavior*. As we have noted, hardly a store manager in Pago Pago was unable to recount the effects of television advertising on purchasing: how a product sat on the shelf for a year, and then sold out in a week when television began to pitch it; or how people began to buy processed foods their parents would never have known about; or how young people began to look for the decorated sweat shirts or mod clothes worn by mainland teenagers. More basically, television was furnishing role models. In Samoa as elsewhere, it must have been helping to socialize children, preparing them for what would be expected of them in adulthood. How does a boy treat a girl? Does a policeman act like the cops on "Hawaii Five-0" or "Police Story"? How large does crime bulk in adult life? Some of the answers to questions like those were clearly coming from television.

Still more basically, television was surely contributing to a new system of *values* among the young Samoans. This is par-

ticularly important because the television seen in Samoa represents for the most part a foreign culture and foreign values, and
thus reinforced the American cultural invasion already apparent in business, government, and technology. Therefore it becomes both interesting and important to know the extent to
which television has modified the traditionally conservative and
resilient Samoan culture, and how much it has contributed to
the process of change.

But in field research one does what time, resources, and access permit. Nearing the end of our examination of school television in Samoa, we should have liked to put ETV in perspective
of television's total effect in and out of school. That was beyond
our resources and time, however, and we concentrated on finding out something about the changes in cultural values that
were under way in Samoa, and to which television was making
a contribution of unknown magnitude.

The Inkeles and Smith Study of "Becoming Modern"

In 1974 Alex Inkeles and David H. Smith published a study
that set a new standard for measuring individual changes during the "modernization" of a culture. Following along the approach demonstrated by Gabriel Almond and Sidney Verba
(1963), Daniel Lerner (1963), and Howard Schumann (1967), Inkeles and Smith conducted highly sophisticated sample surveys
of adult males in Chile, Israel, Argentina, India, Nigeria, and
East Pakistan (now Bangladesh). They assumed that certain
qualities and values (such as openness to new experience, readiness for social change, the ability to form and hold opinions of
one's own, information seeking, and a feeling of efficacy in political and social life) distinguish individuals in a modern industrial society, and that this set of characteristics would indicate
the direction of movement in industrializing societies. They
then devised scales to measure each of these qualities and set
them against demographic and behavioral measures. The result
is an impressive study of emergent "modernity," as defined by
these authors against a background of industrialism.

It would have been interesting and illuminating to apply these same tests to the Samoan culture, but there were certain arguments against doing so. For one thing, perhaps the central force described in the Inkeles-Smith model was experience in the factory, and Samoa has virtually none. For another, the chief correlates Inkeles and Smith found in relation to their measures of "modernity" were education, factory experience, and the use of mass media. But for our purposes, the most meaningful group to study was the young people, in their last year of secondary school, just about to enter on careers in adult life, and this ruled out two of the three most important Inkeles-Smith variables, for all the members of this group would have had about the same amount of education and little or no experience working in a factory. Furthermore, we had no measure of change over time, since the chief baseline available to us was Richard Bauldauf's study based on data gathered before the Inkeles-Smith scales were published. Beyond these reasons, there is the hard fact that we had neither the funds nor the time to apply the Inkeles-Smith study to Samoa over a five-year time span and for all the age groups it would have been appropriate to cover.

Nevertheless, the results of that study are encouraging to us when we set them beside our own results. The set of attitudes and behaviors that Inkeles and Smith identify with modernity are represented in the American entertainment television that so quickly became popular in Samoa. Therefore, we were dealing with essentially the same general kind of impact as they studied (though not, to be sure, in an industrializing state). More important, Inkeles and Smith found, as did Lerner before them, that the mass media were among the most important forces in bringing about such attitudinal and behavioral changes, which agrees with our conclusion that American entertainment television was at least partly responsible for the rapidly changing way of life.

Still, we make no claim to having tried to measure modernity. Rather, we have tried to gain some little insight into the impact on an ancient culture of the favorite Western entertainment medium. In this, we were fortunate in having some earlier field-work in Samoa that dealt with characteristics of the traditional culture and thus gave us an opportunity to measure ongoing change.

Earlier Studies of Values in Samoa

Two studies of cultural values in Samoa have aided us in our study of the years 1964–79. One is an undated research report by Jarrell W. Garsee and Alfred P. Glixman, which is based on data that Garsee gathered while he was on the staff of a church in Samoa. In either 1964 or 1965, then, he administered Gordon's survey form for measuring interpersonal values (Gordon 1963) to 139 seniors in the high school of American Samoa (since renamed Samoana). Subsequently, comparing his results with Gordon's measurements of mainland high schools, he and Glixman found that Samoan students were significantly less independent, more conforming, and more benevolent than mainland American students. Their measures are not directly comparable with the ones we used, but it is worth noting that we found Samoan students becoming significantly more *independent* and *less* willing to conform between 1972 and 1977. The implication is that they had moved closer to mainland American values and farther from their traditional ones since the mid-1960's.

The second value study we used (Baldauf 1975) was a more ambitious one, conducted by the author as doctoral fieldwork when he was in charge of tests and measurements for the American Samoa schools in 1972 and 1973. He was interested in the relation between overt manifestations of acculturation (such as language and behavior) and covert ones (such as attitudes and values). To obtain a satisfactory measure of values, he first adapted Charles Morris's "Ways of Life" (Morris 1956), but then found that a 76-item "Inventory of Cultural Values," derived largely from Ryan's "Values Inventory" (1973) was more useful for his purpose. He designed the inventory to measure nine dimensions of value: competition, success, education, work-pleasure, change, family, authority, independence-conformity, and materialism. Each of these dimensions was represented by eight items, half negative, half positive, to allow for the Samoans' reluctance to respond negatively. He correlated the responses on these dimensions to a number of other measures, including achievement, language used at home and in other situations, dress, age, family size, religion, ownership of TV, residence in Western Samoa or the United States, and years in school with ETV.

Baldauf's study was carefully done and has been deservedly admired. Its chief importance to us was that it offered a baseline against which we could measure the change in values among American Samoa teenagers over a five-year period during which American entertainment television had become very popular in Samoa. Therefore, we retained most of his items, added some questions on media use and demography, and designed a study to make possible these comparisons:

1. A comparison of the values of American Samoans in 1972 and 1977. (What was the trend of change over time?)

2. A comparison of the values in 1977 of the Western Samoans and the American Samoans. (In a sense this was a time comparison too, because both American influence and American television had come more quickly and more intensively to American Samoa than to Western Samoa.)

3. A comparison of the values in 1977 of people in areas of Western Samoa with access to television and people in areas with no access. (Because the signal from KVZK-TV could not easily be picked up in large parts of Western Samoa, people in those areas did not have television sets. We hoped that this comparison, within a homogeneous culture where the main difference between groups was only the presence or absence of television, would tell us something about how much television had to do with any change in values.)

We administered our revised instrument (after testing) to 227 high school seniors on the island of Tutuila in American Samoa and to 245 secondary school students of equivalent age on the islands of Upolu and Savaii in Western Samoa. We analyzed the results by item, applied factor analysis, and were able to make from the factors six indexes that appeared to be both clearly interpretable and consistent. These were:

1. Conservatism. (The largest factor for both the American and the Western Samoa samples. Examples of the items: "Old ways of doing things are best"; "Laws are made for the good of everybody and everyone should be forced to obey them"; "I feel that family life is the most important part of things I do."*)

2. Success. (Examples: "I want to be a success"; "Other things may be important to some people, but being successful is very important to me.")

3. Work Ethic. (Examples: "I would rather work on something interesting than rest or play"; "Play is fun, but work is more satisfying"; "The only reason to go to school is because you have to." The third item is negatively related to the first two.)

4. Materialism. (Examples: "Having lots of money is very important to me"; "There are things I want to have and do which require money, and that is why I think money is important.")

5. Independence-Conformity. (Examples: "I like to make my own plans"; "I obey some laws but not others.")

6. Competitiveness. (Examples: "You should try to be a winner in games and sports"; "It is better to agree with people than to argue with them"; "It is wrong to beat others at things like getting good grades in school." The first item is negatively correlated with the second and third.

Even though neither the family nor the attitude toward authority appeared as strong factors in our analysis, we made indexes for them because they seemed to us to be value centers we needed to know about:

7. Authority. (Examples: "I do not like taking orders from anyone"; "We should respect only those leaders who deserve our respect"; "Some of our laws should be respected, others should not.")

8. Family. (Examples: "Most activities should be centered

*The indexes are given in their entirety in Appendix C.

around the family"; "My family is important to me, but not more important than some other things.")

Thus we had eight measures on which to compare Baldauf's sample with two samples of our own.

The Findings

In the figure on p. 166 we have put the results of the basic comparisons we were able to make. These are:

1. Values held by American Samoa teenagers in 1977 compared with values held by American Samoa teenagers in 1972.

2. Values held by Western Samoa teenagers compared with values held by American Samoa teenagers, both measured in 1977.

3. Values held by American Samoan teenagers in 1972 compared with values held by Western Samoa teenagers in 1977. The reason for making this comparison is that television came later to Western Samoa, and it seemed worth finding out whether the values held in the Western islands in 1977 might be similar to those held five years earlier by American Samoans of the same age.

4. Values held by teenagers in the parts of Western Samoa where the television signal was supposed to be available compared with values held by Western Samoans of the same age in areas where the signal was not thought to reach. For reasons that will be explained later, the supposition about the availability of signal proved unreliable, and for that reason we obtained additional data on the Western Samoa sample and made a fifth comparison of the following kind:

5. Values held by Western Samoa teenagers who made regular use of television compared with values held by those who seldom or never watched the medium.

We have simplified the figure by listing only the comparisons where differences were significant or near-significant. A difference of .05 or less (meaning that the result obtained would not have been likely to occur oftener than five times out of 100 by chance alone) is usually considered statistically significant. Dif-

Value index	(1) American Samoa 1972 compared with American Samoa 1977	(2) American Samoa 1977 compared with Western Samoa 1977	(3) American Samoa 1972 compared with Western Samoa 1977	(4) Western Samoans inside and outside area of supposed access to TV, 1977	(5) Western Samoa TV viewers compared with non-viewers, 1977
CONSERVATISM	Less conservative in 1977 (.05)	American Samoans less conservative (.01)			Non-viewers near-significance in being more conservative (.10)
SUCCESS	Less success-minded in 1977 (.01)	American Samoans less success-minded (.01)			Viewers near-significance in showing more respect for success (.10)
WORK ETHIC			Western Samoans more respect for work ethic (.05)		Viewers near-significance in showing more respect for work ethic (.10)
MATERIALISM					Viewers more materialistic (.05)
INDEPENDENCE	More independent in 1977 (.01)	American Samoans more independent (.01)	American Samoans more independent (.001)		
COMPETITIVENESS	Slightly more competitive in 1977 (.10)	American Samoans more competitive (.01)			
AUTHORITY	Less respect for authority in 1977 (.05)	American Samoans less respect for authority (.001)	Western Samoans more respect for authority (.001)		Non-viewers more respect for authority (.001)
FAMILY	Less respect for family in 1977 (.01)	American Samoans less respect for family (.01)			

Differences between groups of Samoa teenagers as measured by eight value indexes, 1972–1977

ferences between .05 and .10 approach significance and therefore sometimes suggest a trend in the data; we have listed these
near-significant differences also.*

Column 1 of the figure shows clearly that significant changes
took place between 1972 and 1977 in the values of American
Samoa twelfth-graders. Five of the eight differences between
1972 and 1977 samples were significant, and a sixth approached
significant. Over the five-year period American Samoa teenagers became:

> Less conservative
> Less enamored of success
> More independent, less inclined to conform
> Less inclined to respect authority
> Less inclined to value the family

The trend that was near significance suggested that they also
became more competitive. The differences in attitudes toward
work ethic and materialism were not significant.

The comparison between the 1977 American and Western
Samoa samples (column 2 of the figure) showed even more substantial differences. The same six comparisons were statistically
significant, four of them at a higher level of significance than in
the 1972–77 comparison. The Western Samoa sample was:

> More conservative
> More inclined to value success
> Less independent, more willing to conform
> Less competitive
> More inclined to respect authority
> More inclined to value the family

As in the 1972–77 comparison, evaluations of the work ethic
and materialism did not show significant differences.

These first two comparisons indicate that American Samoa
teenagers had been moving toward Western values and away

*The raw figures for all comparisons on each of the indexes appear in Appen-
dix C, Table C.2.

from the traditional values of Samoan culture. If such a change had really been taking place, however, we ought to be able to demonstrate it by comparing the 1972 value measurements in American Samoa with the 1977 measurements in Western Samoa. In 1972, the American Samoa twelfth-graders should have held values more like the traditional ones represented in Western Samoa; during the next five years they would have moved farther from those values, nearer to Western viewpoints. That is precisely what we find in column 3 of the figure.

In a sense, all these first three comparisons are time comparisons. Western Samoa in 1977 was at an earlier stage of acculturation to the kind of values so evident in American Samoa as the 1970's drew to a close. The Western islands had had less contact with the aggressive American culture that was so prominent in the American islands. They had had less and later experience with American television. Therefore, it is not surprising that their scores were in fact much like the American Samoa scores of five years earlier. As column 3 in the figure shows, there were only half as many significant differences between Western Samoa in 1977 and American Samoa in 1972, as there were between the two in 1977. There was no significant difference between Western Samoa in 1977 and American Samoa in 1972 in conservatism, success-mindedness, materialism, competitiveness, or respect for the family.

We can be quite confident, therefore, that the direction of change was toward:

> Becoming less conservative
> Valuing success less
> Becoming more independent
> Becoming more competitive
> Feeling less respect for authority
> Ascribing less importance to the family

This suggests the impact of Western culture on a traditional culture. But it must be taken in context. Even though the family had lost some of its importance, it was still very important in

1977 (to 76 percent of the young respondents in Western Samoa, 64 percent in American Samoa). Even though young people were becoming less conservative, they were still quite conservative (74 percent for Western Samoa, 60 percent for American Samoa). Even though they valued success somewhat less, more than 80 percent, on the average, valued it highly. Even though the work ethic seemed under attack, still about three-fourths of all the young people held to it. (These figures can all be read in the appendix.) And therefore the changes we have reported were all relative changes. The resilient Samoan culture has long proved its ability to absorb outside influences and come to terms with them.

Thus far we have been talking about the impact of a Western culture on a traditional one. This impact has come from trade, tourism, political relationships, and many other sources. The measures we have reported have told us nothing about how much, if any, of the impact has come through exposure to television. This is what we hoped to find out from the comparison of television and non-television areas in Western Samoa.

The signals from station KVZK in Pago Pago can supposedly be received only in certain parts of the Western islands. By selecting approximately half the sample from the places where television could be picked up, we had hoped to create an experimental setting in which all conditions would be the same except for television. The culture is homogeneous throughout the Western islands. There is about the same amount of contact with Western visitors, Western traders, Western products, Western politics, and Western religious representatives everywhere in Western Samoa. In theory there should have been only one consistent difference in the experimental conditions: one part of the sample should have been exposed to western entertainment television, and the other part should not. Therefore, any difference in values we found would probably be related to television.

But when the results came in they were not what we expected. There were no significant differences between the television areas and the non-television areas.

When we studied the results and talked with our interviewers, however, we began to suspect why no greater differences had shown up. Interviewers told us that it was not true, in many cases, that young people in the so-called non-television areas really had no access to television. Many of them went to visit relatives in television areas like Apia, and stayed a long time in their relatives' homes. Some young people were sent to school in areas where there was television. In some areas where television could supposedly not be received, ingenious methods were used to overcome difficulties and bring it in. In other words, observers suggested (and our own survey results appeared to confirm) that there were no such sharp divisions between television and non-television samples as we had assumed in basing our design on areas.

We therefore sent our interviewers back with a new set of questions designed to find out precisely how much exposure people actually had to television. We found that the division between teenagers who watched and did not watch television was by no means as simple as the division between television reception and non-reception areas. So we divided the sample into those who habitually viewed television at least two nights a week and those who watched it not at all or less than two nights a week (the one-night-a-week group was very small, for if young people had access to television they typically watched it a great deal). Column 5 of the figure shows what we found. Because the number in this second survey was rather small, only two of the differences were significant, but three others approached significance, and the differences were in the expected direction. That is, the teenagers who watched television were farther than the non-viewers from the traditional value position, closer to the foreign values represented by the responses in American Samoa.

So the evidence at least suggests that exposure to Western entertainment television did make some difference, apart from the other influences that also encourage such change. This finding, as we have said before, should not be over-interpreted. Even the Western Samoa teenagers who watched television regularly were still overwhelmingly on the side of traditional values, not Western values. All we have found is an indication of change, and that television apparently has had something to do with that change—not that television was the sole mover or even the prime mover. Other powerful social and economic influences have clearly also had an impact on traditional culture.

A Note on Language and Values

All respondents were permitted to decide whether to respond to the inventory of values in its Samoan- or its English-language version. The majority of the Western Samoan students preferred the Samoan version, the majority of American Samoan students preferred the English version. But 40 American Samoan students chose to take it in both languages, dividing about half and half on which language they filled out first. In the questionnaires turned in by this bilingual group, we found that 18 items were answered differently by at least 10 percent of the sample according to which language they were responding to. The interesting feature of this finding was the direction of the difference. When a student answered a questionnaire first in his native language, and if his answer differed from his answer to the English version, he was three times as likely to answer in the way his *culture* would prescribe. If he first answered the English version, on the other hand, and if his answers differed from his answers to the Samoan version, he was twice as likely to answer in the direction of the foreign culture. This seems to support what has long been suspected, that language carries some cultural traits with it, and that cultural change, other things being equal, tends to go with language change.

In Retrospect

It is clear that the values of the Samoans had changed in important ways by the end of the 1970's. It is less clear how much entertainment television had to do with these changes, or even whether there would have been any difference in the rate of change if American entertainment television had never been introduced along with school television into American Samoa.

Does viewing this kind of television merely repeat, or reinforce, or extend the influence of a foreign culture already exerting an impact through so many other parts of life? We do not have enough evidence to say. Yet perhaps we can say something about the three hypotheses most commonly stated concerning the influence of television.

1. *Television makes no difference.* The cultural impact through other experiences is so powerful that the presence or absence of television neither slows nor hurries the process of change.

2. *Television helps to make a difference.* It acts chiefly as an eloquent and attractive pitchman, a model of behavior, for a broader cultural invasion.

3. *Television makes a very great difference.* It is capable of fundamental cultural change with or without support from other cultural impacts.

Of these three hypotheses, it is easy to reject the first one—no difference. When the Western Samoa sample shows no recognizable pattern of change in comparison to the American Samoa sample until it is divided into viewers and non-viewers, and then the viewers show quite clearly the same differences we saw in the other comparisons—in other words, when we can transform a meaningless pattern of differences into a meaningful one merely by introducing the variable of television viewing in place of television access—then we can hardly say that television makes no difference.

By the same token, on the basis of what we have found we cannot say that television is capable by itself of making a great cultural difference. All of us have had the experience of being asked in far countries about the heroes and stories of American popular television, but when a Frenchman asks us, as one of our colleagues from Hawaii was recently asked on a visit to Paris, "Connais-vous McGarrett?" (McGarrett being the hero of the long-running TV crime drama "Hawaii Five-0"), that is hardly any reason for the former members of the French Academy to turn over in their graves. Perhaps becoming familiar with McGarrett may leave some cultural imprint, but nothing in our data from Samoa indicates that such an experience is likely to have much impact by itself.

The hypothesis that best fits what we have seen in Samoa, the one with which we are most comfortable, is the second: that entertainment television contributes as an agent and a reinforcer of broader cultural forces. It is a most attractive agent, and the commercial network programs—the principal carriers of the lower-middlebrow culture that is most often thought of as the invader when critics speak of a cultural "invasion"—have proved to be far more attractive to Samoa viewers than have the noncommercial programs. But how much these programs contribute to cultural change must depend on the individual and a great many factors in the surrounding situation.

NINE

The Cost of Educational Television in American Samoa

IN TRYING to come up with a reasonable set of figures for the costs of educational television in American Samoa, we have been forcibly reminded of the qualification made by the Wolf Management economists in their 1969 report, "Economic Development Program for American Samoa":

> There are many opinions and estimates and few hard "facts" in American Samoa. The largest body of published data covering the territory consists of the Annual Reports submitted by the GAS [Government of American Samoa] to the Secretary of the Interior. The statistics contained in the reports are the individual responsibilities of the directors of the departments and the heads of the offices represented therein; but analysis of the data too often reveals inaccuracies, inconsistencies, and guesswork.
>
> Of necessity, we had to use available published and unpublished information in this report. In many instances, the "statistics" used were unverifiable; in others, the available data was insufficiently detailed for analysis or projection. In the interest of accuracy, we were sometimes forced to retabulate source data; at other times we have had to revise published and unpublished material; and occasionally we have had to develop data of our own (Wolf 1969: xi).

Unfortunately, this is true as well when it comes to calculating the cost of educational television in American Samoa. The necessary data for a full and accurate calculation cannot be obtained directly from government records, which are designed chiefly for budget accounting. It would clearly take a media economist or cost accountant to sort out the appropriate data, and even then—because television costs have been so entangled with other educational expenditures—one would have to make an extraordinary number of assumptions in allocating various expenditures to television. Moreover, the number of changes in the use of television after 1972 and the state of flux in television policy in the period after 1967 make cost studies all the more difficult.

Nevertheless, for the early period we have had the benefit of the study mentioned earlier by the educational economist John Vaizey, who visited Samoa as a member of a UNESCO team in 1966. Vaizey's task in allocating expenditures among accounts was made somewhat easier by the fact that television was then in only its second year and the whole system was less complicated. But he used the method of estimating capital costs in favor at the time—that is, figuring depreciation at a steady rate per year, dividing that rate by the number of years of expected life of equipment, and then adding to the result a social discount or notional annual interest rate—rather than the method of annualizing capital costs that has since come to be preferred (as set forth, for example, in Jamison, Klees, & Wells 1978: 25ff; see also Coombs & Hallak 1972; Carnoy 1975; Carnoy & Levin 1975; and Jamison 1977). We have therefore taken the liberty of adapting his figures so as to annualize the capital costs. We have also attempted to separate out the expenditures on evening home television so as to concentrate on school television.*

Costs in 1966

Tables 36–38 present Vaizey's estimates of the capital and operating costs of the Samoan television and a breakdown of those two types of cost into the more conventional categories of production, transmission, and reception.

Not all of this cost was for ETV in the schools. Vaizey allocated 25 percent of capital costs to non-school television, and

---

*Obviously we would not want Professor Vaizey to be held responsible for any of the changes we have made.

TABLE 36
Capital Costs of the American Samoa Television System
as of January 1966
(*Thousands of dollars*)

Type of cost	Amount
Transmission	
Transmitters, towers, antennas	541
Studio equipment	525
Microwave	49
Videotape recorders	314
Translators	7
Television building and installations	653
Aerial tramway to transmitter site	195
SUBTOTAL	2,284
Reception	
Receiving systems	15
Receivers and accessories	82
SUBTOTAL	97
TOTAL	2,381[a]

SOURCE: John Vaizey, in Wilbur Schramm, Lyle Nelson, William Odell, Seth Spaulding, and John Vaizey, "Educational Television in American Samoa," in *New Educational Media in Action: Case Studies for Planners* (Paris, 1967), 1: 38.
[a] Does not include the costs of school buildings, buses, and jeeps. All but about $500,000 of this total ($300,000 for local labor, $200,000 for shipping) represented mainland expenses.

$10,000 to $15,000 out of operating expenses for "acquisition and shipping of programs for evening viewing" (Vaizey, in Schramm et al. 1967: 38). The latter figure is an insignificant part of a $1,400,000 operating budget, and the allocation of capital expenses was intended to cover some of the other operating costs—engineering salaries, announcers, electricity, etc.—for the evening program. The figure of 25 percent came from the original plan that "up to one quarter" of the television time could be used for "other than school programs." In 1966 nowhere near one quarter of air time was used for evening television, and in adjusting his depreciation and interest figures in such a way as to charge non-school television with one quarter of all the investment, Vaizey was making allowance for operat-

TABLE 37

Operating Costs of the American Samoa Television System in Fiscal 1966

(*Thousands of dollars*)

Type of cost	Amount
Materials	
Production (general)[a]	89
Engineering[b]	102
Administrative[c]	19
SUBTOTAL	210
Other outlays	
Salaries (excluding teachers)[d]	553
Phone, electricity, rent	133
Other services[e]	18
SUBTOTAL	704
Television teaching costs	
Elementary:	
8 studio teachers	72
4 research teachers	32
2 assistant television teachers	8
2 clerk typists	3
1 classroom text preparer	5
High school:	
8 studio teachers	72
1 studio teacher (typing)	4
2 research teachers	16
3 Samoan studio teachers	13
Printing and reproduction for classroom use	60
SUBTOTAL	285
TOTAL	1,119

SOURCE: Same as Table 36.

[a] Includes photography, studio production, art, teaching aids, library materials, videotapes and reels, film rentals and purchases, audiotapes, and records.

[b] Mainly replacement parts.

[c] Office supplies, custodial supplies, dues and subscriptions, etc.

[d] Includes salaries, terminal leave payments, transportation of people and materials.

[e] Includes office machine maintenance, and acquisition and shipping of materials for evening viewing.

TABLE 38

Estimated Costs of Production, Transmission, and Reception in the
American Samoa Television System as of January 1966

(*Thousands of dollars*)

Type of cost	Production	Transmission	Reception[a]	Total
Investments[b]	1,239	1,045	97	2,381
Studio equipment	525			525
Videotape equipment	314			314
Buildings	400	253		653
Transmitters, etc.		541		541
Microwave		49		49
Translators		7		7
Tramway, etc.		195		195
Receiving systems			15	15
Receivers			82	82
Operating costs	805	349	45	1,199
Production	89			89
Engineering	40	50	12	102
Administration	12	7		19
Salaries (non-teaching)	300	220	33	553
Phone, etc.	70	64		134
Television teaching costs	285			285
Other services	9	9		18

SOURCE: Same as Table 36, p. 40.
NOTE: Figures have been rounded.
[a] Does not include the cost of electricity, which may have been a significant sum, since the receivers were never shut off, for fear of damage from moisture.
[b] This figure is not adjusted for use of the installation for out-of-school programming; the adjustment is made in current costs. Capital charges are diminished by 25 percent to take account of the use of the system for non-school programs.

ing expenses that accounting records did not permit him to separate out, and also perhaps looking forward to the time when
evening programming would bulk larger in Samoan television.
Having made these assumptions about the cost of evening television as a part of total television cost, Vaizey calculated the cost
of ETV in 1966 at $216 per year per student, about $0.59 per student hour. Accepting his allocation of 25 percent of capital expenses to non-school television, and using the current formula
for annualization, we arrive at an estimate very close to his:
about $226 per student per year, $0.62 per student hour.

It may be useful to say how we reached that estimate. We attempted to annualize the capital investment amounts, using the formula

$$\frac{r(1 + r)^n}{(1 + r)^n - 1}$$

where r equals a 10-year average life of equipment and n equals the social discount rate of 10 percent that Vaizey adopted based on the local advice he got in 1966. Substituting these in the formula we obtain

$$\frac{.1(1.1)^{10}}{(1.1)^{10} - 1} = .16275$$

Applying this factor to the total capital investment reduced by one-quarter ($1,785,750), we get an annualization figure of $290,631. Adding this to the specified operating costs ($1,199,000) gives a total operating cost estimate of $1,489,631.

There were 6,600 students at that time. Therefore the annual operating cost per student was a few cents under $226, and at 365 hours of television a year (the estimate Vaizey got from officials in Samoa), the cost per student hour would be a fraction of a cent under $0.62 an hour. These figures are almost twice what the Bronson team estimated would be necessary to add television to the educational system.

Costs in 1972

Our 1972 cost estimates were not put together by a professional educational economist and therefore must be viewed with great caution. Still, we need to have some idea of what the ETV system was costing at the time the decision was made to cut it back sharply and when the evening entertainment schedule was being expanded.

Putting together a realistic cost estimate for 1972 involves reallocating and shifting from account to account in order to separate expenditures properly related to television from those that are not. Table 39 shows the television accounts in the official budget for fiscal 1972.

TABLE 39
Budget Allocations for the American Samoa Television System, 1972

Item	Capital and replacement	Operations	Total
TV instruction	$ 2,000	$ 449,954	$ 451,954
TV production	18,760	400,680	419,440
TV engineering	249,500	599,131	848,631
Out-of-school service	4,800	111,769	116,569
TOTAL	$275,060	$1,561,534	$1,836,594

But these figures do not give us a usable budget for school TV. For instance, some proportion of general overhead for the educational system must properly be charged to television (e.g. part of the time of top administrators was necessarily devoted to television problems), just as some of the activities under "TV instruction" are properly chargeable to classroom instruction rather than to television (e.g. television teachers made lesson plans for an entire course, not merely for the television part of it). Costs also must be apportioned among classroom television, evening home television, and early childhood education (ECE).

Likewise, the engineering expenses need to be divided. These and other operational questions were discussed at length with school and television administrators, and a set of assumptions was made (see Schramm 1972–73, report no. 7). After the necessary shifts are made and the operational costs are broken down into production and distribution costs (which fit the existing accounts better than the more common division into production, transmission, and reception), the direct costs of the television system look like this:

Type of Instruction	Production	Distribution	Total
School TV	$860,411	$163,100	$1,023,511
Evening TV	390,821	51,815	442,636
Early childhood education	90,716	5,762	96,478
TOTAL	$1,341,948	$220,677	$1,562,625

If these estimates are anywhere near correct, then American Samoa must have been spending about $1,500,000 a year on all television operations and about $1,000,000 on classroom television. To that must be added a capital cost. We had some trouble deciding how to handle that item. The budget line for capital and replacement was particularly large in 1972 because the original equipment was aging and showing the effects of eight years of exposure to humidity and salt air. The estimate we received—of a $3,000,000 investment in capital equipment (not including school buildings, of course) up to that time—may be low, because it is easy to take replacement and repair costs out of engineering. But since that was the best estimate available, we decided to annualize $3,000,000, using the same 10 percent social discount and the same formula as with the 1966 figures, obtaining an annual capital expense of $488,250.

At the suggestion of the school officials and broadcasters, we then divided these charges by the proportional amounts of material sent to the three groups of users (65.5 percent for classrooms, 28.3 percent for homes, 6.2 percent for ECE groups). That gives us an estimate of annualized capital expense of $319,803 for school television, $138,175 for evening television, and $30,271 for ECE. So with both direct costs and capital expense figured in, the American Samoa system was spending in the neighborhood of $2,050,000 for television in 1972, and a little over $1,343,000 of that was for ETV. (Figures are rounded to the nearest thousand.) With a school enrollment of 8,100 the per-pupil cost was $165.84, which we can round to $166.*

The problem of estimating cost per student hour is difficult because by then some teachers were deciding on their own whether or not to use television, and the amount of available television was in process of being reduced. The estimate we got from teachers and administrators centered around 270 hours a

---

*This estimate of per-pupil cost is very close to that of Jamison and Klees (1975), who used the same data but categorized costs slightly differently and assumed different lifetimes for some items of capital.

year (which we suspect may be high). But assuming that estimate is close to the mark, then the cost per student hour would
have been about $0.61.

In Retrospect

Thus it appears that the cost of ETV per student was significantly less in 1972 than in 1966 ($166 vs. $266) but the student
hour cost was about the same ($0.61 vs. $0.62). We should expect the cost per student to be less because in 1972 there were
more students. We should expect the hourly cost not to reflect
the greater number of students, however, because at that time
fewer hours of ETV were being broadcast.

We must not forget that the value of the dollar changed between 1966 and 1972. The differences are more spectacular
when that change is taken into account. Here are the same comparisons in 1967 dollars:

Year	Cost per student	Cost per student hour
1966	$233	$0.64
1972	$131	$0.48

How do these Samoan figures compare with high school television costs elsewhere? They are rather high. In current dollars,
with less television, a larger system, and a mainland rather than
Samoan salary scale, Hagerstown, Maryland, had a significantly
lower cost per pupil-hour in 1972 than Samoa ($0.61 in Samoa
vs. $0.46 in Hagerstown). El Salvador served some 48,000 stu-
dents at a student-hour rate of $0.14; and the Mexican telesecun-
daria, with 29,000 students and a minimum of equipment and
facilities, was supplying ETV for $0.07 per student-hour (Jami-
son, Klees, & Wells 1978: 242).

Still, had the Samoan system at the height of its production in
1966 been serving a larger school population, the costs would
have compared not unfavorably with these. Using the 1966 figures we discussed and the same annualization rate, and assuming a school enrollment of 13,200, double the actual enrollment

in 1966, the annual cost per student would have been in the neighborhood of $117, and the cost per student hour about $0.32. If the system had been used to serve *ten* times as many students (66,000), the cost per student would have fallen to about $35, and the hourly cost to about $0.10. These estimates are iffy, and require a number of assumptions (for example, that major additions to the transmission system would not be required, and that the only costs of adding new students would be reception costs), but they show, at least, that the system could have operated far more economically for a larger population.

TEN

Lessons from the Samoa Experience

SOME FIFTEEN years have passed since KVZK-TV went on the air and a tiny group of islands in the South Pacific became the setting for perhaps the world's most ambitious project to use television as a means of bringing about a rapid transformation of an entire school system. A bold experiment it was, and one with significance for both developed and developing nations seeking to improve and extend their educational programs.

In the preceding chapters we have seen how the idea developed, how it was implemented, and how forces within and outside the system eventually brought about a virtual abandonment of the project. Before we turn to what lessons can be drawn from Samoa's experience, however, it might be well to have in mind where things stood when we completed this study, that is, at the beginning of the 1979–80 school year.

Anyone taking a casual glance at the station schedule in the fall of 1979 might conclude that instructional television was alive and well in American Samoa—that it was, in short, still playing a significant role in the Samoan school system. But such a first impression would be deceiving.

True, the station was still broadcasting approximately 56 hours a week of school television. But virtually none of it was new local programming. It consisted almost exclusively of reruns of old, locally produced shows, some as much as six to ten years old, and such mainland imports as "Sesame Street" and "The Electric Company." More significantly, these telecasts no longer provided the "core of instruction," as they did when the project was fully operational. Direct instructional broadcasts were now limited to three subjects at the elementary level: oral English, along with English sound drill; social studies; and language arts. Beyond that, television's classroom role had been largely reduced to that of a supplemental or enrichment service, to be used when and if a teacher decided it was appropriate.

A look at the remainder of KVZK-TV's schedule is also instructive, especially for those developing countries contemplating the introduction of television for educational/informational and similar purposes. Instead of the evening service envisioned by Governor Lee—an occasional travel film or an old movie— Samoa's three channels were providing 174 hours of U.S. network programming a week. Instead of a small ancillary service intended to arouse interest in, and support for, daytime instructional programming, the evening schedule had taken on a life of its own; in fact had become the dominant feature of Samoan television. And commercial prime-time programming was significantly influencing Samoan lifestyles, attitudes, and values, as we have seen.

But what of the schools and the educational system itself? There, an equally striking change occurred in the 15 years of our study. In 1979 Samoa's children were attending modern schools, a marked contrast to the inadequate, makeshift "structures" of 1961. And the record leaves little doubt that television, together with the new approach to education that accompanied it, was the catalyst in this transformation.

At the close of the 1970's, American Samoa had 26 consolidated elementary schools (as compared with 56 poorly equipped village schools in 1961), four high schools, and a two-year community college. Education had long since been made universal and compulsory from the age of six to the age of sixteen, equality among schools had been pretty well achieved, and Fia Iloa, the special school for the children of U.S. citizens and privileged Samoan youngsters with some mainland schooling, had been abolished.

When Governor Lee first turned his attention to the Samoan

public schools in 1961, the average per-pupil expenditure was $50, disgracefully lower than in any state or territory under the American flag. In fiscal 1980, the figure was approximately $1,041, still well below the U.S. average, but a remarkable improvement in 19 years' time. So it is fair to say that the project, whatever its failures, did work important changes in the Samoan public school system, though the changes were neither as swift nor as decisive as those who launched it had hoped for.

Test results have been presented and analyzed in the preceding chapters. In essence they provide a significant body of evidence that the introduction of television did improve the standard of English language in the schools. But it is equally clear that the result fell far short of achieving a standard comparable with mainland schools, an objective that in any case probably was unattainable.

Of special importance, especially in terms of the long-term program, is the leveling off and decline of test scores at the eighth-grade level, a development that coincides with the most severe cutbacks in the use of classroom television. Although that drop was not large in any one year, the cumulative effect was significant, and this is plainly a development that needs to be closely monitored.

Finally, it is clear from the evidence that within a matter of years television became less an instrument of education, as originally planned, than a means of adult entertainment. By the early 1970's, as we have seen, the three channels were essentially operating as extensions of the U.S. commercial networks (plus PBS), rather than as part of a broad overall educational program. On a related front, again contrary to expectations, Western Samoa and other nearby island states chose not to accept KVZK-TV's classroom programming, but the station's evening entertainment shows were enthusiastically welcomed. TV antennas sprouted up almost as quickly on the main island of Western Samoa as they did in American Samoa.

At the beginning of this volume we suggested that school television in American Samoa was neither wholly a success nor wholly a failure. And in the succeeding chapters, as we followed ETV through its vicissitudes, we found both good and bad to report. But our impression remains that the way to look at the Samoan development is not in terms of good and bad, but rather in terms of the lessons to be learned from the experience. In short, what can another country, considering the use of television for instruction, learn from what took place in Samoa?

In the first place, we know that students can learn from television. There need no longer be any doubt about that. But we know also that television is not the only effective teaching medium. There are less costly ones, like textbooks, radio, and sound tapes. There are some, like films, that may be more or less expensive depending on how they are used. There soon will be much more expensive ones, like computers. And there are means of instruction that in most cases would already be in place—like teachers. Therefore, the choice of ETV over something else, or in combination with other things, is not a choice to be made quickly or lightly, but only after the most careful consideration of specific needs,costs, and alternatives.

Furthermore, although the instructional effectiveness of television is not in question, ETV is more effective for some particular mental skills to be learned, some subjects, some students, and some conditions, than for others. Therefore, the uses to be made of it must be carefully planned in advance, and introduced at a pace that allows them to be tried and tested and perfected before extending the service. Any country considering the introduction of television for instruction needs to be wary of a plan for introducing it quickly or throughout an entire school system at once. There is always an overpowering urge to use the equipment because it is there. Hardware always outruns software, so that studios and transmitters cry out for use before educators are ready to use them.

It is essential for planners to keep in mind that content and method, more than signals, are going to determine whether ETV meets the educational goals set for it. Perhaps the greatest challenge facing a new ETV system is to bring the educational technology up to the electronic technology. The new user seldom realizes how long and slow a process this is, quite different from setting up a transmitter and turning on the current. Therefore, any plan to introduce ETV faster than one grade, or one or two subjects, at a time should be looked at with skepticism.

Again, although television can teach—and is probably the most "complete" teaching medium we have available—it is not a complete instructional system. What is built around it, what use the teacher is allowed to make of it, what other learning experiences are to be provided the student, are matters of first importance. Introducing ETV to carry any large part of the task of instruction is therefore really introducing a system of instruction, and the whole system, the whole combination of resources to be available to the teacher and learning experience to be available to the student, must be considered and planned together— which is another reason to move slowly and put resources into that part of the task comparable to the resources put into the electronic machinery of the system.

In the second place, the Samoa experience demonstrates that television makes an impact on a school system apart from and beyond its contribution to students' learning. This is one of the most common conclusions from observing the introduction of ETV in developing countries, but Samoa illustrates it most dramatically. Television was a major reason to build consolidated schools throughout the islands, to put new impetus behind teacher training, to bring about some important reorganizations and communication improvements in the system, to encourage (after 1972) a climate of experimentation with new teaching methods and materials, to stimulate an infusion of money into the budget so that the annual expenditure dramatically increased. In brief, television was a prime mover in transforming a primitive school system under a colonial type of administration. Television did not do it all, of course, but it certainly was instrumental.

However, television used for instruction also makes an impact on teachers. This requires a user, first, to make a key decision at the start about just how television is to be used, then to introduce it with considerable care, and not least, to expect changes in teachers and be prepared to be responsive to those changes.

The most important decision is whether the television teacher or the classroom teacher is going to be in charge of classroom instruction, or how the responsibility is to be divided between them. Samoa went about as far as it is possible to go toward putting television in charge. The substance of the instruction was to be on television; the lesson plans were made in the studio; the classroom teachers were called follow-up teachers and assigned to follow the lesson plans designed to reinforce what was learned from television. Niger did somewhat the same, but used slightly trained monitors rather than teachers in the classroom. The difficulties inherent in the Samoa strategy are obvious. Our conclusion is that these difficulties are almost overwhelming when ETV is used in the classroom, particularly in the higher grades. If television is used to extend education where there are no schools, where people study at home or in groups informally organized, then it is feasible for control to be at the television end. But in the classroom, with experienced teachers (even not well-trained teachers), successful control by studio is dubious.

At the opposite end of the scale is the use of television for enrichment only, at the pleasure of the classroom teacher. This has worked well in systems where the level of teacher training is high. For a developing country whose most urgent need is not to enrich instruction but to raise its general level substantially, the challenge is to find a strategy between total teaching and enrichment—something that might be called *selective* instruction, in which television is used for the educational tasks that will especially aid the teachers and help the students, for which programs can be carefully prepared and will be welcomed in the classrooms. But not too much television, not for tasks that could be done as well or better by other means, and not with the kind of approach that threatens the teacher.

This implies that classroom teachers must be partners in planning what is to be taught. They must be partners in the enterprise of planning what should go on television, and so far as possible how it should be taught. Then they will be more helpful as partners in appraising and revising it. They will also cease to feel threatened by it and not bottle up their dissatisfactions until too late, as happened in Samoa.

One of the most important lessons to be learned from Samoa is that teachers change with the experience of television in their classrooms, and the change is especially dramatic and noticeable in the case of experienced teachers who are not highly trained. The classroom teachers in Samoa, after two years of television, were quite different in their command of the art, in confidence, and in aspirations. In a developing country this change can be healthful. It is equivalent, as some observers and some present Samoan administrators have said, to a substantial amount of formal training. But it also presents a delicate problem of adjusting to change. The amount and quality of television that may have been suitable at the first were no longer suitable in Samoa after two years. If the ETV leaders in Samoa had recognized the growing ability of classroom teachers to take charge, and had seen fit to give them more responsibility and also to provide fewer and better programs centrally, some of the later difficulties might have been avoided. Failure to recognize the changing situation had two effects on different groups of teachers. For one group, it exacerbated their dissatisfactions; for the other, it encouraged them to become apathetic about their own part in the process and more dependent than they should have been on the lesson plans and programs from the studio.

Instructional television, newly introduced, also has an impact on the community surrounding the school, particularly if entertainment television is not available. Some of this impact may result in civic improvement. For example, without the coming of television, it might have been a long time before electricity became available throughout American Samoa. Television undoubtedly stimulated economic growth and employment. It helped bring the government closer to the people on matters of mutual concern. And a top leader in the Western Samoan government told one of the authors of this book that he credited anti-litter campaigns run on American Samoan television with a new environmental consciousness in his country.

But the very size and impressiveness of television make it a political football easy and tempting to kick. Many of the things that happened to ETV in Samoa, for example, were not the result of television at all, but rather of political changes and political currents swirling around it. Another lesson to be learned from the Samoa experience, therefore, is the importance of bringing community leaders and parents into the planning from the outset, so that it will be *their* system, understandable to them and aimed at some of their felt needs.

The Samoans' ambivalence toward the goals of the educational system—their desire to have their children trained to participate fully in the American culture and at the same time their deeply felt resistance to anything except Samoan culture and Samoan language—needed to be resolved early in terms of practical decisions concerning what should be taught in the schools and how the schools should operate. The question of the language of instruction is a very sensitive one. Several times we have conjectured whether Samoan education might have done a better job for Samoan students if English had been the second language throughout elementary school. Such a problem deserved most careful consideration, but the decision could never have been taken without community participation and concurrence.

In another respect, too, television introduced for instruction is likely to have a community impact. Once the transmitters are on the air, it is almost impossible to keep educational television from spreading into entertainment television. In Samoa, as we have noted, a few entertainment programs from American networks were introduced early in the project to attract people to evening television, which was envisaged as being mostly adult education, news, practical information on health and agriculture, and the best of Samoan culture. The few programs became two channels of American commercial television and a third one of American public television. The adult education and the local shows became completely overshadowed. And watching the two commercial entertainment channels became a national addiction. The leaders of a country preparing to introduce ETV must look forward to what could happen and decide whether they want their evening programs to be "Bonanza," "Kojak," and "Police Woman," or something else.

Finally, a lesson to be learned from Samoa is that miracles must not be expected. Well planned and well used, ETV will contribute powerfully to the process of teaching and learning. Used out of school it will extend the opportunities of learning to students who have no schools or who must study at home. Used in school it will bring expert instruction in subjects where no qualified teachers are available and supplementary teaching and illustrative experiences to classrooms that are unlikely otherwise to have them. It will make large enrollments easier to handle. But it will not bring about an instant change in a school —or even a swift change—for the school as an institution is highly resistant to change. A realistic expectation is that ETV, well used, will produce not a miracle, but rather a measured, steady, consistent improvement.

How might the Samoa experiment have gone differently?

Let us say again that we have been enormously impressed by the goodwill, the generous amounts of money, and the vigorous and dedicated effort that went into this project. If the venture did not turn out as successfully as its sponsors had hoped, it was not due to a lack of any of those inputs. In its early stages, we saw no one in a responsible position who did not want the project to succeed. Just the opposite. A high proportion of the statesiders who worked in Samoa and the advisers who helped plan and guide the programs built up a deep affection for the Samoan people and gave freely of their time and effort when they might have found working elsewhere less stressful and more remunerative. With few exceptions, those in top positions, from Governor Lee, who started it all, to the remarkable Chief Pula, who became the first Samoan to head the Department of Education, gave their hearts and their full efforts to making the project work. The Samoan teachers and principals, although sometimes hurt by what had happened to them and later dissatisfied by what they perceived as happening to classroom instruction, were nevertheless loyal and well intentioned. Certainly, the U.S. Congress and the Department of the Interior were far from parsimonious in the financial support they gave. If the project accomplished less than anticipated, it was not the fault of any of these individuals or groups; it was due rather to the succession of decisions and assumptions that shaped the project itself, and to the setting in which it was forced to operate.

Readers of this book will have their own ideas, from the preceding chapters, of what went wrong and what circumstances caused the difficulties. As we look back over the history of events, however, we are inclined to suggest a very humble, basic explanation: everyone was simply in too much of a hurry!

One can hardly fault the U.S. government for wanting to move swiftly to make up for a long period of neglect. One can hardly fault the Samoan people, concerned over the education of their children, or the Department of Education and their advisers, who saw how much there was to do, from wanting to get on with it as quickly as possible. Yet one thinks of a series of ifs—

—*If more time could have been taken with the original decision.* Governor Lee made efforts to get competent advice, and did get some very good reports, and some excellent advice from the National Association of Educational Broadcasters, the chief professional group in the field. Yet the records suggest that the decision to use television really preceded any thorough exploration of the chief alternatives. The advisers were asked primarily whether television was feasible, not whether it was best for Samoa, or how fast and in what form to introduce it. In hindsight, it is possible to envisage some decisions at this initial stage that might have avoided trouble later.

—*If hardware preparation had not been permitted to outrun the planning and preparation of software.* Television engineers and the electronics industry were ready; it is possible that the experts in the use of educational television were not quite so ready, at that early time of ETV, as they may have thought they were. They were assuming, in effect, that an experienced mainland teacher in front of a television camera could be effective without detailed planning for the Samoa situation; they were assuming that television could carry the core of teaching for an entire school system; that detailed study of curricular needs and teaching methods for Samoa could be postponed until more time was available, and they could depend on stateside experience in those areas; that they could get along without textbooks, and that teachers from the mainland could substitute a weekly mimeographed selection of exercises and questions. In the rush to get ready to go on the air in October 1964, when the new television was ready, an enormous burden of responsibility was placed on the people who had to do the programming. They had backbreaking loads of 10 to 20 programs each per week; they had very little advance preparation for this job, and under the pressure of time even the summer curriculum workshop had to be shortened. The state of the art in ETV in 1964 and the state of these educators' knowledge of Samoa and Samoans were not up to that challenge. This, too, is easy to say in hindsight: what if television could have been put in cold storage for a year and that time spent on studies of needs, methods, and content? But the start of software activities was delayed while work on hardware went ahead; and then there was the tremendous drive from the government not to delay any longer paying an overdue educational debt to Samoa.

—*If there had been time to bring the classroom teachers in.* This was part of the plan—to get their advice, give them some training, prepare them for what they should expect. It would have helped greatly. But there was no time.

—*If there had been time for a thorough meeting of minds with the community leaders on the goals of education.* The governor consulted the high chiefs, which is the way things are done in Samoa, but the consultations were mostly on whether to use television, not on the basic problems of how and for what purpose to use it. If the goals of education could have been discussed frankly and fully, the Americans in charge of television might have understood better the distinction between the chiefs' strong desire to give Samoan children a better education and their reluctance to have them "Americanized"; and the possible conflict between those two goals might have come out into the open and been better anticipated by both sides. For there clearly was some ambivalence in the goals. As a result of not clearly understanding the project from the beginning, the chiefs and parents were impatient with the schools for not preparing their children to be better leaders of Samoa, or even to work in America if they wanted to, and still they created a situation which made that accomplishment as difficult as possible. Furthermore, if the community had felt from the beginning that it was really participating in setting the goals of education, some of the later political problems might have been eased. And the language question— should Samoan be the first or the second language in elementary school—was never adequately or properly aired.

—*If the decision had been to introduce television one grade at a time, rather than in all subjects and all grades by the beginning of the second year.* This would have allowed teachers and producers to concentrate on a much smaller load of programs and to perfect them before moving on to the next load. It would have eliminated the disorder of a school system in which there was little differentiation by grade, and programs had to be completely redone each year because the average at each grade level was annually changing. It would have immensely improved program quality and permitted the recording of one year's programs for use in succeeding years. The reason given for not introducing television at this measured pace sounds specious—that Samoans want all their children to "go forward together" and would be unwilling to wait so long for the benefits to reach the whole system. The alternatives to this procedure, and the probable advantage in quality and effectiveness, would appear to be something that could be explained to parents and leaders; it has caused no trouble elsewhere. The real reason would seem to be the political pressure to get the show on the road—quickly!

—*If there had been time to try out and test programs.* We have said that too little was known, either about television or about Samoa, to get by without trying out and testing. One reason for not doing this was the intolerable load of program production, resulting from the decision to introduce ETV throughout the school system at once. The other was a negative reaction to testing on the part of the advisers. They said, quite properly, that the new system should not be evaluated until it had been in use for one school generation—12 years. In the meantime, however, they were missing information on program effectiveness, student progress, and teacher change that would have been priceless to them. There was no attempt, in those pre–"Sesame Street" years, to introduce formative research, which, dollar for dollar, is probably the most productive research a broadcaster can engage in. By the time they got around to testing and attitude studies, much damage had been done and much time wasted.

—*If there had been time to find out what changes were taking place in the classroom teachers in the first half-dozen years of the project, particularly in the first two or three years.* How much was actually known about the change in teachers' attitudes and abilities during these years is not clear to us. There must have been danger signs. But the rush to get programs on the air (a completely new set each year), to extend television to more levels, the need to handle the little problems and malfunctions that occur in any large media system, to bring in and orient a new set of teachers each year, the desire to "get on with the show"—and, needless to say, the lack of opportunity for television teachers to spend much time in the schools—these made it very hard to step back and look at subtle changes in the classrooms. Some observers of the Samoa scene feel that if the change in the teachers could have been detected and acted on when the project was only two or three years old, the project would still be thriving today. But it was not only this factor; behind it as behind everything else was the great rush to hurry on, to do too big a job in too short a time, to meet the responsibilities imposed by planners and sponsors, to make do without research or extensive observation, that made it hard to be informed, hard to be flexible enough to meet the needs for unexpected change.

—*If there had been time to consider more carefully what might be the ultimate results of bringing in, with government money, a few American commercial network entertainment programs for evening broadcast.* Later developments along this line were planned by consultants from commercial television, but the first ones were not. They were intended to attract audience to educational programs for adults. We do not know whether anyone at that early time foresaw a year when three channels of Samoa television would be occupied from late afternoon until late evening with television from American networks, or thought that this use of the educational station might have any effect on Samoan values.

So the Bold Experiment might have turned out differently. It is easy to say so now, but it must have been inordinately difficult to foresee the results of the crucial decisions at the time they were made. Fundamental decisions on Samoan television are due now, and the project may still rise, in different plumage, from the ashes. Meanwhile, the Experiment stands as a case study in what to do and what not to do for any developing country that is thinking of using television to improve its educational system, and any affluent country that is thinking of helping to support such a project.

Appendixes

Supplementary Data on Tests and Opinion Surveys

TABLE A.1

Stanford Achievement Test Scores of Teachers and Teacher-Candidates, 1932

Category	Average score	Grade equivalent	Category	Average score	Grade equivalent
Paragraph			Geography	65.0	5.3
meaning	57.9	4.6	Physiology,		
Word meaning	67.7	5.5	hygiene	73.1	5.9
Dictation	76.6	6.3	Arithmetic		
Language usage	76.9	6.3	reasoning	80.2	6.1
Literature	64.8	5.2	Computation	90.3	8.1
History, civics	59.0	4.6	AVERAGE	71.2	5.7

SOURCE: Mark M. Sutherland, "A Study of Teacher Training in American Samoa," M.A. thesis, University of Hawaii, 1941, pp. 46–47.

TABLE A.2

SRA Achievement Test Scores of American Samoa Elementary and High School Teachers, 1972

(*Grade equivalents*)

Category	Samoan elementary teachers (N = 209)	High school teachers Samoan (N = 32)	High school teachers Non-Samoan (N = 7)
Social studies	6.7	8.3	12.4
Science	7.6	8.9	12.4
Language arts	7.7	8.9	11.9
Mathematical reasoning	6.5	7.5	11.3
Mathematical concepts	7.9	9.5	11.5
Computation	10.1	10.8	10.6
Mathematics (total)	8.3	9.6	11.1
Reading comprehension	5.9	7.6	11.7
Vocabulary	5.9	7.8	12.1
Reading (total)	5.9	7.7	12.1
AVERAGE	7.2	8.7	11.9

SOURCE: Department of Education files, Pago Pago.

TABLE A.3
Stanford Achievement Test Scores of American Samoa Students in Grades 4–12, 1935
(Raw scores; N = 532)

Age (years and months)	N	Paragraph meaning	Word meaning	Dictation	Mathematical reasoning	Computation	Average score	Educational age (years and months)
10.6	36	5.9	10.6	13.9	17.5	27.9	15.2	6.10
11.6	55	12.5	14.5	22.5	25.5	38.9	22.8	7.10
12.6	83	17.8	20.2	28.8	31.8	42.9	28.3	8.3
13.6	80	18.5	22.1	30.7	36.0	45.8	30.6	8.6
14.6	94	23.5	25.1	37.9	43.0	52.9	36.5	9.0
15.6	77	24.5	27.6	39.8	41.2	51.2	36.9	9.0
16.6	72	29.6	37.3	51.7	51.9	56.3	45.4	9.7
17.6	35	32.9	43.0	56.3	58.2	60.3	50.2	9.11

SOURCE: Same as Table A.1, p. 46.
NOTE: Scores are listed cumulatively. Therefore the column that deserves special attention is the educational age, compared with the chronological age.

TABLE A.4

Stanford Achievement Test Scores of American Samoa Students in Grade 9, 1954

(*Grade equivalents*)

Category	Public schools (N = 227)	Private schools (N = 37)
Paragraph meaning	4.3	5.9
Word meaning	4.6	5.2
Spelling	7.1	8.4
Language	5.8	7.9
Arithmetic	6.7	7.7
Arithmetic computation	8.0	9.2
Social studies	5.2	6.4
Science	4.7	5.8
Study skills	5.7	5.7
AVERAGE	5.6	6.9

SOURCE: Department of Education files, Pago Pago.

TABLE A.5

Stanford Achievement Test Scores of American Samoa Students in Grades 3–6, 1971

(*Grade equivalents*)

Category	Grade 3 (N = 860)	Grade 4 (N = 815)	Grade 5 (N = 705)	Grade 6 (N = 581
Word meaning	1.8	2.2	2.6	2.8
Paragraph meaning	1.7	2.1	2.7	3.0
Vocabulary	1.7	2.0		
Spelling	2.1	2.5	3.6	3.8
Word study skills	1.9	2.5	2.7	2.8
Language			3.1	3.2
Arithmetic	2.2	2.5		
Computation			5.0	5.5
Arithmetic concepts			3.6	3.8
Science and social studies			3.2	3.4

SOURCE: Department of Education files, Pago Pago.

Appendix A

TABLE A.6

Stanford Achievement Test Scores of American Samoa Students
in Grades 3–7, 1972

(Grade equivalents)

Category	Grade 3 (N = 767)	Grade 4 (N = 855)	Grade 5 (N = 724)	Grade 6 (N = 664)	Grade 7 (N = 405)
Word meaning	2.1	2.6	2.6	3.0	3.1
Paragraph meaning	2.0	2.3	2.7	3.2	3.4
Vocabulary	2.0	2.3			
Spelling	2.5	2.8	3.6	4.3	4.6
Word study skills	2.3	2.9	2.4	2.9	2.9
Language			3.3	3.5	3.6
Arithmetic	2.4	2.6			
Computation			5.0	5.7	6.0
Arithmetic concepts			3.6	4.2	4.5
Science and social studies			3.3	3.3	3.5

SOURCE: Department of Education files, Pago Pago.

TABLE A.7

SRA Achievement Test Scores of American Samoa Students
in Grades 7–12, 1971

(Grade equivalents)

Category	Grade 7 (N = 399)	Grade 8 (N = 407)	Grade 9 (N = 416)	Grade 10 (N = 487)	Grade 11 (N = 392)	Grade 12 (N = 360)
Social studies	4.2	4.9	5.4	5.4	6.1	6.3
Science	4.8	5.7	5.7	5.8	6.4	6.6
Language arts	4.2	5.2	5.8	5.8	6.6	7.0
Mathematics	5.4	6.1	6.6	6.5	7.1	7.3
Reading	4.3	4.6	4.9	4.8	5.8	6.0
AVERAGE	4.6	5.4	5.8	5.6	6.4	6.8

SOURCE: Department of Education files, Pago Pago.

TABLE A.8

SRA Achievement Test Scores of American Samoa Students in
Grades 8–12, 1972

(*Grade equivalents*)

Category	Grade 8 (N = 407)	Grade 9 (N = 624)	Grade 10 (N = 512)	Grade 11 (N = 405)	Grade 12 (N = 343)
Social studies	4.5	5.0	5.7	5.9	6.5
Science	5.0	5.5	5.9	6.4	6.8
Language arts	5.0	5.4	6.1	6.4	7.3
Mathematics	6.1	6.6	7.0	6.9	7.7
Reading	4.2	4.3	4.8	5.5	5.8
AVERAGE	5.0	5.4	5.9	6.2	6.8

SOURCE: Department of Education files, Pago Pago.

TABLE A.9

Difference in SRA Achievement Test Scores After Four Years of High School,
American Samoa Graduating Classes of 1975 and 1976

(*Growth scores*)

Group tested and size	Reading	Language arts	Mathematics	Social studies	Science
Class of 1975					
As grade 8 (N = 418)	240	257	352	268	258
In grade 12 (N = 430)	303	340	372	349	303
DIFFERENCE	63	83	20	81	45
Class of 1976					
As grade 8 (N = 418)	243	273	316	259	271
In grade 12 (N = 307)	311	336	364	360	303
DIFFERENCE	68	63	48	101	32
Average difference over four years	66	73	34	92	39

SOURCE: Department of Education files, Pago Pago.

TABLE A.10

Performance of American Samoa Students in
Grades 3–6 on English- and Samoan-Language
Versions of a Mathematics Test, 1971

	Average percentage of items correct	
Grade	English version	Samoan version
3	63%	71%
4	75	85
5	59	65
6	72	65

SOURCE: R. M. Thomas et al., "Study of Unmet Educational Needs in American Samoa," Department of Education, Pago Pago, 1974–76, pp. 76–77 (mimeo).

TABLE A.11

Performance of American Samoa Students in Grade 12 on the
Michigan Test of English Language Proficiency (MTELP),
1966, 1968, 1970, and 1971

(Percent scoring over 70)

School	1966	1968	1970		1971	
Fagiatua		1%	5%	(83)	3%	(80)
Leone	7%	6	3	(103)	7	(99)
Manu'a	0	0	6	(34)	3	(35)
Samoana (non-accelerated)	8	5			6	(113)
Samoana (accelerated)		74			89	(35)
Samoana (accelerated and non-accelerated)			24	(160)		
Fia Iloa	68					

SOURCE: Department of Education files, Pago Pago.
NOTE: Figures in parentheses indicate the total number of students tested. Sample sizes not available for 1966 and 1968.

TABLE A.12
Analysis of Variance for Text Tables 22 and 23

Source of variance	Sum of sq.	df	Mean square	F	P
ANOVA summary, ages 7, 9, 11, and 13, by experience 0, 1, and 2					
Age	22,425.486	3	7475.160	32.52	<.01
School experience	15,287.194	2	7643.597	33.26	<.01
Age × experience	2,896.139	6	482.690	2.10	<.05
Within groups	13,789.834	60	229.831		
ANOVA summary, ages 9, 11, and 13 by experience 0, 1, 2, and 3					
Age	11,348.917	2	5674.459	20.786	<.01
School experience	17,615.222	3	5871.741	21.508	<.01
Age × experience	4,975.864	6	839.311	3.038	<.05
Within groups	16,379.997	60	273.000		

TABLE A.13

Opinions of Educational Television Held by American Samoa Elementary and High School Teachers, 1972

(*Percent agreeing or strongly agreeing*)

Survey item and response	Grades 1–4 (N = 125)	Grades 5–8 (N = 92)	Grades 9–12 (N = 32)
TV is used too much in our schools.	55%	60%	70%
TV is used the wrong way in our schools.	22	27	46
Many students do not understand TV lessons.	41	35	56
Schools depend too much on TV for presenting and developing the major content of instruction.	52	58	63
TV should only be used to introduce basic skills, concepts, and information with the development left up to the classroom teacher.	53	69	66
Students are just plain bored with TV.	44	38	68
TV teachers do not seem to know the level of understanding of the students they are teaching.	67	69	71
TV does not leave classroom teachers enough freedom to use their own ideas in teaching.	52	63	61
Classroom teachers should be given complete freedom to decide whether or not to use TV.	52	64	90
TV lessons are very helpful in teaching:			
Mathematics	81	71	54
Science	77	79	61
Social studies	82	77	69
Language arts	85	74	57

SOURCE: Department of Education files, Pago Pago.

TABLE A.14a

Opinions of Educational Television Held by American Samoa Teachers
and Administrators for Grades 1–8, 1972–1974 and 1976

(*Percent agreeing or strongly agreeing*)

Survey item	1972 (N = 246)	1973 (N = 157)	1974 (N = 230)	1976 (N = 171)
TV is used too much in our schools.	54%	50%	45%	39%
TV is used the wrong way in our schools.	22	13	21	10
TV does not leave classroom teachers enough freedom to use their own ideas in teaching.	55	43	24	40
It is harder to maintain discipline when you teach with TV.	[a]	36	36	30
Students learn more by use of TV in a course than they would without it.	[a]	39	47	26
Through TV you can teach more during the year because you cover more material.	[a]	61	64	48
Classroom teachers improve their teaching methods by observing the TV teacher.	[a]	68	67	39
Students ask fewer questions when we use a TV lesson.	[a]	54	53	52
A serious obstacle to learning with TV is that students cannot ask questions until the program is over.		62	57	63
Students are just plain bored with TV.	39	35	38	31

TABLE A.14a (continued)

Opinions of Educational Television Held by American Samoa Teachers and Administrators for Grades 1–8, 1972–1974 and 1976

(*Percent agreeing or strongly agreeing*)

Survey item	1972 (N = 246)	1973 (N = 157)	1974 (N = 230)	1976 (N = 171)
TV teachers do not seem to know the level of under- standing of the students they are teaching.	65	51	59	58
TV lessons are very helpful in teaching:				
Social studies	78	81	82	72
Mathematics	72	90	74	63
Language arts	81	86	77	83
Oral English		84	88	89
Science	77	81	75	28

SOURCE: Department of Education files, Pago Pago.
[a] Not asked in 1972.

TABLE A.14b

Opinions of Educational Television Held by American Samoa Teachers and Administrators for Grades 1–8, 1972–1974 and 1976

(*Percent*)

Survey item and response	1972 (N = 246)	1973 (N = 157)	1974 (N = 230)	1976 (N = 171)
Generally speaking, how much have TV lessons helped you in your teaching this year?				
Very much or Quite a lot	71	57	67	41
Do you feel that children are learning more this year than last year?				
More (as opposed to less or same)	[a]	51	52	11

SOURCE: Department of Education files, Pago Pago.
[a] Not asked in 1972.

TABLE A.15

Opinions of Educational Television Held by American Samoa
Upper Elementary and High School Students, 1972

(*Percent*)

Survey item and response	Grades 5–8[a] (N = 1,927)	High school (N = 1,624)
I can learn better when we have/don't have a TV lesson.		
Have	56%	24%
Do you want to have TV lessons in school next year?		
Yes	54	23
How many TV lessons do you want in mathematics each week?		
Five	49	9
Four	12	3
Three	12	15
Two	10	22
One	8	11
None	9	41
How many TV lessons do you want in social studies each week?		
Five	36	10
Four	14	6
Three	15	16
Two	13	24
One	10	12
None	12	32
How many TV lessons do you want in science each week?		
Five	37	7
Four	13	6
Three	15	13
Two	14	22
One	11	14
None	11	39

SOURCE: Department of Education files, Pago Pago.

[a] Levels 5–7 in 1972.

TABLE A.16
American Samoa Teachers' Opinions of Educational Television by Level of Education, 1976

(Percent agreeing or strongly agreeing except as noted)

Survey item	High school (N = 27)	High school + < AA degree (N = 25)	AA degree (N = 22)	AA degree + 30 hrs. (N = 49)	AA degree + 45 hrs. (N = 35)	4-year college degree (N = 23)
TV is used too much in our schools.	38%	44%	41%	41%	32%	35%
TV is used the wrong way in our schools.	11	8	5	8	6	26
TV is very helpful in mathematics instruction (disagree and strongly disagree responses).	11	20	14	18	26	31
TV is very helpful in teaching oral English.	85	92	95	84	95	78
Students are just plain bored with TV.	30	24	32	36	23	48
TV does not leave classroom teachers enough freedom to use their own ideas in teaching.	44	36	36	36	46	31
The level of instruction is generally too difficult in TV.	26	28	28	31	19	44
Students ask few questions when we teach with TV.	52	44	54	39	58	70

SOURCE: Department of Education files, Pago Pago.

TABLE A.17

Opinions of Educational Television Held by American Samoa Students in
Grades 5–8, 1972–1974 and 1976

(*Percent*)

Survey item and response	1972 (N = 1,927)	1973 (N = 1,292)	1974 (N = 2,099)	1976 (N = 2,330)
I can learn better when we have/ don't have a TV lesson.				
Have	56%	56%	59%	55%
Don't have	44	44	41	45
Classes with TV are harder than/easier than/about the same as classes with no TV.				
Harder		38		23
Easier		34		38
Same		27		38
I like classes with TV less than/ about the same as/more than classes with no TV.				
Less		37		32
Same		24		35
More		38		33
Do you want to have TV classes in school next year?				
Yes	54	69	58	55
No	46	27	42	36
Don't care		1		7

SOURCE: Department of Education files, Pago Pago.

TABLE A.18

Opinions of Educational Television Held by American Samoa Students in
Grades 5–8 in Pago Pago Bay Area and Remote Schools, 1976

(Percent)

Survey item and response	Bay area[a] (N = 638)	Remote[b] (N = 216)
TV lessons this year are better than/about the same as/not as good as they were last year.		
Better	29%	31%
Same	44	52
Not as good	22	16
I can learn better when we have/don't have a TV lesson.		
Have	55	65
Don't have	45	34
Do TV classes give students enough time to ask questions or to express their own opinion?		
Yes	36	41
No	42	45
No opinion	22	14
I like classes with TV less than/about the same as/more than classes with no TV.		
Less	33	24
Same	31	32
More	34	43
Do you want to have TV classes in school next year?		
Yes	55	66
No	36	28
Don't care	7	5
How many TV classes would you like each week in:[c]		
Mathematics		
Five	18	24
None	33	16
Social studies		
Five	25	20
None	25	11
Science		
Five	16	13
None	41	31
Language arts		
Five	16	21
None	41	28
Oral English		
Five	28	34
None	37	15

[a] Pago Pago and Matafao schools.
[b] Olosega, Manga-o-Alava, Ofu, Faleasao, Silioga schools.
[c] Maximum and minimum responses only.

Survey of Teachers' and Administrators' Preferences on the Use of Educational Television

THIS SURVEY consisted of two sets of questions. First, the teachers and administrators were asked to select from among five alternative uses of in-school TV by subject, Plans A–E:

Plan A. TV should *present and develop* the main parts of the course. (This meant using TV in about the same way as it had been used.)

Plan B. TV should only *introduce* basic skills, concepts, and information, with the development left up to the classroom teacher. (This meant using less TV in most courses.)

Plan C. TV should only be used to *add enrichment* (nonessential concepts and information. (This, like Plan B, meant using less TV in most courses.)

Plan D. TV should not be used at all in the particular subject.

Plan E. Other ways TV might be used (as suggested by the respondent).

The responses to this set of questions are shown in Table B.1.

The second set of questions asked the teachers and administrators to select their preferences from among four different types of support the school system should furnish in the event Plan A, Plan B, Plan C, or Plan D was adopted for the next school year. The support programs were labeled Alternatives A–D:

Alternative A. Course materials provided should be about the same as this year. This includes lesson plans, student worksheets, and as many books and audiovisual materials as the Department of Education can afford.

Alternative B. The only course materials provided should be lesson plans and as many books and audiovisual materials as

Appendix B

TABLE B.1

Teachers' and Administrators' Preferences Among Proposed Ways of Using Television, 1972

		Percentage of teachers		Percentage of administrators	
Preferred use of TV by subject	Grades 1–4[a] (N = 127)	Grades 5–8[b] (N = 96)	High school (N = 38)	Elementary (N = 23)	High school (N = 11)
Language arts[c]					
Plan A	61%	47%		65%	
Plan B	25	33		26	
Plan C	6	9		2	
Plan D	6	7		—	
Plan E	2	3		4	
Science					
Plan A	56%	59%	21%	57%	27%
Plan B	31	26	32	35	36
Plan C	5	8	18	9	27
Plan D	6	3	24	—	9
Plan E	—	3	5	—	—
Social studies					
Plan A	61%	54%	26%	43%	18%
Plan B	23	30	21	35	27
Plan C	8	6	39	13	55
Plan D	8	7	8	9	—
Plan E	1	2	5	—	—
Mathematics					
Plan A	66%	53%	13%	35%	36%
Plan B	23	28	32	39	18
Plan C	5	9	18	13	45
Plan D	5	7	37	13	—
Plan E	1	2	—	—	—

NOTE: See accompanying text for Plans A–E. Note also that this table differs from Table 10 in the text in separating teachers from administrators instead of combining them. Some columns do not add to 100 because of rounding.

[a] Levels 1–4 in 1972.
[b] Levels 5–7 in 1972.
[c] Not offered in high school

the Department of Education can afford. Student materials, such as worksheets, should be made and reproduced in each school.

Alternative C. The only course materials provided should be a brief course (unit) outline with a list of objectives, and as many books and audiovisual materials as the Department of Education can afford. Each school should make its own lesson plans and worksheets.

Alternative D. The only course materials provided should be as many books (with teachers' editions) and audiovisual materials as the Department of Education can afford.

The responses to this second set of questions are shown in Table B.2.

TABLE B.2

Teachers' and Administrators' Preferences Among Types of Support Programs Depending on the Way Television Is Used, 1972

Preferred type of support by use of TV	Percentage of teachers			Number of administrators	
	Grades 1–4[a] (N = 127)	Grades 5–8[b] (N = 96)	High school (N = 30)	Elementary (N = 23)	High school (N = 11)
TV as at present (A)					
Alternative A	68%	61%	38%	14	6
Alternative B	22	24	16	7	2
Alternative C	11	15	47	2	3
TV for introduction only (B)					
Alternative A	59%	47%	28%	12	5
Alternative B	29	39	24	7	4
Alternative C	12	14	47	4	2
TV for enrichment only (C)					
Alternative A	52%	43%	25%	13	5
Alternative B	21	33	25	3	4
Alternative C	24	16	31	4	1
Alternative D	3	8	19	2	1
No TV at all (D)					
Alternative A	55%	44%	19%	10	5
Alternative B	17	33	9	2	2
Alternative C	25	15	38	7	3
Alternative D	3	8	34	2	1

NOTE: See accompanying text for Alternatives A–D.
[a] Levels 1–4 in 1972.
[b] Levels 5–7 in 1972.

Surveys of Values in American Samoa

TABLE C.1

Intercorrelations of Six Value Scales, American Samoa, 1972

Value	Competi- tion	Success	Change	Family	Indepen- dence	Materi- alism
Competition	—	.01	.01	N.S.	.01	.05
Success		—	N.S.	.01	N.S.	N.S.
Change			—	−.05	.01	N.S.
Family				—	−.05	N.S.
Independence					—	N.S.
Materialism						—

SOURCE: Richard B. Baldauf, "Relationships Between Overt and Covert Acculturation in American Samoa," Ph.D. dissertation, University of Hawaii, 1975, p. 47.

TABLE C.2

Factors and Item Loadings for American Samoa Value Study, 1977

Item number	Loading	Item
		Factor 1. Conservatism
6*	.64143	I think it is more important to follow custom than to be free to do what one chooses.
40*	.63660	Old ways of doing things are the best.
36*	.55687	Children should learn to do things the way their parents did them.
30*	.48347	I feel that family life is the most important part of things I do.
70	.47521	Playing games is fun, but the greatest fun is winning.
60*	.43862	Laws are made for the good of everybody and everyone should be forced to obey them.
64*	.40463	Only a fool does not follow the wishes of the majority.
47	−.39637	I like to choose an activity and beat someone at it.
8	.36288	It is better to agree with people than to argue with them.
43	.36226	I do not like to choose an activity and beat someone at it.

TABLE C.2 (continued)

Item number	Loading	Item
20	.34561	It is wrong to beat others at things like getting good grades in school.
50	.32714	I like to do things the same way other people do them.
45	−.32714	You do not learn the most important things in school.
73	.30940	While a person's family is important he should be much more concerned with himself.
13	.30741	Having lots of money is very important to me.
		Factor 2. Success
33*	.64143	Other things may be important to some people, but being successful is very important to me.
23*	.47325	I think success is very important.
37*	.47230	Getting good grades in school gives me a lot of satisfaction.
63	.45526	We should respect all our chosen leaders.
10*	.43582	I want to be a success.
35*	−.41662	My family is important to me, but not more important than some other things.
24	.39920	I think it is important to put business before pleasure.
61	−.38036	I am not interested in being successful; there are more important things in life.
44	.34633	There are things I want to have and do which require money, and that is why I think money is very important.
49	.34631	I am very interested in being successful.
17	.34348	We should welcome the idea that the world must change, rather than wishing it would not change.
22	.32894	Too much importance is placed on getting good grades.
18	.31400	I think members of a family should do some things together, but also do some things with others.
36	−.30737	Children should learn to do things the way their parents did them.
		Factor 3. Work Ethic
14*	.51213	I would rather work on something interesting than rest or play.
54*	−.48350	The only reason to go to school is because you have to.
27*	.45381	We should try something new only when we know that it is better than the old ways of doing things.
66*	.41779	Play is fun, but work is more satisfying.

TABLE C.2 (continued)

Item number	Loading	Item
74*	.41221	I am interested in trying to do things better than most people.
45	−.38260	You do not learn the most important things in school.
56	.36455	There is nothing more important to people than their family life.
30	.35266	I feel that family life is the most important part of things I do.
21*	.34797	It is important for a student to get a good report card.
67	.34696	I am usually independent when it comes to making decisions.
57	.34158	New ways are usually better than old ways.
71	.33274	Our country cannot improve without a great deal of change.
49	.33258	I am very interested in being successful.
68	−.30754	If you dislike a class, you should not worry about getting a bad grade in it.

Factor 4. Materialism

41*	.68186	Nice things and money are not very important to me.
13*	−.59292	Having lots of money is very important to me.
28*	.56750	I do not care much about having money and expensive things.
44*	−.47645	There are things I want to have and do which require money, and that is why I think money is important.
5*	−.39057	I would like to have many fancy and expensive things.
48*	.37959	Owning lots of things and having lots of money only ties you down.
9*	.36114	I do not need money to be happy; in fact, money just makes happiness harder to find.
32*	−.35890	Useful, beautiful and expensive things, as well as the money to buy them, are very important to me.

Factor 5. Independence

46*	.53880	I like to make my own plan.
31*	−.48621	I enjoy working for the sake of work apart from money or fame.
65*	.48423	I obey some laws but not others.
15*	.41104	Some of our laws should be respected; some should not.
72*	−.34039	In one way or another, I hope to continue my education as long as I live.

TABLE C.2 (continued)

Item number	Loading	Item
11*	.33161	I feel I should pay more attention to my family than anything else.

Factor 6. Competitiveness

3*	−.61818	You should not always try to be a winner in games and sports.
25*	.59348	You should try to be a winner in games and sports.
20*	−.47040	It is wrong to beat others at things like getting good grades in school.
55	.39985	It is more important to have fun in life than to be successful.
8*	−.35452	It is better to agree with people than to argue with them.
17	.34251	We should welcome the idea that the world must change, rather than wishing it would not change.

NOTE: Asterisk indicates an item used in the index for this factor. Two other clusters of items did not emerge as factors, but each group correlated highly, and we included them as indexes because they dealt with values of considerable importance to the Samoan culture. One was Index 7, Authority, consisting of the following items:

15. Some of our laws should be respected; others should not.
28. We should respect only those leaders who deserve our respect.
36. I believe in obeying laws, even though I might not like them.
53. I do not like taking orders from anyone.
62. Laws are made for the good of everyone, and everyone should be forced to obey them.

The other was Index 8, Family:

11. I feel I should pay more attention to my family than to anything else.
19. I think members of a family should do things together, but also spend a lot of time with others.
32. I feel that family life is the most important part of things I do.
37. My family is important to me, but not more important than other things.
54. Most activities should be centered around the family.

TABLE C.3

Effect of Language on Judgments of 40 American Samoa Students Taking Value Test in Both Samoan and English, 1977

	Number of items	
Direction of value judgment	Test in Samoan	Test in English
Not significantly different	66	66
Traditional	13	5
Western	5	13

Sample Home Television Schedules of KVZK-TV, American Samoa, 1966-1980

Sample Week of KVZK's Home Television, 1966

Monday, March 7

7:00 P.M. Mickey Mouse Club
7:30 What's New
8:00 Let's Learn English
8:15 Top of the News
8:35 Cheyenne
9:30 Top Star Bowling
10:30 News Digest

Tuesday, March 8

7:00 P.M. Mickey Mouse Club
7:30 What's New
8:00 Olaga Manuia (Healthy
    Living)
8:35 Hawaiian Eye
9:30 Cultural Affairs
10:30 News Digest

Wednesday, March 9

7:00 P.M. Mickey Mouse Club
7:30 What's New
8:00 Let's Learn English
8:15 Top of the News
8:35 Andy Williams Show
9:30 Public Affairs
10:30 News Digest

Thursday, March 10

7:00 P.M. Mickey Mouse Club
7:30 What's New
8:00 Film Shorts
8:15 Top of the News
8:35 Adventures in Paradise
9:30 Cultural Affairs
10:30 News Digest

Friday, March 11

7:00 P.M. Mickey Mouse Club
7:30 What's New
8:00 Let's Learn English
8:15 Top of the News
8:35 Disney Cartoon Parade
9:30 Bonanza
10:30 News Digest

Saturday, March 12

7:00 P.M. Great Adventure
8:00 Olaga Manuia (Healthy
    Living)
8:15 Disney Movie
10:00 America
10:30 Light Time

Sample Evenings of KVZK-TV's Home Television, 1967–79

Tuesday, March 15, 1967

Channel 2
7:00 P.M. Friendly Giant
7:15 News (in Samoan)
7:30 You Are There
8:00 Soifua Fa'asamoa (Samoan Living)
8:30 Garry Moore Show
9:15 News (in English)

Channel 4
7:00 P.M. News (in English)
7:15 Friendly Giant
7:30 Twentieth Century
8:00 What's New
8:30 Cheyenne
9:15 News in Review (English)

Tuesday, March 16, 1971

Channel 2
5:00 P.M. Sesame Street
6:00 What's New
7:00 Talofa Tamaiti (Welcome Children)
7:10 Man and His World
7:35 ABC News
8:05 News in English
8:20 The Great American Dream Machine
9:50 Thirty Minutes with . . . .

Channel 4
5:00 P.M. Sesame Street
6:00 Misterogers
7:00 Talofa Tamaiti
7:10 Flintstones
7:35 ABC News (English)
8:05 News in Samoan
8:25 Ta'u Mai (Tell Me)
8:55 Olaga Manuia (Healthy Living)
9:15 Bonanza

Tuesday, March 5, 1974

Channel 4
3:45 P.M. Misterogers
4:15 Sesame Street
5:15 Electric Company
5:45 News in Samoan
6:00 News in English
6:15 ABC News
6:45 Big Time Wrestling
7:45 Adams Chronicles
8:45 NBC Tuesday Night at the Movies
10:15 Police Story
11:15 Johnny Carson Show

Tuesday, March 11, 1975

Channel 4
7:15 P.M. NBC Nightly News
7:45 NBC Premiere Movie
9:45 Police Story

Channel 5
3:15 P.M. Misterogers
3:45 Villa Allegre
4:15 Sesame Street
5:15 Electric Company
5:45 KVZK Evening News
6:15 Zee Cooking School
6:45 Olaga Manuia (Healthy Living)
7:00 Sports Corner
7:15 Big Time Wrestling
7:45 America
8:15 Arabs and Israelis
8:45 PBS Special of the Week

Tuesday, March 16, 1976

Channel 2

3:00 P.M. Misterogers
3:30 Sesame Street
4:30 Electric Company
5:00 Zoom
5:30 Gettin' Over
6:00 Consumer Survival
6:30 Washington Week in Review
7:00 Book Beat
7:30 Big Time Wrestling
8:30 Masterpiece Theatre
9:30 Tala'ese'ese (News)
10:00 Images of Aging

Channel 4

3:40 P.M. Days of Our Lives
4:40 Wild, Wild West
5:30 Tala'ese'ese (News)
6:00 NBC Nightly News
6:30 Josie and the Pusi
7:00 Movin' On
8:00 Police Woman
9:00 Dean Martin
10:30 Tonight Show

Tuesday, February 21, 1978

Channel 2

3:00 P.M. Sesame Street
4:00 Electric Company
4:30 Misterogers
5:00 Villa Allegre
5:30 Lowell Thomas Remembers
6:00 Infinity Factory
6:30 KVZK Evening News
   (repeat)
7:00 On Island
7:30 Performance at Wolf Trap
9:00 Hollywood Television
   Theatre
10:30 Over Easy

Channel 4

3:00 P.M. To Say the Least
3:30 Days of Our Lives
4:30 Another World
5:30 KVZK Evening News
6:00 NBC Nightly News
6:30 Hollywood Squares
7:00 Wheel of Fortune
7:30 NBC Special
8:30 NBC's Big Event
10:30 NBC Tuesday Movie of the
   Week

Channel 5

7:30 P.M. Happy Days
8:00 Laverne and Shirley
8:30 Three's Company
9:00 Soap
9:30 Family

SAMPLE WEEK OF KVZK-TV's HOME TELEVISION, 1980

Monday, February 18

Channel 2

4:00 P.M. Sesame Street
5:00 Electric Company
5:30 Villa Allegre
6:00 Studio See
6:30 3 . . 2 . . 1 . . Contact
7:00 Footsteps
7:30 The Voyage of Charles
    Darwin
8:30 Every Four Years
9:30 Masterpiece Theatre
10:30 Over Easy

Channel 4

4:00 P.M. Days of Our Lives
5:00 The Doctors
5:30 KVZK Evening News
6:00 NBC Nightly News
6:30 Hollywood Squares
7:00 Wheel of Fortune
7:30 Little House on the Prairie
8:30 National Association of The-
    atre Owners Presents the
    American Movie Awards

Channel 5

7:00 P.M. KVZK Evening News
7:30 Laverne and Shirley
8:00 Angie
8:30 Stone
9:30 Family
10:30 Barney Miller

Tuesday, February 19

Channel 2

3:30 P.M. Sesame Street
4:30 Electric Company
5:00 Villa Allegre
5:30 Zoom
6:00 As We See It
6:30 3 . . 2 . . 1 . . Contact
7:00 Korean Hour
8:00 Camera Three
8:30 American Short Story
9:30 PBS Special
10:30 Over Easy

Channel 4

4:00 P.M. Days of Our Lives
5:00 The Doctors
5:30 KVZK Evening News
6:00 NBC Nightly News
6:30 Hollywood Squares
7:00 Wheel of Fortune
7:30 NBC Tuesday Night at the
    Movies
10:30 Tonight Show

Channel 5

7:00 P.M. KVZK Evening News
8:00 Goodtime Girls
8:30 Winter Olympic Games

Wednesday, February 20

Channel 2

3:30 P.M. Sesame Street
4:30 Electric Company
5:00 Villa Allegre
5:30 Studio See
6:00 Once Upon a Classic
6:30 3 . . 2 . . 1 . . Contact
7:00 Pavarotti at Juilliard
7:30 A'oa'oga i Amerika Samoa
  (Education in American
  Samoa)
8:00 Pearl
8:30 Nova
9:30 World
10:30 Over Easy

Channel 4

4:00 P.M. Days of Our Lives
5:00 The Doctors
6:00 NBC Nightly News
6:30 Hollywood Squares
7:00 Wheel of Fortune
7:30 Real People
8:30 Different Strokes
9:00 Hello, Larry
9:30 The Best of "Saturday Night
  Live"
10:30 Tonight Show

Channel 5

7:00 P.M. KVZK Evening News
7:30 Eight Is Enough
8:30 Winter Olympic Games

Thursday, February 21

Channel 2

3:30 P.M. Sesame Street
4:30 Electric Company
5:00 Villa Allegre
5:30 Zoom
6:00 3 . . 2 . . 1 . . Contact
7:00 Taiwan Hour
8:00 The Advocates, in brief
9:30 PBS Special
10:30 Over Easy

Channel 4

4:00 P.M. Days of Our Lives
5:00 The Doctors
5:30 KVZK Evening News
6:00 NBC Nightly News
6:30 Hollywood Squares
7:00 Wheel of Fortune
7:30 Buck Rogers in the 25th
  Century
8:30 NBC Special: Steve Martin
9:30 Quincy
10:30 Tonight Show

Channel 5

7:00 P.M. KVZK Evening News
7:30 Mork and Mindy
8:00 Winter Olympic Games

Friday, February 22

Channel 2

3:30 P.M. Sesame Street
4:30 Electric Company
5:00 Villa Allegre
5:30 Studio See
6:00 As We See It
6:30 3 . . 2 . . 1 . . Contact
7:00 A'oa'oga i Amerika Samoa
(Education in American
Samoa)
7:30 Washington Week in Review
8:00 Wall Street Week
8:30 Milwaukee Symphony
Orchestra
9:30 The Prime of Miss Jean
Brodie
10:30 Over Easy

Channel 4

4:00 P.M. Days of Our Lives
5:00 The Doctors
5:30 KVZK Evening News
6:00 NBC Nightly News
6:30 Hollywood Squares
7:00 Wheel of Fortune
7:30 Doug Hennings' World of
Magic
8:30 NBC Friday Night at the
Movies
10:30 Midnight Special

Channel 5

7:00 P.M. KVZK Evening News
7:30 Winter Olympic Games

Saturday, February 23

Channel 2

2:30 P.M. Zoom
3:00 Villa Allegre
3:30 Once Upon a Classic
4:30 Free to Choose
5:30 PBS Special (repeat of 2/21)
6:30 Washington Week in Review
7:00 Footsteps
7:30 PBS Special
9:00 Mystery

Channel 4

9:00 A.M. Bay City Rollers
9:30 Godzilla/Globetrotters' Hour
10:30 Fred and Barney Meet the
Shmoo
12:00 Daffy Duck
12:30 P.M. Casper and the Angels
1:00 NBC Golf
2:30 NCAA Basketball
5:30 Fagufagu Atu (Becoming
Aware)
5:45 KVZK Weekend News
6:00 NBC Nightly News
6:30 American Samoa Red Cross
Chapter
7:00 NBC News Special
7:30 CHiPs
8:30 BJ and the Bear
9:30 Prime Time Saturday
10:30 Tonight Show

Channel 5

4:30 P.M. American Bandstand
5:30 ABC's Wide World of Sports
7:00 The Ropers
7:30 The Love Boat
8:30 Wrestling from Hawaii
9:00 ABC Saturday Night Movie

Sunday, February 24

Channel 2

3:30 P.M. Amazing Grace Bible
  Class
4:00 Rev. Rex Humbard
5:00 Oral Roberts and You
5:30 Mafutaga Fa'ale-tusi-Paia
  (Bible Study)
6:00 Pavarotti at Juilliard
6:30 Music and the Spoken Word
7:00 Sauniga Lotu (Church
  Service)
7:30 Nova
8:30 American Short Story
9:30 Masterpiece Theatre
10:30 Christopher Closeup

Channel 4

1:00 P.M. NBC Golf
3:00 Sportsworld
4:00 NBC Special
5:30 Manatu fou mo le faama'i
  lepela (New Findings
  on Leprosy)
5:45 KVZK Weekend News
6:00 NBC Nightly News
6:30 Meet the Press
7:00 Disney's Wonderful World

Channel 5

3:30 P.M. Winter Olympic Games
6:00 All-Star Wrestling
7:00 Winter Olympic Games

APPENDIX E

Sample Sizes, 1970-1979

Group	1970	1971	1972	1973	1974	1975	1976	1977	1978	1979
Standardized tests:										
Students										
Grade 3		860								
Grade 4		815	855							
Grade 5		705	724							
Grade 6		581	664							
Grade 7		399	405							
Grade 8	483	530	418	[a]	470	718	733	653	[b]	601
Grade 9	495	416	624							
Grade 10		487	512							
Grade 11		392	405							
Grade 12		360	343	[a]	361	430	307	373	[b]	376
Opinion surveys:										
Teachers										
Grades 1–8			246[c]	157[c]	230[c]		171[c]			
Grades 9–12			32							
Students										
Grade 5			618	402	589		570			
Grade 6			939[d]	311	560		561			
Grade 7				579[e]	542		617			
Grade 8			370		408		582			
Grade 9			519							
Grade 10			395							
Grade 11			327							
Grade 12			340							

Group	1970	1971	1972	1973	1974	1975	1976	1977	1978	1979
TOEFL tests	437						373	401		
MTELP tests		417							379	
Swains Island study			57							
Values study:										
American Samoa			306					227		
Western Samoa								323		
TV area								168		
Non-TV area								155		
Viewers								114		
Non-viewers								106		

[a] Tests not administered in 1973.
[b] 1978 results not reported because of irregularities in test administration.
[c] Includes administrators.
[d] Level 6: combined grades 6 and 7 in 1972.
[e] Level 7: combined grades 7 and 8 in 1973.

Works Cited

Works Cited

WE HAVE USED the following abbreviations in the text citations: DOE, Department of Education, American Samoa; FY, United States, House of Representatives; NAEB, National Association of Educational Broadcasters.

Almond, Gabriel A., and Sidney Verba. 1963. *The Civic Culture: Political Attitudes and Democracy in Five Nations.* Princeton, N.J.

Baldauf, Richard B. 1975. "Relationships Between Overt and Covert Acculturation in American Samoa." Ph.D. dissertation, University of Hawaii.

Barry, Marilyn. 1976. "ITV Attitude Survey." Report to the director of education, files of Department of Education, Pago Pago. Mimeographed.

Berry, Paul. 1965. "Education by Television in American Samoa." Report of the Hudson Institute for the Office of Research and Analysis, U.S. Agency for International Development. Washington, D.C.

Bronson, Vernon. 1966. "Notes on the Problems and Considerations Involved in Planning the New Educational System in American Samoa. Talk to new teachers, files of Department of Education, Pago Pago.

———. 1968. A System Manual for the Staff and Faculty, files of Department of Education, Pago Pago. Mimeographed.

Carnoy, Martin. 1975. "The Economic Costs and Returns to Education," *Economic Development and Cultural Change*, 23 (2): 207–48.

Carnoy, Martin, and H. M. Levin. 1975. "Evaluation of Educational Media: Some Issues," *Instructional Science*, 4: 385–406.

Carroll, Timothy. Undated. Memorandum to James Fellows, files of National Association of Educational Broadcasters, Washington, D.C.

Clark, Lloyd. 1972. "Results of Instructional Television Survey." Memorandum to Milton deMello, director of education. June 1, files of Department of Education, Pago Pago.

Cobb, Roy D. 1967. "Education in American Samoa." Opening remarks to visiting U.S. educators. May 22, files of Department of Education, Pago Pago.

Coleman, J., E. Q. Campbell, C. J. Hobson, J. McPartland, Jr., A. M. Mood, F. D. Weinfeld, and R. L. York. 1966. *Equality of Educational Opportunity.* Washington, D.C.

Coombs, P. H., and J. Hallak. 1972. *Managing Educational Costs.* New York.

deMello, Milton. 1973. "History and Recommendations." Report to Department of Education, department files, Pago Pago. November.

Department of Education, American Samoa. 1932, 1962–79. Annual reports to the governor of American Samoa.

———. 1970. "Non-comprehensive Use of TV in the High Schools of American Samoa." Report from the assistant director of education for secondary instruction and the television instruction supervisor for the Secondary Division to director of education. March.

———. 1971. Report of the Task Force to Study the Role of ITV in the Samoan School System.

———. 1973a. Attitudes Survey. Vol. 1: Summary Report. Vol. 2: Survey Responses. May. Mimeographed.

———. 1973b. "ETV in American Samoa," August. Mimeographed.

———. 1973c. "Philosophy of the Department of Education." Report to the public by the director of education.

———. 1974. Attitude Survey. Report from the program director for instructional development to the director of education.

———. 1976. Attitude Survey. Report from the program director for instructional development to the director of education.

Direct. 1976. "Samoa:" A Blow to Expectations," 3: 19ff. Published by Le Centre d'Information et d'Échanges-télévision de l'Agence de Coopération Culturelle et Technique, Paris.

Everly, Hubert V. 1961. "Education in American Samoa." Report to the Committee on Interior and Insular Affairs, U.S. Senate. July 17.

Fiedler, Martha L. 1967. "ETV Goes Way Out—And Brings the World to Samoa," *American Education,* March. Published by U.S. Department of Health, Education and Welfare, Washington, D.C.

Garsee, Jarrell W., and Alfred P. Glixman. 1967. "Samoan Interpersonal Values." Published by the Church of the Nazarene. Mimeographed.

Gillmore, David. 1977. "Education in American Samoa: The Way It Was; the Way It Is," *Journal of the National Association of Educational Broadcasters,* March–April, pp. 30–39.

Gordon, L. V. 1963. *Manual for Survey of Interpersonal Values.* Chicago.

Gores, Harold B. 1963. "New Schools for American Samoa: A Planned Program for a New Educational System." Educational Facilities Laboratories, Inc. New York.

Grattan, F. J. H. 1948. *An Introduction to Samoan Custom.* Apia, Western Samoa.

Gray, John Alexander Clinton. 1960. *Amerika Samoa: A History of American Samoa and Its U.S. Naval Administration.* Annapolis, Md.

Harley, William G. 1969. Letter to Governor Owen Aspinall, Feb. 17, files of National Association of Educational Broadcasters, Washington, D.C.

Harwood, B. Thomas. 1968. "Efficiency of the Oral English Program in American Samoa with Implications for Other Areas of the School Program." Memorandum to George Pittman, South Pacific Commission, files of Department of Education, Pago Pago. June 11.

Hawaii. 1970–73. Series of 25 reports of "task forces" under University of Hawaii contract with Department of Education, American Samoa, department files, Pago Pago.

Hornik, Robert C., Henry T. Ingle, John K. Mayo, Emile G. McAnany, and Wilbur Schramm. 1973. "Television and Educational Reform in El Salvador." Final report, Institute for Communication Research, Stanford, Calif. August. Mimeographed.

Husén, T., ed. 1976. *International Study of Achievement in Mathematics.* Stockholm and New York.

Inkeles, Alex. 1978. "The International Evaluation of Educational Achievement: A Review of International Studies in Education," *Proceedings of the National Academy of Education.* Washington, D.C.

Inkeles, Alex, and David Horton Smith. 1974. *Becoming Modern: Individual Change in Six Developing Countries.* Cambridge, Mass.

International Association for the Evaluation of Educational Achievement. 1973–76. *International Studies in Education.* 9 vols. Stockholm and New York.

Jamison, Dean. 1977. *Cost Factors in Planning Educational Technology Systems.* UNESCO International Institute for Educational Planning, Fundamentals of Educational Planning Series, no. 24. Paris.

Jamison, Dean, and Steven Klees. 1975. "The Cost of Instructional Radio and Television for Developing Countries," *Instructional Science,* 4: 333–84.

Jamison, Dean, Steven Klees, and Stuart Wells. 1978. *Cost of Educational Media: Guidelines for Planning Evaluation.* Beverly Hills, Calif.

Kaser, Thomas. 1965. "Classroom TV Comes to Samoa." *Saturday Review,* June 19, pp. 58–59, 72–73.

Keesing, Felix Maxwell. 1956. *Elite Communication in Samoa: A Study of Leadership.* Stanford, Calif.

Lee, H. Rex. 1966. "Planning Communication Facilities for Public Education." Address to the Conference on Biomedical Communication of the New York Academy of Science, U.S. Public Health Service Audiovisual Facility, New York, April 6.

———. 1967a. Report of the governor of American Samoa to the U.S. Department of the Interior.

———. 1967b. "Education in American Samoa." Address to Third International Conference on Educational Radio and Television, Educational Broadcasting Union, Paris, March 16.

———. 1968. "Television for Educational Reform: The Samoan Model," *Compact*, October, pp. 23–26.

Lerner, Daniel. 1963. *The Passing of Traditional Society: Modernizing the Middle East*. Glencoe, Ill.

Leton, Donald. 1972. "Testing in American Samoa." Report under the University of Hawaii contract with Government of American Samoa. Honolulu.

Long, Oren E., and Ernest Gruening. 1961. "Study Mission to Eastern (American) Samoa." Report to Committee on Interior and Insular Affairs, U.S. Senate. July 17.

Mayo, John K., Robert C. Hornik, and Emile G. McAnany. 1976. *Educational Reform with Television: The El Salvador Experience*. Stanford, Calif.

Mead, Margaret. 1934a. *Coming of Age in Samoa: A Psychological Study in Primitive Youth for Western Civilization*. New York.

———. 1934b. "Social Organization of Manu'a," in Bernice P. Bishop Museum Bulletin no. 76. Honolulu.

Morris, Charles W. 1956. *Varieties of Human Values*. New York.

National Association of Educational Broadcasters. 1962. "The Uses of Television to Reorganize and Upgrade the Educational System of American Samoa." Report to Governor H. Rex Lee. January.

Nelson, Lyle M., Wilbur Schramm, Lark Daniel, William Minnette, Spencer Ross, and Lee Morris. 1970. "Report of Visiting Team to Study Education in American Samoa," Office of Foreign Contracts, University of Hawaii.

Niyekawa-Howard, Agnes. 1971–72. "Report of Bi-Lingual Education Task Force, Office of Foreign Contracts, University of Hawaii.

Pittman, George. 1969. Memorandum to Roy D. Cobb, director of education, files of Department of Education, Pago Pago. Jan. 23.

Ryan, T. A. 1973. "Value Conflict in Elementary Schools in Hawaii." Report of U.S.O.E. Project No. 9-0528, School of Education, University of Hawaii, Honolulu. Mimeographed.

Sanchez, Pedro. 1955. "Education in American Samoa," Ph.D. dissertation, Stanford University.

Schramm, Wilbur. 1972. Swains' Island Testing. Memorandum to Milton deMello, director of education. Dec. 27.

———. 1972–73. "Learning in American Samoa: A Review of the Test Results." Eight reports: (1) Quick reference table of scores. (2) Some key questions concerning standardized testing and improvement in the schools of American Samoa. (3) Has the standard of oral English improved in the schools since 1963? (4) The locally made tests, 1971–72. (5) The language of instruction. (6) The attitudes toward the instructional television. (7) Costs of instructional television. (8) What the reports say. Institute for Communication Research, Stanford University.

———. 1973. "ITV in American Samoa—After Nine Years." Institute for Communication Research report, Stanford University. March.

Schramm, Wilbur, Lyle M. Nelson, William O. Odell, Seth Spaulding, and John Vaizey. 1967. "Educational Television in American Samoa," in *New Educational Media in Action: Case Studies for Planners*. International Institute for Educational Planning. Paris.

Schumann, Howard. *Economic Development and Individual Change: A Socio-Psychological Study of the Comilla Experience in Pakistan*. 1967. Occasional Papers in International Affairs, no. 15. Harvard University Center for International Affairs. February.

Science Research Associates. 1972. "Using Test Results: A Teacher's Guide." Chicago.

Siegel, Barry. 1979. "Television: It's Changing Life in Samoa," *Los Angeles Times*, June 14, p. 1.

Stoltz, Jack H. 1967. "Educational TV in a Pacific Paradise," *California Teachers Association Journal*, October, pp. 18–22.

Sutherland, Mark M. 1941. "A Study of Teacher Training in American Samoa," M.A. thesis, University of Hawaii.

Tate, Gloria M. 1971. "English in Pacific Island Primary Schools," *South Pacific Bulletin*, 2d quarter.

Thomas, R. M., T. F. Titiali'i, C. W. Harris, and M. L. Harris. 1974–76. "Study of Unmet Educational Needs in American Samoa," files of Department of Education, Pago Pago. Mimeographed.

United States, Congress. Act of February 20, 1929. 455 Stat. 1253.

———. House of Representatives, Committee on Appropriations. Hearings of Subcommittee on Supplemental Appropriations, FY 1962, 181–97.

———. House of Representatives, Hearings Department of Interior and related agencies, FY 1973, 1053–1097; FY 1964, 728–77; FY 1965, 1396–1435; FY 1966, 1202–1247.

Wallace, Bryson. 1964. "English Language Teaching in Samoa," *Language Learning*, 14 (3 and 4): 3–4, 167–72.

Westinghouse Learning Corporation. 1971. "Report on the Diagnostic Survey of Education in American Samoa." Palo Alto, Calif. Jan. 26.

Wolf Management Services. 1969. "Economic Development Program for American Samoa." Report to the governor, American Samoa. Feb. 19.

World in Figures. London, 1976.

Wright, J. S. 1964. "Education," in *Building a New Samoa*. Publication of the Office of the Governor, American Samoa.

Index

Achievement tests, 16, 108–11, 121–25, 201–5
Adult education, 36, 38
Advertising, TV, 151
Agriculture, 14
Ali'i, 8, 12
Almond, Gabriel, 160
Alternatives to ETV, 40–42, 187
American Samoa: population, 6–7; society, 7–9; political status, 9–13; economic setting, 13–15; early educational system, 15–24. *See also* Culture
Aspinall, Owen, 10, 78–80, 152
Aunu'u Island, 6
Authority, Samoan view of, 164, 167–68

Balch, Richard, 70, 80
Baldauf, Richard, 161, 163
Barnett, Frank, 10, 152
Betham, Mere: as director of education, 10, 88; on Samoan schools, 22–24
Block, Clifford, 63
Book Depository Library Act, 38
Bronson, Vernon: as head of NAEB team, 32–37, 51, 56, 70, 73; on language of instruction, 34–35, 57–59; on failure of ETV, 76–77

Chiefs, Samoan, 8, 11–12, 32, 194–95
Churches, 16
Clark, Lloyd, 83
Cobb, Roy D., 10, 62, 73, 75–76
Cocoa, as export, 14
Coleman, James, 139
Coleman, Peter Tali, 10f
College, community, 185
Competitiveness, Samoan view of, 164, 167–68

Conceptual learning, 56
Congress, U.S.: appropriations for education, 31, 38, 193; and commercial TV, 60–61
Conservatism, Samoan view of, 164, 167–69
Cooney, Stuart, 70
Copra, as export, 14
Costs of ETV, 41, 47, 174–83
Culture, Samoan: impact of TV on, 3f, 44–45, 158–60, 171–72; family relationships, 8–9; and Samoan language, 20, 139; relevance of proposed curriculum, 29, 33, 135–36; and educational viewpoint, 43, 191, 194–95; studies of values in, 162–71, 219–22; effect of English language, 171
Curriculum: and irrelevant textbooks, 19, 29, 34; NAEB team's recommendations for, 33, 53; centralization of, 33, 67; and Samoan culture, 33, 135–36; lack of planning for, 54–57, 71–72; role of English language, 58–59. *See also* Language of instruction

deMello, Milton, 10, 74, 81–82, 86–88
Department of Education, *see* Education, Department of
Department of Interior, U.S., 11, 14, 17, 37–38, 193
Direct, articles on Samoan TV, 89, 148

Early childhood education, 180–81
Eastern Samoa, *see* American Samoa
Economy, 13–15
Education, Department of: directors of, 10, 21; control of TV removed from, 60, 89, 152; and opposition to TV, 74–76, 80–82, 86–89

Educational system, *see* Schools; Television, educational
Educational television, *see* Television, educational
Electricity, 42, 46, 68, 190
Elementary schools: rote learning in, 2, 21, 141; consolidation of, 3, 28, 35, 38f; villages responsible for, 15, 23, 28; early history, 15–18, 21–24; new buildings, 46–47, 185; use of television, 48–49, 84–85, 92–106, 145
Elliott, John C., 10
El Salvador, ETV in, 67, 95–99, 104, 140, 182
Emigration, 7, 9, 20, 30–31
English language: and Samoan culture, 20, 62, 139, 171; teachers' lack of fluency in, 21, 29, 66, 107–8; NAEB team's recommendations for, 34–35, 57; Bronson's ambivalence toward, 57–59; Pittman-Tate method for teaching, 58–59, 72, 113, 116, 118; TV helpful in teaching, 106, 108, 146, 186; used in standardized tests, 109–26; effect on student progress, 132, 139, 141–44, 147
Everly, Hubert V., 27–30, 77–78
Ewing, James A., 10
Exports, 14f

Fales: description, 2, 16, 23; and new schools, 39, 46
Family: in Samoan society, 8–9; Samoan view of, 164–65, 167–68
Fellows, James, 79
Fia Iloa school, 18, 77, 86–87, 133–34, 185
Fong, Hiram, 64
Fono, 11–12, 82
Fort, L. M., 10

Garsee, Jarrell W., 162
Gates Reading Survey, 112–13
Gillmore, David, 57, 70
Glixman, Alfred P., 162
Goals, educational: need for, 33, 36, 43; ambivalence toward, 191, 194–95
Government, U.S., *see* United States government

Governors, list of, 10
Gruening, Ernest, 27

Hagerstown, Maryland, ETV in, 1, 93–94, 104, 182
Harley, William G., 32, 79
Harold, John W., 10, 75
Harwood, B. Thomas, 114–15
Haydon, John M., 10, 80f, 152
Hawaii: Samoans emigrating to, 7, 9, 20, 30–31; University of, 74, 80, 86
High schools: beginnings, 18–20; instruction in English, 28; reforms for, 31, 38–39; new buildings, 39, 47, 185; opposition to TV in, 81–87, 99–100; achievement tests, 122–25, 145, 204–5
Holmes, Lowell D., 32
Home television, *see* Television, entertainment
House of Representatives, Samoan, 12

Independence, Samoan view of, 164, 167–68
Inkeles, Alex, 138, 160–61
In-service education, 34, 36, 41, 52, 57, 69–70
Interior, U.S. Department of, 11, 14, 17, 37–38, 193

Johnson, Lyndon B., 64
Judd, Lawrence M., 10
Junior high schools, 18, 35, 38, 99

Keesing, Felix, 8
Kennedy, John F., 3, 15
Kessler, William J., 32

Landownership, 8
Language of instruction: English as, 16, 20, 28–31, 43, 58–59, 66; as sensitive issue, 66, 141–44, 147, 191; effect on student progress, 132, 139, 141–44, 147
Learning, conceptual, *see under* Rote learning
Lee, H. Rex: as new governor, 3, 11; and existing school system, 15–16, 19–22, 24, 107; ETV introduced by, 25–43, 56–57, 59, 62, 75; on entertainment TV, 60–61, 150, 185; and opposition to TV, 77f

Legislature, Samoan, 11–12
Lerner, Daniel, 160
Lesson plans, TV, 55, 69
Leton, Donald, 128
Lewis, Richard, 39
Libraries, 72
Long, Oren E., 27
Lowe, Richard B., 10

Mackenzie, Vernon, 151n
Magnuson, Warren, 60
Manu'a islands, 6
Matai system, 8, 11–12, 32, 194–95
Materialism, Samoan view of, 164, 167
Mathematics tests, 110–11, 125, 128, 135, 145, 206
Mead, Margaret, 8, 153
Medical care, 9
Michigan Test of English Language Proficiency (MTELP), 206
Missionaries, 16
"Modernization" study (Inkeles), 160–61
Morris, Charles, 162
Mount Alava, 35, 45

National Association of Educational Broadcasters (NAEB), 31–37, 39, 53–54, 57, 78–79. *See also* Vernon Bronson
National School Lunch Act, 38
Natural resources, 13
Newspapers, 154
Niger, ETV in, 2, 64, 189

Opinion surveys: teachers and students, 83–86, 92–106, 208–17; home audience, 153–58

Pago Pago harbor, 15, 45
Phelps, Phelps, 10
Pittman, George, 55, 58, 62, 70, 107, 113
Pittman-Tate method, for language instruction, 58–59, 72, 113, 116, 118
Polynesians, 7
Population, 6–7, 9, 14, 20
Preschool program, 36, 142
Program schedules: ETV, 48–53; home TV, 223–29
Pula, Chief Nikolao, 10, 21, 88, 192

Radio, 41–42, 154, 156
Reading tests, 109–13, 119–22, 128
Reid, John Lyon, 39
Reller, Theodore, 39
Rose Island, 6
Rote learning: as instructional method, 2, 21, 141; vs. conceptual teaching, 56, 69, 111; and instruction in English, 143
Rothschild, D. A., 10
Ruth, Earl B., 10, 152
Ryan, T. A., 162

Samoan language: and Samoan culture, 7, 20, 139; vs. English as language of instruction, 28–31, 43; NAEB team's recommendations for, 34–35, 57; use of in Western Samoa schools, 135, 144
School attendance, TV influencing, 62
Schools: consolidation, 3, 28, 35, 38–39; early history, 16–21; per-pupil expenditures, 27–28, 186; recommendations for, 27–37; expansion, 47; TV as impetus for money for, 67, 146, 185. *See also* Elementary schools; High schools
Schumann, Howard, 160
Science Research Associates, Inc., *see* SRA achievement test
Senate, U.S., Committee on Interior and Insular Affairs, 27
Senators, Samoan, 12
Senter, M. J., 10, 75
Shanks, Robert, 63
Shepoiser, Lawrence H., 32, 39
Siegel, Barry, 151n
Smith, David H., 160–61
Southern California, University of, 78
Spencer, H. S., 10
SRA achievement test: given to eighth graders, 108, 124, 204–5; given to twelfth graders, 122, 124–25, 145, 204–5; given to teachers, 122, 201; cultural bias of, 135
Standardized tests, 109–13, 121–25, 131–36, 201–6, 230
Stanford achievement tests, 109–11, 121, 201–4
Students: effect of English, 20, 132, 139, 141–44, 147; changes in, 71; on TV usefulness, 84, 92–106, 211,

213–14; academic performance, 107–26, 127–47; values, 163–73
Studio, television, 3, 45–46
Success, Samoan view of, 164, 167–69
Swains Island, 6, 117–21

Task force of University of Hawaii, 74, 86
Tate, Gloria, 58–59
Taufa'ahua Tupou IV, King, 44
Taulele'a, 12
Teacher training institute, 18. *See also* In-service education
Teachers, mainland, 26, 40–41, 76–77, 82
Teachers, Samoan: training, 2, 16, 32, 33, 40–41, 107, 142; lack of fluency in English, 21, 29, 66, 107–8; and curriculum, 54–55, 59–60; as follow-up teachers, 55–56, 65–66, 72–74, 136–37, 189; changing attitudes, 56, 70–74, 83–86, 90, 103, 196–97; TV providing training for, 57, 69–70, 188, 190; lack of involvement, 65–66, 136–37, 189–90, 194; on TV usefulness, 83–86, 92–106, 208–10, 215–17; test scores, 109, 111, 122, 201. *See also* In-service education
Teachers, studio, 4, 60, 71, 88; demands on, 52–55, 72, 194
Television, educational: in developing countries, 1–2, 63, 67, 95–99, 104, 140, 182, 189; speed of introduction of, 3–5, 44, 71–72, 187, 195–96; Lee's introduction of, 25–43, 56–57, 59, 62, 75; NAEB team's recommendations for, 32–37; planning for, 35, 53–57, 61, 64–65, 189–91; alternatives to, 40–42, 187; cost, 41, 47, 174–83; indirect contributions of, 42, 46, 67–68, 146, 185–86, 188, 190; as core of instruction, 48, 55, 194; schedule of programs, 48–53; for teacher training, 52, 57, 69–70, 87; teachers' lack of involvement in, 65–66, 136–37, 189–90, 194; hardware outrunning software in, 67, 193–94; opposition to, 75–91, 152;

for enrichment, 82, 84, 185, 189; teacher and student surveys on, 83–86, 92–106, 208–14; and student achievement, 107–26, 144–45; lessons of Samoa experience, 184–97. *See also* Curriculum; Language of instruction
Television, entertainment: Lee on, 60–61, 150, 185; impact, 148–73; shift to, 148, 186, 191–92; audience survey on, 153–58; and Samoa values, 159–60, 169–73; lack of planning for, 197; sample program schedules, 223–29
Television studio, 3, 45–46
Test of English as a Foreign Language (TOEFL), 125
Textbooks, 19, 21, 29, 34, 55
Trace, J. R., 10
Tulafale, 8
Tuna canneries, 14
Tutuila Island, 6

Udall, Stewart L., 26–27, 31
United States, Samoans emigrating to, 7, 9, 30–31
United States government, 3f, 60–61; Samoans' dependence on, 9, 11, 13–15; support of ETV, 31, 37–38, 193
University of Hawaii, 74, 80, 86
University of Southern California, 78

Vaizey, John, 40–41, 175–78
Values: TV affecting, 159–60, 169–73; studies of, 160–73, 219–22. *See also* Culture, Samoan
Verba, Sidney, 160
Villages, responsibility for schools, 15, 23, 28
Vocational education, 18, 31, 81–82

Wallace, Bryson, 107
Western Samoa, 12–13, 135, 144; TV reception, 35, 149, 151, 153, 186; values in, 163–71
Wolf report (1969), 81, 174
Work ethic, Samoan view of, 164, 167, 169
Wright, J. C., 10, 75